THE HEART GROWN BITTER

A chronicle of Cypriot war refugees

PETER LOIZOS

Lecturer in Social Anthropology
London School of Economics and Political Science

CAMBRIDGE UNIVERSITY PRESS

Cambridge
London   New York   New Rochelle
Melbourne   Sydney

Published by the Press Syndicate of the University of Cambridge
The Pitt Building, Trumpington Street, Cambridge CB2 1RP
32 East 57th Street, New York, NY 10022, USA
296 Beaconsfield Parade, Middle Park, Melbourne 3206, Australia

First published 1981

Printed in Great Britain at The Pitman Press, Bath

Library of Congress catalogue card number: 81-10037

British Library Cataloguing in Publication Data

Loizos, Peter
The heart grown bitter.
1. Cyprus – Politics and government
2. Cyprus – History
I. Title
956.45'04   DS54.9

ISBN 0 521 24230 4
ISBN 0 521 28546 1 Pbk

CONTENTS

ILLUSTRATIONS

Note. All captions to the photographs refer to land-holdings in 1969. Most of the people mentioned increased their holdings between 1970 and 1973. For the reason these figures were not updated, see Appendix 1, p. 191. The majority of these photographs were taken by the author, the remainder either by Dr Willy Guy (nos. 8, 9, 22, 29, 30) or persons unknown.

PREFACE

This book describes how some of the Greek Cypriot inhabitants of Argaki, a village in western Cyprus, became war refugees and how they experienced the first year and a half of dislocation. They fled from Argaki in August 1974, when the village was bombed by aircraft from Turkey. Not long afterwards, Turkish troops occupied the village. The Turkish Cypriots of Argaki, some fifty persons, remained in the village, as did some thirty elderly Greeks. The book has two chief aims. First, to record how people initially experienced the dislocation of becoming refugees, and secondly, to commemorate the village of Argaki and its people.

Argaki villagers were the subject of my earlier work, *The Greek gift: politics in a Cypriot village*, so since their prewar life has already been described in some detail the people who form the subject of this book are more fully known than are most refugees. The first section of the present book reviews that life again, with rather different emphases. Because my father is from Argaki, my attachment to the community owes as much to sentiment and family ties as to the fact that I also studied it as an anthropologist. So that the reader can take full account of this, I have started the book in a more personal style than is usual; a second reason for this is that the formal impersonality of *The Greek gift* seemed inappropriate for the subject matter of this book.

The first chapter, which describes how I first visited Argaki, when I was not yet an apprentice anthropologist, is the most personal. As the book progresses, this element recedes, but never completely vanishes, although most of the writing is narrative, with interpretative asides. It has been written for a wider audience than a conventional anthropological study: there are few technical terms, and only rarely does the main text refer to scholarly works. Some readers may wish to consult the appendices on methods and general theoretical issues.

Many of the events related in the book were directly observed by me, although others were not. The first chapter is written from observations made while on a personal visit in 1966. The second blends events noted during the period of my major field research (January 1968–April 1969) with an account of the past as the villagers then perceived it, and with information from documents. But it has been written after more than ten years' reflection on the village – it is not an account of how I saw things in 1969. From 1969 to 1973 I made four short visits to Cyprus; chapter 3 is based partly on things seen and heard then (or earlier) and partly on things heard later, from the villagers as refugees. Chapters 4, 5 and 6 are all reconstructions, based on what I was told by the participants in 1975. I was not in Cyprus for any part of 1974, the year described in these chapters. Chapters 7, 8 and 9 are chiefly the events I observed in Cyprus in April 1975, and in the months from September to December of that year, but they inevitably rely also on information about things that happened when I was not there.

ACKNOWLEDGEMENTS

Like its predecessor, this book was written with the generous support of the Nuffield Trust and the Social Science Research Council. My colleagues at the London School of Economics enabled me to take a term of research leave in 1975.

Many people have contributed to the work. First, the people of Argaki, who were unfailingly generous, and tolerant of my intrusions into their distress. I hope none of them regrets this, particularly the Diakourtis, Pipis, and Protopapas families, whose members bore the heaviest burdens of my visits. During the field research, Michael Attalides was strongly supportive in many ways.

At various times during the writing I received encouragement from Chris Curling, Caroline Ifeka, Melissa Llewellyn-Davis, Ioan Lewis, and Barry Paskins, and from participants in a seminar at Bristol University. From Sue Allen-Mills, John Davies, Lynn Hieatt, Joe Loudon, Stephen Morris, Jonathan Parry, and Paul Stirling I received more helpful editorial advice and hard work than an author should need. Gill Shepherd has both encouraged me throughout and given valuable editorial advice; since she has done this while remaining married to me, she deserves a rather special kind of thanks. Although there would have been no book without the efforts of all these people, none of them shares my responsibility for its inadequacies or for any particular statements in it.

I am indebted to George Skotinos for his permission to reproduce his painting 'Pentedaktylos' on the dust-jacket, and to Dr Willy Guy for allowing me to use a number of his photographs. Dave Ellsworth printed most of the photographs in the book, and Jane Pugh drew the maps. The manuscript was expertly and cheerfully typed by many people, but chiefly by Pat Blair, Ann Fry, Hilda Jarrett, Barbara Vernon, Joan Wells, and Marie Williams. I gratefully acknowledge the permission of Routledge and Kegan Paul to quote from the poem which appears on p. 27; to Penguin for permission to quote (p. 77) from Thucydides: *The Peloponnesian War*, copyright the translator, Rex Warner,

1954; and to Jonathan Cape for permission to quote (p. 155) from *Selected Poems of Nazim Hikmet*, translated by Taner Baybars (distributed in the United States by Grossman Publications).

Part I

PEACE

Chapter 1

ARRIVAL

August 1966

First sight of Cyprus was alarming and took me by surprise. It was about 5:30 a.m. and when I came on deck the Paphos coast loomed large on the port side as the boat made for Limassol. It was the bare, parched quality of the yellow hills that immediately disturbed me, for it seemed that in so inhospitable a landscape no one could live at all, let alone live at ease. Perhaps Cyprus was an awful rural slum, in which people would be suffering vastly simply to survive? From a few miles out to sea the sparse, dark trees on the hills seemed to offer little sustenance; I did not then know the olive and the carob and just how nourishing in their different ways they are. After watching the shoreline for a while without seeing anything more encouraging than sheep, I went below to make sure my baggage was in order.

My father, a Greek Cypriot, had left Cyprus in 1930 and never been back. I had grown up with my Scots-Irish mother in England, knowing little of my father, Cyprus, or things Greek, except that my surname was proof of a link to all three, and that my mother had some interesting things to say on these subjects. In recent years I had got to know my father a little better and had become intrigued by his stories of his childhood on the island, how he had become one of the first communists there and how this had led to his clash with the Church and subsequent self-imposed exile.

I was twenty-nine and without knowing quite why had just resigned from a good job in the BBC. I was attracted to the idea of research in social anthropology, which had grown out of earlier exposure to some of its writings and practitioners. Once on a Moroccan holiday I had passed a haunting hour in a village off the tourist routes and had left feeling that I should have stayed to find out about its people, who seemed innocent of the industrial revolution and who clearly found me as exotic as I found them. Perhaps my father's village in Cyprus would seize my imagination in the same way? My visit to Cyprus now was exploratory – if everything went well, I might study anthropology in London, and one day return to the island to do research.

When my father heard I was going to Cyprus he was delighted, and gave me a list of old friends and a rough guide to the closest members of his family. He assured me I would receive a warm welcome, and enjoy my visit. For me the whole notion was exciting, but unnerving. It all seemed very unlikely, somehow, that after spending half a lifetime in England and America, being treated in most respects as a fairly standard Englishman, I could really arrive in Cyprus and expect a number of Cypriots to treat me as a relative. I rather expected to be given a lukewarm welcome, to stay a few days with some people who would do their best to ignore the fact that we were total strangers, and then, with embarrassed relief on both sides, to set out for a walking tour on my own.

By now the peasant ladies who had moaned and vomited in the cabin areas for three days and nights were reviving and pressing in great numbers against the various exit points on the rails. Half a mile out to sea, we were to await the arrival of small boats with immigration officers. Clearly it would take hours; it was extremely hot, and like a proper young Englishman I was above milling about in a crowd of hysterical Mediterraneans when it was quite obvious that pushing and shoving would make little difference to who got off the boat first. To prove my superiority to myself (since I was the only person interested in the problem), I stretched out on a bench, and started to doze.

'There's a policeman come aboard and he's looking for you.' I opened my eyes to see who it was that the policeman might be seeking. Perhaps some of these short dark men were gun-runners or smugglers. There was no one around except a young Englishman I'd been drinking with a few nights before. He said it again, only to me. 'What does he want?' 'I don't know, but he's asking everyone if they know where Peter Loizos is.' He went away to see to his baggage.

Explanations sorted themselves rapidly in my head, none of them very pleasant. Because of my father's communist past, the authorities were going to turn me back. Or, because of my English citizenship, the independent government, men who had won their freedom by a bloody campaign against the occupying British army, were now going to humiliate me in the name of my ambiguous background. What indeed had I done to help Cyprus in her hour of need? And now I thought I could simply arrive for a holiday with a British passport, and do what I liked? I would be taught a lesson.

'Peter Papa-Loizou?' A policeman, three stripes, a pistol on his hip, dressed in very smart tropical cream drill, appeared. He had a thin moustache, like Ronald Colman, and very steady, somehow familiar, brown eyes that gave nothing away. What was going to happen now? 'Yes. That is, Peter Loizos.'

'I am your cousin Lefteris.' He was smiling now, and grasping my hand, pulling me towards him and embracing me, with formal kisses first one cheek, then the other. I knew this was not a good time to be very English about men kissing each other, and I also knew where I had seen the eyes before – in the shaving mirror. They were remarkably like my own, and indeed with a similar moustache, a suntan and a slightly different hairstyle, I could have passed as his brother. We also appeared to be the same age.

'Where are your luggages? I take you off the boat.' We got the bags, and he led me to the rail. Immigration officials were coming up on to the boat from a small craft below, and my cousin had a word with one of them, who then took a cursory look at my passport and stamped it. Saying goodbye to the acquaintances of the last few days, I followed my cousin down on to the ladder. Since it would clearly be hours before the rest of the passengers would get ashore, I could see that having Cypriot cousins was going to prove advantageous. But then it occurred to me that many of the *real* Cypriots on the boat must have had Cypriot cousins too, and they were not getting any help. 'How can you get me off so easily?' 'The immigration man knows me – we are friends.' He went on to explain that only a few of 'our family' had come to meet me, because it was a long way from the village, there were few cars available, and there was a lot of work on at this time in the fields.

We came ashore and passed through the customs in short order, it again being apparent that the officials knew Lefteris, and I was virtually waved through. We came out of the customs shed, and a dozen people surrounded us.

My cases were seized by some, my hands pumped by others, my cheeks kissed by all. Introductions were made, and even though I had tried unsystematically to form some picture of who my various relatives were, this collapsed straight away. There was a small woman who seemed in charge; she turned out to be one of my father's sisters, Aunt Stylou Pipis. It was hard to tell whether she was fifty or seventy years old; she was dressed all in black, with a cowl over her head, and had a huge hook nose and very bright eyes. She had seized me in the mêlée and pulled my face down to her level, so that I was bent double. She then bestowed a number of wet kisses on me. Although this was uncomfortable and I felt embarrassed to be nuzzling in the folds of her black garb, my strength (which should have been greater than hers) seemed to have gone. Perhaps it was something to do with the necklock she had on me.

Other people of different ages and sizes were standing about looking very friendly. The three youngish men who knew some English had found that I spoke no Greek at all, and the others were discovering this for themselves as I stood gaping, failing to make the appropriate Greek replies to comments such as:

> I am your first cousin, Tomas. You are welcome.
> I am Maroulla, the wife of your cousin Lefteris. You are welcome.
> I am your uncle Ioannis, the brother of your father. You are welcome.

Eventually, when translated introductions had been made, and everyone had now seen that, although willing to look as if I knew what was going on I clearly didn't, they looked expectantly at me. Something had to be said or done now, and yet I had no idea what, being quite swamped simply by the fact that I had all these relations and that they seemed spontaneously pleased to see me. This made me also pleased to see them but, since we could not talk very much, here we were standing around grinning foolishly.

Mutterings in Greek. 'We go to the cars?' 'Yes, of course.' 'Perhaps you are hungry?' 'Oh no, I just had breakfast on the boat.' 'But it is time to eat.' Eventually we went to Lefteris' house near by, and had a snack of refreshingly cold red water-melon, iced beer, and a white cheese called *halloumi*. It was about 100 degrees Fahrenheit, and I was completely unused to the heat, so this snack made me feel much better. Lefteris was trying to persuade everyone to stay for a proper meal, and this would, I learned a few days later, have developed into a ceremonial affair lasting at least three hours, with three types of meat dishes, bottles of light local brandy, beer, fruit, cheese; a feast by my standards, or indeed anyone else's. Eventually, Lefteris' offer of hospitality was overruled, and it was decided that we should set out for Argaki. I think I was consulted about this, but I was being extremely careful not to commit myself to anything which might be burdensome for everyone else, since I was highly aware that for reasons I could not understand my slightest whim was likely to be taken very seriously. Besides, I was genuinely keen to get to the village, and also thought I could see on one or two faces a certain guardedness, a watchful quality that suggested that beneath the enthusiasm for my arrival and the apparently timeless spirit of mutual exploration, there were the pressures of normal workaday life. Since I had no idea of how rich or poor these people were, what jobs they did, or how difficult it was for them to get time off, I felt that the sooner the ceremonies were over, the better for them.

We set off in three cars and were soon outside Limassol and into the barren countryside which had so intimidated me from the boat. But now it was a landscape with figures and, even if it was semi-desert, people managed to live here and express warmth and pleasure which belied the arid hills, the dust, the scrub, and the parched, chemical feel to the land. I was in a car with my cousin Andrikos and my Uncle Kouvaros. My uncle had many questions about my father, whom I greatly resembled, he said. Andrikos translated questions and answers. It was said that we would have to stop off in Nicosia to see Eleni, who had been unable to come to the boat; she was another cousin, the daughter of my father's dead brother Zenon. He had been a wealthy man, for many years *muktar*, headman of the village. But Eleni, his only surviving child, lived in a 'big house' in the capital; having been educated in England some ten years previously, she was now the senior school inspector in Domestic Science, at the Ministry of Education.

Her house was certainly large – an off white two-tiered rectangle which would have occupied the space taken by two or three English terraced houses. There was fragrant jasmine around the door, making me almost drunk in the late afternoon, and someone had just sprinkled the garden with water, which, as it evaporated, cooled the air. In the house another little old lady in black gave me a very careful looking-over, agreed that I resembled Prokopis, my father, and explained that we would have to wait for Eleni to arrive. Our party seemed a little subdued in this huge cool house, but we sat and drank home-made lemonade until my cousin came.

With Eleni I again had the odd illusion that I was looking at a version of myself in disguise, or, at the very least, at a sister. The similarity about the eyes was the most forceful resemblance. We stood and stared at each other for some time. After some politeness in English, she asked me why I had come, in a way that suggested she was quite puzzled. I explained as best I could – curiosity, a wish to get to know the island and my family. Hard to explain. I didn't go into the more personal feelings I had about understanding my parents by this journey; it hardly seemed the right time.

It was getting dark, and Eleni explained (in English) that the villagers had had a long journey to fetch me from the boat, and that it was still a forty-minute drive back to the village, where there would be a 'feast'. She was apologetic because she would not be able to come to it, and because her husband was not there to greet me. But she hoped I would come and stay in their house for as long as I liked when I 'grew tired of the village'. I thanked her and we set out again.

Even in the thickening dusk I could see a decided change in the landscape as we drove west out of Nicosia. The yellow barren hills of the Limassol district were repeated for the first ten miles, but then quite suddenly gave way to marked-off fields of rich red-brown earth, reminding me of Devon. Trees, dark green and suggesting fruitfulness, were planted in packed rows. These proved to be orange groves. But the light went, and I could sense only that we continued over an equally promising landscape.

We reached Argaki, which seemed dark and silent. There were weak street lamps – sixty-watt bulbs fixed high up on telegraph poles – which barely revealed the mud-walled houses on the narrow streets. I was dazed and didn't take in much else. Although I now know we must have passed through the well-lighted and crowded coffee-shop area, I have no reliable recollection of doing so. We followed the randomly winding irregular streets and finally turned into an apparent dead end. There were a few people sitting outside my Aunt Stylou Pipis' house on chairs, and when we stopped I was unprepared for the idea that we would now meet any more.

I was wrong. At first I thought that the whole village must have been inside the house. There were, my rapid count informed me, some seventy persons of all ages. In the courtyard a long table – several tables laid end to end – had been set with food and drink of all kinds. It could accommodate only about twenty of us but this seemed to worry no one. Pakis, who had taken over from his brother Andrikos the role of chief interpreter, explained that all these people were my relatives, and that was why they were there. The *whole* village? No, just my *close* relatives. 'We did not invite the second cousins, because the house is small and they are perhaps one hundred and fifty, perhaps two hundred . . . later you can meet them all when we go to the coffee shop.'

This was why they had been mildly apologetic at the quayside about the allegedly small numbers of those who had come. Eventually I was to get straight just who they were and where they all came from. My father had had two brothers and four sisters who had all married. Between them they had produced twenty children who had survived to adulthood. This is an important qualification in Cyprus; one of my aunts had exactly one living child to show for thirteen pregnancies. Most of these cousins had by now married. Six married uncles and aunts put twelve persons into the room. Fifteen married cousins added thirty more, making forty-two. The five unmarried younger cousins brought it to forty-seven. Then there were large numbers of small children, assorted in-laws, neighbours, and odd people who had dropped by to see if I had news of their relatives in England. My grandfather had been one of eight, and most of *them* had had large families; from this, the second cousins became 'hundreds' – and hence were necessarily absent tonight.

People had been waiting a long time to eat, and now they started. I found my plate piled high with all kinds of ceremonial foods – stuffed vine leaves, roast goat meat, lamb, chicken, red-gold roast potatoes, salad with piquant coriander, macaroni stuffed with mincemeat (which alone would have made a very acceptable meal in London). Whenever I made a small hole in the food on my plate, an aunt would seize a particularly juicy chicken leg or chunk of goat, and swoop it down on to my plate. If I cunningly tried to control this cornucopia I was urged on with the words 'phage akoma ligho' (eat a little bit more), or more imperatively 'phage Petro' (eat, Peter). My glass was being continually refilled as well. It took me some time to realise that whenever I picked it up, everyone else picked up theirs. In Cypriot village company, you do not drink alone, in your own time, or simply when you feel like it. You drink ceremonially together, and each round emphasises the collective nature of the event. Since I did not understand this, and was also the guest of honour, my bad manners were being redefined and overlooked, and instead I was being treated as a kind of toastmaster or pacemaker, even though I was not making any toasts.

But these were being made for me. 'To our much-loved cousin Peter who has come to get to know us'. Of course I couldn't drink to myself. 'To our relative Prokopis, so many years in England'. This was all right. The technique was that when all were holding their glasses raised in front of them, towards some notional centre of the table, the toast 'Eh-ee-vah' was pronounced, a version of 'your health', and the glasses clinked in the middle. Sometimes everyone clinked glasses with everyone else, saying their names. 'Eh-ee-vah Tomas, Mikailis; eh-ee-vah uncle Kouvaros; eh-ee-vah cousin', and so on.

Pakis, on my right, was bearing the brunt of the ceremonies since he was translating all the remarks addressed from all sides of the room to me, as well as my numbed and fumbling attempts to reply in the spirit of the event. Unless you are remarkably unselfconscious it is extremely difficult to take part – let alone occupy centre stage – in a ceremony when you have no idea what is expected. Nor can you simply watch how others do it, as you might watch which knife they pick up; that will take you so far, but all sorts of things in ceremonial occasions are simply not symmetrical. If guest tries to imitate host it may add to confusion: it is for the host in England to say 'Shall we go and eat now?', and for the guest diffidently to agree. So although the food and brandy after my journey were helping to make me relax, I was also trying to respond to the very large and generous efforts being made towards me by choosing the appropriate kind of behaviour. Everything that was said to me needed a reply, and not just an 'oh, really' or a 'how nice', but an answer as warmly and elegantly phrased as the question. Since I have a strong sense of occasion it did not seem right that all the action should be going one way. It was also clear from some of the things that were being said that the people around the table were making very deliberate attempts to make me feel at home. Tomas, the oldest of my cousins and obviously one of the most influential members of the company, now made a short speech:

> We all wish to express our pleasure that our uncle Prokopis, who has been away abroad so many years, has sent us his son, our relative, to get to know us, so we can show him hospitality.

There were also numerous comments about how like my father I looked, and how like various persons around the table, and many questions about my father's health.

Pakis, the translator, had throughout the meal prompted me tactfully with the names and relationships of people who were addressing me through him.

> Your uncle Tchanggos, the man on my right . . . the husband of your father's sister, Klykou, wishes to say something to you. He says: 'You are welcome to the village and when you write to your father send him many greetings from his childhood friend . . . ' [and so forth].

Now he said to me that he thought I must make some kind of a speech. What happened next surprised even me, and looking back it seems that on a quieter level it had been in preparation for some time. I began,

> When I was a small boy at school in England, I did not look particularly Greek, and because, as you know, I was brought up by my mother, I did not speak any Greek, only English, like any Englishman. And yet I had a long Greek name, Papaloizou, and this name caused me a great deal of trouble. For some reason the English children found it odd that I should look so English and yet have a name which to the English seems funny. So they used to tease me about it, and of course, like any child, I didn't like being teased. It used to get me into trouble and fights. For many years I carried this name around wondering why my mother hadn't done the sensible thing and given me an English name, so I could be exactly like everyone else. Now, coming here after so long and meeting you all for the first time, I feel all those difficult childhood years were worth while.

This speech (which, though apt, was also from the heart) produced a strong effect on the people at the table, some of whom were visibly moved, and all of whom were very attentive, while Pakis relayed the contents in Greek. Further things were said to make me feel even more at home, and the one that I have never forgotten was the dialect proverb which Tomas produced: 'Opios eschi dhendro, eschi schios.' This was probably the first respectable sentence of the dialect that I learned. It means 'whoever has a tree has shade'; whoever has kinsmen has protection.

Chapter 2

ARGAKI

1900–1970

Casual impressions, 1966

The villagers who had so graciously and ceremoniously received me were to preoccupy me for the next fifteen years, but I did not know that in 1966, and my six weeks in Cyprus were an extraordinary holiday. While others worked, I took my ease; since I could not speak Greek, and during the day the men who spoke English were out at work, what I learned then about the village must have been largely through impressions on my senses.

Much was conveyed through sound. At first I used to wake early, before dawn, hearing women calling shrilly, and fearing that dreadful quarrels were breaking out on all sides, so harshly strident were their tones. Gradually it became clear that these were neighbours calling over courtyard walls, or mothers chiding children. Men did not yell so often, but they started up their tractors at 4 a.m. so that they could get in a good stint in the fields before the midday heat. Dogs howled all night, inciting each other to frenzied competition, and the many cockerels delivered their *pronunciamentos* well before daybreak. As if to make up for this, there was in the noon heat a great silence, with only the buzz of flies to mark time passing, while in the evenings crickets and household doves were pleasing minstrels.

My senses of taste and smell were also stimulated. The aroma of the local food, which fortunately I found delicious, pervaded the village throughout the day, for the farmers ate when it fitted in with their work, rather than at set times. There were also other scents – of the dried mud-and-straw bricks of the houses and courtyards, and of the near-by animals, which were pleasingly fresh after the acrid fumes of my city life.

The surfaces of the village were usually hotter and rougher than I was used to; only the centre of the village was paved, and in summer the pathways out to the fields were hard and stony. The wood of the older doorposts and window-shutters had a curious dryness not to be found in

11

London. Only the occasional plastic table-top or a newly built house with its dead straight lines, plane surfaces, and sharp edges reminded me of industry.

But it was through my eyes that I had to do most of my learning about the village. It was not a conventionally pretty village, and tourists never visited it. It was in the plains, and not on the sea. The houses were made

The approach to Argaki from Kato Kopia.

of either dull mud bricks or a charmless red brick. Unless you looked at it in a rather special way, it looked drab and flat, hot and dusty, with neither the striking terraced settings of the mountain villages, where five or six houses appeared to stand one upon another like acrobats, nor the whitewashed nestling compactness of some villages in the Kyrenia foothills, like Karmi and Bellapaïs.

The way to see the village at its best was to get high up on someone's roof, and then look at small areas of houses, concentrating on arbitrary sections, where several different planes criss-crossed each other, with a courtyard wall running at an oblique angle to the roof of another house. The eye had to concentrate and pile up the dwellings one upon another, as a telephoto lens would do, in order to discover the complex textures.

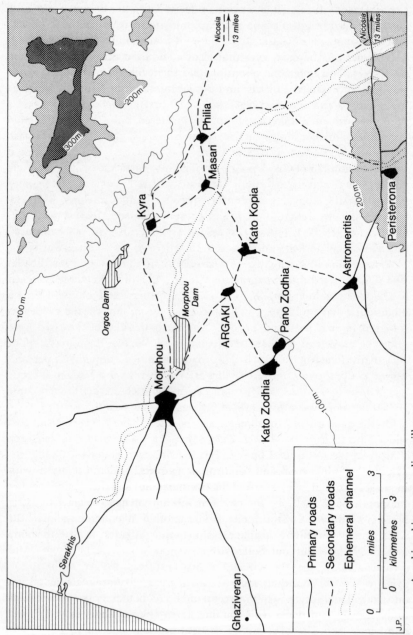

Argaki and its surrounding villages.

13

Early in my first visit I set out to get to know the region. Nicosia in summer was a bright place in a dry yellow-dun plain, which must be why its Greek name is Levcosia, from the root *levkos*, white. Starting towards Morphou from Nicosia, one first drove for fifteen miles across shorn wheatfields and limestone outcrops, and then, from the first sight of the sea, the land started to turn darker, as more and more pumps watered citrus groves and summer vegetables. The first pumps to be seen had a bore the size of a bicycle pump and watered only small patches of vegetables, but five miles further on they were bigger than an English drain-pipe and watered whole fields and orchards. The road passed through a number of Greek police checkpoints, particularly at Peristerona village, where, brought to fame by postcards, a Turkish minaret stands photogenically alongside a church spire, suggesting a closer harmony between the two religions than had actually existed. Most of the Turks had by then left Peristerona. Just before Astromeritis ('the place of stars') the main road forked, and the left turn swung up south towards the Troodos mountains, which were clearly in sight all the way from Nicosia. The right fork led into Astromeritis village and, when it emerged, turned to the west, giving both a view of the northern end of the Kyrenia mountain range and also a sight of the sea. From now on the earth was coloured in rich reds and browns, and on both sides of the road were groves of grapefruit, orange, and lemon trees, some of them mature, but also many fields of saplings. The road continued through Upper and Lower Zodhia, two large, rich villages, and then after a few more bends reached the first houses of Morphou, an orange-rich market-town of some 10,000 persons, and a by-word in Cyprus for new wealth.

On the outskirts of Morphou a keen eye might have just seen a signpost which said in English: *Argaki. Kato Kopia. 3 mi.* The road doubled back sharply to the right, as if back to Nicosia, to where indeed it finally led. The road was less good, but still fast, along open fields and orchards with some scattered houses starting half a mile out from the edges of the compact village itself. To the east was a large corrugated metal building like a warehouse, for the packing of carrots and potatoes, which was communally owned by Argaki. It stood in sight of an even larger one owned by the village of Kato Kopia, Argaki's nearest neighbour and greatest rival.

But before this building was reached the road to Argaki swung off left into the village, which was framed by the Kyrenia mountains fifteen miles to the north, towards Turkey. Passing a sandstone primary school on the right, and then fifteen or twenty houses on each side, one reached the centre of the village – the coffee shops. Although I shall call this centre 'the square' it was not square-shaped, but rather an irregular space where four routes came together; each of the four had itself been fed a little earlier by tributary pathways, so one felt as if all thoroughfares were focused on the square. While the church, some fifty yards away, was the spiritual centre of Argaki for the Greeks, the square was the social and economic centre, where three main coffee shops were sited, at which, from boyhood onwards, the men spent most of their leisure time. They drank the first coffee of the day there at any time after 5 a.m., before going off to work in the fields or elsewhere, and it was there that they sat after the evening meal, occupied with newspapers, cards, backgammon, radio, television, conversation, or nothing more demanding than clicking their worry-beads. The village telephone was there, and a co-operative grocery; butchers worked there publicly on Friday and Saturday, so that everyone saw how much meat a man bought for his family. All the buses left from the square – the school buses, the Morphou shuttle, and the Nicosia pullman.

The square was the secular centre for the men, very much a man's world, and women did not like to be seen there. If they had to wait there for transport they stood silently to one side with downcast eyes. If they had to walk through it they tried to make sure they were wearing their thick stockings. Mainly they went out of their way to avoid it, and would take a detour rather than pass through a space containing several hundred men. I myself at first felt like the shyest village maiden when I stood in the square, and sometimes to leave my quiet walled and shuttered house, to come down among these dark incomprehensible men, seemed harder than to face Argos, that giant with a hundred eyes. Most of the men claimed we were blood relatives, and tested me to see if I had yet learned their names. The task was made all the more difficult because, as I was to discover, at least thirty-two of them were called Yiorgios, twenty-one called Haralambos ('Light of Joy'), and fourteen called Christodoulos ('Servant of Christ'). Later a time would come when I knew the nickname of each man, and could tell as my eyes scanned the coffee shops who was not from the village. But then I could not, and simply felt foolish when I failed these tests of identity. They could name me, but I could not name many of them.

When I chanced to come into the square and sit down at a coffee shop, then someone very quickly would offer me a coffee or a fruit drink and move nearer, to converse. A small number of Argaki men knew English, from service in the army, or work on one of the British bases, or from labour migration to Britain. So the questions began: 'Where in England do you live?' 'What is your job?' 'How much is the salary?' 'Are you married?' In village custom if one did not wish to reply one simply smiled and said nothing, as if the question had not been asked. But of course I did not know this either, and felt there was something intrusive about such questions.

Part of Argaki's main square, at noon.

Serious inquiries, 1968

Accommodation and apparel

I returned to the village in January 1968 with fifteen months' grounding in social anthropology, to study the community as thoroughly as I could. The Greek I had learned in London proved too Athenian for me to converse with most people; only those who had a good bout of secondary education, and had thus learned 'proper' Greek, could communicate with me, so for a month or so, until I had grasped the essentials, they had to translate from Cypriot village dialect into my halting Greek. In the first months I was again dependent on my eyes and again found it painfully difficult to venture into the coffee shops and be accosted by unidentifiable relatives. One remedy was to deal with people in ones or twos, and I found a coffee shop away from the main square where only old men with little to do passed their days. The best therapy for my agoraphobia (in the most literal sense), was, I found, to take the life histories and genealogies of these men, very slowly, in very simple words. When not doing this, there was the pleasure of walking about and using my eyes, but by now I had read a good deal about rural Cyprus and other similar places, and had a better framework with which to make sense of what I saw.

It was easy to recognise several different types of house. First there was a very simple kind, a single dwelling unit made almost entirely of dun-brown mud bricks, with sunbleached wooden shutters flanking the glassless window-frames. The door was made of a few thin wooden planks, the floor was of beaten earth, while a rickety unpainted table and a couple of light iron beds, like army issue, comprised the furniture, along with a dresser. Such a house stood in a small untidy yard, with an irregular dried mud wall topped with cut thorn bushes. A few goats and chickens might be consuming scraps in the yard. The people sitting at the door were usually very old, dressed in black clothes, the men wearing baggy trousers hanging between the legs in many folds, and the women in long black skirts, long-sleeved black blouses, and headscarves. With few exceptions the old people in Argaki looked scruffy and poor, and often their clothes had food stains on them. If they had any savings tucked away, they were careful to give no hint of it.

There were also simple mud-brick houses arranged in a more complicated way, with an upper storey, or several rooms around a single entrance. The doorways in these houses had stone jambs and lintels, expensive materials worked by craftsmen. Sometimes over these doors was a date formed in crudely wrought iron. The windows also had stone frames, and even glass panes. Through an open doorway one could see past the high surrounding walls into the courtyard and the house itself, obtaining a glimpse of storehouses with piles of dried beans, and yellow melons hanging in the rafters.

It soon became clear that these two variants of the mud-brick house represented the extremes of wealth. The bigger houses, with two storeys and many rooms and outbuildings, were owned by families with a lot of land, a lot of animals, a lot of things that needed storing. The very simple houses were those of the poor. There was no point in their adding on more 'rooms' – there would have been nothing much to put in them. Between the two extremes, the mud-brick construction allowed for a great range of types and styles, to suit any need. If the family owned a large enough site, it could go on adding bits at will; or it could divide the site between two of its children, and, like cellular fission, make two units where one had been before.

In the 1940s, the villagers had become a little wealthier, and started to build a different kind of house. In particular, as tractors came to replace large draught animals, the traditional walled-off courtyard was abandoned. Mud bricks were still used, but they were now given a smooth coat of plaster, about an inch thick, which in turn was whitewashed. Often these houses consisted of four rooms around a central 'hall', into which front and rear doors led. But instead of a beaten earth floor, they had glazed concrete. As time went on, people began to build kitchens, with plumbed-in cold taps and a built-in concrete washing-up area around the sink; they also now had a single unshaded electric light bulb hanging in each room.

From the mid 1960s the third 'generation' of village house was built in a new industrially made red-fired brick, and looked as modern as anything to be seen in a postwar British 'new town'. One cheap variant had a sloping red-tiled roof, but was rather four-square and box-like. The more attractive and expensive type was oblong, with a stylish flat roof, like other Mediterranean house-styles, and its finish was in smooth white, not red, bricks.

Argaki: generations of houses.

But these new houses were, in my opinion, strange in one respect: they had little or nothing about them which made them part of an *agricultural* village. True, the new houses each had a small garden filled with persimmon, mandarin, and lemon trees, and other flowering or fruiting plants – for, in spite of their 'perms', *romantika* magazines and new gentility, the farmers' daughters still had green fingers. But the new houses did not stand in walled courtyards, there were no draught animals, the pigs and goats had disappeared. There was no longer an agricultural need for larger houses. Moreover, building land had become very expensive, and the big courtyard of the past could contain three or four of the red box-houses. Although most of the new houses did not please my eye, their owners liked them well enough, and they would last much longer and require less upkeep than the mud-brick ones. They were hotter in summer and colder in winter than the old houses, but there were solar heaters for water, gas fires, and electric fans. I only once heard anyone from Argaki regret the passing of the old houses, and that was a schoolteacher who lived in Nicosia.

The changes to be seen in the house styles were also reflected in other things, such as clothes. The clothing of the elderly was entirely different from that of the young, as if two quite distinct groups of people, or people from two very different historical periods, had got mixed up together. It was not as if the young of today would in thirty years' time wear what their fathers were wearing now – the different clothes were not part of a life-cycle of movements from one style to another linked one.

Old men often wore heavy boots which came to the top of the calf; these looked unfashioned, as if they had been cut and sewn for men who cared not a bit for appearances, but only for long, hard use. Above such boots there would be a few inches of brown skin, and then the first lampblack folds of heavy cloth, the falling edges of *vratches* (breeches), the baggy trousers celebrated by English writers on the Levant. Instead of two slim tubes around the legs, *vratches* hung like a loose kilt, with many extra tucks and folds. They were made by taking a strip of doubled cloth eight yards long and two feet wide and winding it skilfully round and round the hips in folds, gathered in a little at the crotch. Above the waist was worn a rough white long-sleeved shirt, and over it a black waistcoat. Around the head there was often a strip of cloth, called a *kourouli*, loosely tucked up, and worn to keep the sweat from falling into the eyes, variants of which could be found all over the Middle East and Asia.

The men of middle years tended to look as if they had been outfitted from clothes the British Army no longer had much use for, and since many of them had soldiered in this army in the Second World War, it seemed as if they wished to keep the memory of that membership alive. They might wear a khaki woollen stocking cap, particularly in winter, a battle-dress tunic in khaki or dark serge, or a European sports jacket, usually rather worn. Khaki or dark slacks ran down to a lighter, parade-ground army boot. ·

As the British, the latest bearers of European influence, had come to affect the towns of Cyprus, the youngest men in Argaki favoured tailored slacks, styled shirts, and 'sharp' two-piece suits with light town shoes. They appeared both 'European' and 'urbane' at the same time. But European influence was not entirely new: the Greek words for both 'shirt' (*poukamiso*) and 'trousers' (*pantalonia*) seemed derived from French origin-als, and certainly 'Frankish' clothes had for a hundred years or more in the Greek world been a sign both of a certain modish 'modernity' and perhaps of a certain moral failing, a falling from Greek customary grace.

When, about 1940, the first Argaki youngster had worn a short-sleeved shirt, it had raised quite a few eyebrows. It had been Varellas, a shepherd turned livestock merchant; his son-in-law, my cousin Tomas, said, in praise of him, 'He was always ahead of the times.' It must always have been a gamble in the village to be the first to try anything new, because inward-looking communities tend to produce such a high degree of conformity. Perhaps everyone would laugh at you, but perhaps they would rush to copy you in a few months, or a year. Perhaps the one response would be followed by the other.

The women too exhibited at least three 'generations' of clothing style. Elderly women and those who had suffered bereavement wore a black headscarf, hiding all their hair, and tied tightly around the brow and under the chin, with black cotton or wollen tunics from neck to wrist and waist, and a skirt which went to the ankles, with long stockings beneath it. Only the face and the hands were free from black covering.

The middle-aged women, those as yet unmarked by mourning, wore a brown chiffon headscarf trimmed with crimson lace and a white pattern, which allowed a few strands of hair to appear. It was not tight around the brows and chin, and sat above the nape of the neck, on top of the head. It was called a *tchemberi* (kerchief). The colour and pattern seemed the same all over the village, a minor puzzle in itself. These women wore dark skirts, reaching to just below the knees, usually brown, though other dark shades were also worn. They might wear coloured blouses or ones with dark floral prints, usually with a half- or three-quarter-length sleeve.

The younger married women and unmarried girls liked floral print dresses, with quarter-length-sleeves which revealed most of the upper arms, and opened to show a small triangle of flesh at the neck. Their skirts, styled to suggest a slender waist, might stop just above the knee; their blouses could be pink, white, or light blue without causing gossip. They went bare-headed as a rule, and indulged themselves by having their hair done in thick rolled curls or beehive *bouffants*; several young women in the village had learned the art of, and made a modest income by, hair-dressing.

Ploughs and tractors

As with houses and clothes, change was evident in everything to do with working the land. The tractor had easily conquered the flatlands around

Argaki, making really rapid headway after 1945; and so, by 1968, it was unusual to see anyone working with the ox or donkey team and the light wooden scratch-plough, the direct descendant of the Roman *ard*. Those who still happened to have a plough might hitch it to a donkey or two for certain small weeding tasks, but the oxen had gone and the odd ones still kept in Argaki were regarded as curiosities, almost living antiques, like prewar cars in Britain today. The ploughs themselves were still to be found, covered in weeds and nettles in some corner of the courtyard, or hooked up on nails on a mud-brick outhouse wall, the dun wood almost invisible on the dun wall unless you were really looking for it or saw its darker shadow; the single steel tooth (rounded and thin, shaped like a platypus bill) would be rusting. Ploughs like this were still in use only in the foothills and mountain villages, where land was too steep, too stony, or too enclosed by trees and scrub for the tractor; or, more simply, where the farming was too poor ever to carry its cost.

In the past a rich household would have owned a yoke of oxen, while a middling one would have had perhaps one beast and would have sought another household in the same situation, to team up for ploughing. Poorer households would have had to make do with donkeys. Unless one had a substantial land-holding the expense of owning and feeding oxen would not have been worth while.

In Argaki in 1968 the pride of possession which men had felt over their oxen was usually transferred to their tractors. The younger men, and even those below fifty who fancied themselves as coming up in the world, often roared through the village on their tractors much faster than was necessary, especially when they were on their way to the coffee shops, where they would brake very sharply, switch off and spring from the wheel, getting their bottoms onto a chair before the diesel motor had quite died – for all the world like the cowboys they watched in the Morphou movies dropping from the saddle, hitching the horse, and slipping into the saloon all in one movement. Indeed, they boasted to anyone who would listen that the rest of the region called their village 'Little Texas', and they certainly played up to the name in a number of ways.

Cheese and bread

Not that the tractor and its cult could drive out the short-handled hoe, for many of the new and profitable cash crops, such as carrots and potatoes, needed intensive hand weeding. The citrus saplings in their second year needed grafting, which called for skill with a special knife, to slit the graft from a twig with a single deft stroke and bind it with raffia into place. Donkeys were still used for bringing home wild fodder to the goats, of which most households still kept three or four, although the more gentrified families had recently deliberately taken to not keeping them, and telling one so. Most of the donkeys were under the charge of youngsters, women, or the elderly; young and middle-aged men were rarely to be seen leading, much less sitting on, them.

The goats were kept chiefly to provide milk for *halloumi*, the Cypriots' favourite cheese. This could also be made from sheep's milk, but sheep were herded in large flocks by professional shepherds. To make their cheese, the women teamed up with about ten neighbours (who were often also friends and relations) to form a *parea*, a 'company' of people informally associating on good terms. Each woman took it in turns, over a week, to receive from the others sufficient litres of milk to make enough cheese to last for several months. If the women did not pool their milk in this way they would have been unable to produce enough cheese from their own milk supply to make it worth while to carry out the slow and taxing processes involved in making the cheese. Certainly, no woman would have cared to do it every week. The *parea* was the simplest and most sensible form of co-operation to be found in the village, and woe betide the woman who lost her good name by watering her milk, or failing to meet her daily obligations smartly. She would soon find she wasn't welcome in the *parea*. Of course, the day's gossip whirled around these *pareas* much faster than the milk turned into cheese, and, given the semi-secluded status of women in the villages, if the *pareas* hadn't existed, the women would have had to invent something similar.

Although women still made their own cheese, they had virtually stopped making bread. To go from corn to flour to bread in the old way involved a long chain of actions: sowing, reaping, threshing, winnowing, sifting, grinding, kneading, and baking. Just as the scratch-ploughs were now unused, so was the threshing-board, a kind of sled with sharp flints fixed in its base, on which the thresher sat, and which was driven round and round for hours on a circular threshing-floor by a donkey. The heat, dust, and chaff, hour after hour, must have been tedious, and it took many days to thresh enough corn for one household.

The threshing-boards now mouldered in the courtyards. Also forgotten was the hand-mill for grinding the corn. This was a flat stone circle, with a wooden spindle set in the centre, on top of which sat a second domed stone, with a hole in the middle to admit the spindle below. The upper dome was turned on the lower circle by a single handle, and it was slow work. People laughed softly when these old implements were brought to their attention, and would start to describe how bread used to be made. No one now kept it up out of sentiment; no one had a small plot of land for growing corn from which home-made bread could be produced for one day a week. The old methods were demanding of labour, and for most households traditional bread-making was an all-or-nothing affair. There was now a large-scale commercial bakery in Morphou, producing bread that was delivered to Argaki twice daily in a motor-bus, which took only minutes to make the three-mile journey. One woman in Argaki made ninety loaves a day by hand, which she sold to the wealthier families; it cost more than the Morphou bread, but it tasted better too. She and her daughters worked hard to do this, from sunrise to noon. Other people still made their own bread two or three times a year for the big festivals, but now using machine-milled flour. In 1950, 24% of the village land had been under wheat, and another 19% under barley and oats, even though four-fifths of the land was by then irrigated in summer and more profitable crops might have been grown. The old pattern was at the time still in force and the citrus boom had not yet begun, in spite of the example of a few pioneers. But the growing of more profitable cash crops, particularly vegetables and, more slowly, citrus fruits, was every year making the old agriculture based on producing food for the household less attractive. The new money generated by these cash crops allowed tractors to replace oxen, and the way was thus open for many changes in production and consumption. By 1968 very few people grew cereals, and, except for special holidays, all households purchased bread daily.

Living standards

In so many ways living standards in Argaki had improved markedly in the last hundred years. Bit by bit, infant mortality had been brought down, malaria and TB virtually eradicated, doctors and rural dispensaries increased; generally, standards of health, hygiene, and diet, education, and personal security improved. The old days had often been the *bad* old days, as I learned from the life history of a gentle, quiet man who had watched four of his brothers and sisters marry, and each die of TB within a few years of the wedding. They had been treated, sometimes for a year at a time, in the costly private clinics of Nicosia physicians, and field after field had been sold to pay the bills. So he had seen both his family and its considerable fortunes destroyed at the same time. No wonder the villagers dreaded TB; the children of any family hinted to be cursed with it would be avoided as marriage partners by anyone who knew, and would have to accept as a spouse either a poor person, one with some physical or social blemish, or an uninformed outsider. No wonder all parents wanted their children to look plump and robust. Never mind if they got fat; that was healthy. It was the lean and hungry look which augured death.

People had a good sense of the changes which had occurred; at the age of fifty Tomas remembered how he'd had head lice as a boy: 'We *all* did. I remember I was at the barbers, having my hair cut really short just like we do with the kids today, and as he cut it off, I could see little red marks appearing all over my head. We haven't had lice here for years, now.' So too with meat-eating: old men were always eager to tell me how, when they had been young, 'People were poorer, much poorer. We worked from sunrise to sunset just for the price of a loaf of bread; and as for meat! – we ate it *twice a year*, Christmas and Easter, if we were lucky.' By 1968 most Argaki families expected to eat meat at least twice a week, and many did so every day.

Some changes were accomplished very quickly. For example, the villagers used to cook with wood, but it was costly to buy and hard to find near the village. So when in 1962 HajiPavlis, an Argaki merchant, introduced gas bottles and simple burners into the village, every family began using them within a year or two. No more time was wasted in foraging for wood, and since the gas was really cheap, if you didn't take advantage of it, everyone said what a donkey you were. Nevertheless, at Christmas and Easter, when women still baked their own bread in the domed mud ovens in the courtyard, they still needed wood or charcoal.

But other transitions, such as giving up the self-sufficiency of mixed farming and becoming a market farmer, might take twenty years of stopping and starting; and the old patterns still held in the minds of those too old to change their thinking. Aunt Stylou, widow of my father's brother, Zenon, could never get over not producing her own olive oil. In 1950 there were still 2,000 olive trees on the village land: a house which was self-sufficient in oil would have owned ten or a dozen trees. At that time Aunt Stylou had many more than that. But I remember her in 1970 looking at her three *leminzanes* (demijohns), each one holding about twenty-five litres, and grumbling to anyone who would listen that we were half-way through the *second* one, and it was still a long time to go till the olive harvest. At which her son-in-law, a chemistry graduate from Birkbeck (by night), said, 'Come on, mother-in-law: if we run out of oil, we'll just go to the co-op and buy some more. *They* won't run out.' But although this was rational and sensible, Aunt Stylou shook her head over the idea. Well-founded families ought never to need to *buy* olive oil, it wasn't *done*. And the fact that it *was* now done, by everyone, only made it worse.

One other indication that people saw many things as 'getting better' lay in their attitudes towards having children. Their grandparents might have had eight or ten brothers and sisters, or be among the few survivors of a dozen or more pregnancies, but few infants now died in Argaki and young parents were ready to say that four children would be quite enough for them, although there were still some who said, 'We'll have as many as God sends.' Since people hoped and planned to provide their children with a good education, and either a white-collar job or a good land-holding (or, rarely, both), there was no longer a great deal of sense in having very large families.

The youngsters were kept in school for longer and longer (sometimes to their real distress if they lacked aptitude), and almost no one in the village under forty was unable to read or write. Argaki had recently produced two doctors, as well as a dentist, a lawyer, and some senior civil servants, with several more of each on the way. A university education became something the wealthier or brighter youngsters could expect, and it afforded an interesting alternative to being a farmer. It could be paid for on a month-by-month basis, which made it easier in all sorts of ways than buying land; and unlike money, land, or friends, an education could not be lost overnight in a card game or in a drought. The sort of proverb the villagers tended to quote – 'Learn a skill and hang it on the wall until you need it' – doesn't travel very well, but the sense is clear enough.

Social distinctions

When referring to the different social positions of village families, people spoke of *i plousii* ('the rich'), *i archontes* ('the people who run things'), *i kali* ('those who are doing well') or *i metrii* ('the middling people'), and *i phtochi* ('the poor'). These collective plural nouns described families – the men, women, and children of a household; and since women owned property in their own names, often more than their husbands or brothers did, this joint description of a family position was precise. However, in other contexts, people tended to speak as if the occupation of the male household head was a key criterion of family status, with the family's wealth being understood or taken as read; some official documents in the village showed all the household's land in the name of the husband, even though sometimes all of it was legally owned by his wife. In public life, men represented women in most official contexts.

To make sense of social distinctions in the village, I had to go beyond the classifications the villagers used, since they varied from one context, and speaker, to another, and were often attempts to place the speaker above someone else, or to deny the wealth or poverty of another family. For my purposes, and for simplicity, I combined the family land-holdings with the occupation of the male household head, ignoring the occupations of wives (since few wives earned steady wages, or had better-paid jobs than their husbands) and of unmarried sons and daughters.

About 10% of the household heads formed an emergent class, the highly educated, who were now teachers or middle-range civil servants. Their salaries were secure and they also had, often by marriage, solid land-holdings which they worked chiefly by hired day-labourers.

Then there were the farmers proper, who formed 40% of the village, men with enough land to keep them fully occupied. Farming was now so profitable that these men were often at least as well off as the educated group, but they knew they lacked the sophistication of the latter, and were happy enough to give them their daughters in marriage, along with sizeable portions of their land.

About 30% of the householders were skilled men, such as carpenters, builders, plumbers, electricians, mechanics, and the men who owned tractors, bulldozers, trucks, or buses which they worked for hire. They often had useful land-holdings, but needed to sell their labour to make a decent living. Because of this need to work for others, and the related insecurity of competing on the labour market, they felt themselves inferior to the solid farmers.

The remaining 20% of the village inhabitants were labourers and shepherds, men who had their special skills but were not honoured with the title 'skilled', and who earned less, per hour, than the skilled men. The shepherds might manage to make a good living – cheese and milk prices always seemed buoyant – but only by putting in very long days, usually from sunrise to sunset, which constituted many hours in the Mediterranean summer.

Of these Argaki households fewer than 2% had started marriage without some land, and every family owned a house, however modest, so there was no significant group of families with nothing at all. There could be no argument about the differences between those at the top and those at the bottom, on whom the former looked down – all agreed that a large gap existed – but any family could contest vigorously the claims of those close to it in wealth, education, and reputation, and small differences were keenly felt, and counted for much. And even though the rich often had close kin among the poorest, and blood ties were supposed to bind up the wounds of class, nevertheless the poor were very conscious of their poverty, probably all the more sharply so because the village, generally, was prospering. In fact in material terms, this was probably to their advantage – there was a fairly steady demand for their labour on the lands of those men with more land than they could manage themselves. If these employers were wise, they not only paid poor labourers a good wage, but would entertain them with meat and brandy from time to time, to ensure their future availability. But poverty is more than a level of consumption alone, and if the Argaki poor were materially better off than the mountain villagers, they were spiritually at a disadvantage; they were at the bottom in a flourishing, flamboyant community, in which others were prone (when half-way through a bottle of brandy) to bang on the table and remind everyone in the tavern that they had started life with nothing, but through hard work, thrift, and intelligence had got somewhere.

However rich, middling, or poor, a man and wife found their greatest satisfaction less from their own possessions than in the achievements of their children and the marriages that were arranged for them. A family's final resting-place in village public opinion could be established only when its last child had been married off. Were the sons-in-law professionals? White-collar men? Labourers? Farmers? Did the daughters have fine dowry-houses and hundreds of orange trees? Or jerry-built cheapjack houses and just a few seedlings to keep up appearances?

Weddings were *the* social events of the village calendar, and every family was supposed to send one representative and cash gifts of at least several pounds. A good wedding in the early 1970s could bring in over £1,000 in cash presents for the young couple.[1] And if it was a wedding of successful, rising families, the mothers of the bride and groom would sing praise-songs to their own children, and for their own families.

In 1972 my Aunt Stylou Pipis sang such a song at the wedding of her daughter, Peva, who, on becoming a primary school teacher, had been able to take a loan from her professional association to build her impressive dowry house – hence the reference below to 'her golden hand'. Aunt Stylou Pipis singled out in her song the achievements of her four eldest children for attention:

> The astronauts today
> go as far as the moon
> praised be my Maker
> who has given me such joy.
>
> I've had six children
> and they're all educated
> not one below the mark
> they're all outstanding.
>
> I've had six children
> and not one wrong'un
> one is an auditor
> one a land-office man.
>
> And deep down in my heart
> today is greatest joy
> now my Maroulla's come
> my highschool teacher.

---

[1] All references to money in the text are to the Cyprus pound (£), which in 1975 was worth approximately 25% more than the British pound sterling.

For my two daughters
are better than other folks'
I've a highschool teacher
and a primary teacher.

. . .

It was the wish of God
that these two should be one
and she built her house
with her golden hand.[1]

Women, men, and matchmaking

The ways in which women and men regarded each other and the marriage system were very much less visible than houses, clothing, and farming methods, and took much more time to understand; indeed to this day there is much in these matters which still eludes me. It was easy enough to remark the absence of women from 'public life' – the coffee shops and the square – but that might simply have been due to the demands of housework. The deeper meaning of that absence came through to me only slowly, like the ghostly image of the photographic print appearing in the developing bath.

There were, none the less, clues. One evening I was strolling with a young unmarried cousin, and suggested we might visit a certain house. He said he would prefer not to; there might be misunderstandings. I was baffled. Eventually he explained, 'They have an unmarried daughter, and if I go to their house people might think I was interested in her.' Later, I began to notice how, if men approached a house at night, they made a great deal of noise calling out in hoarse, loud voices, or forcefully banging on the wooden doors. If they moved too silently they were up to no good, were prospective thieves of its wealth, its honour, its secrets.

Mealtimes afforded other clues. In most houses the women never spoke to me at meals before I spoke to them, and did not sit to eat with the men but hovered between kitchen and table, bringing new dishes. 'They are shy' was the only explanation I could get, and it made little sense. After meals, men at leisure did not sit and talk to their wives. They left smartly for the coffee shops. There was no question of 'keeping their wives company'; the proper company for a woman was other women, for a man other men. In fact it was said of some men, as a criticism, that they were 'men of the house, with no interest in public life and no opinions to

---

[1] This song is an abridged and revised version of the poem found in Davis 1977:186.

express'. The house was the place where women did most of their work, while men did most of their work 'outside', in the fields, or the towns, or in the politicking, the quest for intelligence, which occurred in the coffee shops while they were 'at leisure'. Neither men nor women were ever really off duty, for as vigilant, thoughtful family members, they were ever on the look-out for those tiny scraps of information which might serve towards the advancement of their own family, or, what was very nearly the same thing, towards the decline of another house. Of particular importance was information relating to marriage eligibility, since the matches made by its children contributed powerfully to a family's mobility. Women were especially prominent in matchmaking, although their husbands were always tactfully drawn into the discussions, and both sexes were used as go-betweens.

Another hint lay in the men's preference that their wives and daughters should not take on paid work, i.e. work for anyone but their family. A man who was doing well, as the sole provider, liked to boast, 'O, my wife has never been out to work.' Many families could not get by in this way, so then the problem was to make sure the women's work was acceptable, preferably in a group with other relatives, or working in the shop of a brother or cousin. Certain jobs were looked down on by all, such as nursing, which involved working among strangers, and coming into intimate physical contact with strangers; the 'service' element carried no honour – quite the reverse.

But despite these indications, my understanding came slowly. During my first visit some of my girl cousins asked if I would take them to the beach – they did not get out of the village much. I agreed, gladly. We set off and then I noticed something apparently wrong. 'Have you brought your costumes?' I asked. No, they hadn't. 'We'll just watch you swim', they said. To me, the whole idea of going to the beach in the August heat was to cool down by swimming, so I was baffled. Stasa, a dreamy girl married to my host and cousin, Pakis, explained:

> A couple of years ago I persuaded my father to take me and my sister to
> the beach, like the city girls do, and we put on bathing costumes. But as
> I was coming out of the water a boy said to me, 'O, you are very
> beautiful', and my father got angry and hit him with a bottle. So we
> don't like to put on costumes now – it makes for misunderstandings.

They laughed. 'Our fathers and brothers are jealous, and a little old-fashioned', they said.

There were other similar stories about Stasa's father, a handsome, serious man, prominent as a leader of the conservative farmers in Argaki. His wife had brought a very great deal of land to the marriage, and he added to it with hard work and shrewd purchases. He had seven daughters to marry off, but no sons to protect their virtue. One day while Stasa was at secondary school, an Argaki boy had told her he liked her; Spiros had got to hear of it, and had beaten the lad quite soundly to show the world that his daughters were not to be treated with less formality and respect than anyone else's. He had done such things two or three times earlier in his life. Yet in other respects he seemed a calm and reasonable man.

Eventually the image became clearer. 'We hope we are Europeans in most things', said an uncle, 'but in matters of honour – that is, where our women are concerned – we are happy to be Middle-Easterners.' This meant to him and others that no Argaki woman could ever properly know socially a man to whom she was not married. Unmarried girls should, where possible, be kept innocent of any contact with boys or men who were not their blood kin, and, since other men were always out not only to have fun but also to destroy the honour of their social competitors, a man should keep his women protected from any dangers of seduction or violation. Men believed that women were so little in control of their animal passions that they were very easily seduced, and that all a really skilful man needed to do to have his way with one was to be alone with her for a while in a quiet place. This view credited men with great powers of persuasion and women with great sexual frailty, but it fitted closely with other local beliefs. Nevertheless, sexual mores were changing, too. For at least a generation it had been common enough for a young man who had entered into a formal engagement to sleep secretly with his beloved in the two or three years before marriage. One of my cousins, a man in middle age, laughed as he recalled how he had outwitted his fiancée's mother, and his own mother, on the morning after the wedding. They came to make the traditional inspection of the nuptial sheets, for proof of the girl's virginity, and were easily satisfied with the drops of chicken's blood they were shown.

Everyone was expected to marry, and families regarded the arrangement of a marriage as a task requiring the most careful consultation and calculation. A marriage was not a matter of two young persons' deciding they wished to spend the rest of their lives with each other – that was merely one final outcome of it. It was more a matter of a family deciding that they had sufficient money and property available to marry off a son or daughter, then of making secret enquiries to narrow down the possible partners to a small number who resembled them in health, wealth, social position, and family honour. Then, and only then, by very delicate and still utterly secret diplomacy, they enquired whether the match was acceptable to the other family. A refusal unless *very* tactfully handled was considered to be a social snub. The family that refused the match was supposed to keep the child in question unmarried for at least a year after the rejection, so initial enquiries had to be managed by a man or woman who would couch a proposed match in such a hypothetical, conditional form that a rejected family could maintain that it had never in fact been interested. Of course, property was a vital consideration in such negotiations and many a promising match broke down over who would give what to whom.

In the old days, parents had made the matches more or less while their children slept. Boys and girls alike were told whom they were to marry, and that was that. Many an elderly woman chuckled as she told me how she woke up one morning and her father said, 'We engaged you last night.' 'To whom, papa?' 'To the son of so-and-so.' 'And', the old lady would add, 'I didn't know what he looked like, or who he was – I had never seen him, and when he came to the house I felt very shy and ran off to hide. In those days we were secluded – *chonoumasteh* – not as today.'

In the 1920s when my father was still living in the village, he had tried to be 'modern'. Since he was a teacher (even though a primary school teacher) he was shown respect by the villagers, and when he went into a coffee shop, all the men, even those old enough to be his father or grandfather, stood up as a mark of this. He was regarded as a modern young man, in touch with things civilised, urban, and carrying some of

The approach to the church, from the square. The Kyrenia foothills are just visible.

the derived authority of the British. However, there were limits. A young woman was sent to the village as a teacher. There was a wedding in the village, and my father, knowing what was modern and progressive in Nicosia, asked the young woman to dance. Greatly to her credit, she accepted. No one had ever seen a man and woman dancing together before, in the European fashion where the man holds the woman, and the astonishment was widespread. My father came off the dance floor feeling he had cut a bit of a dash, only to be seized roughly by his father, the priest, and his Uncle Tirkas, a very hard-nosed old traditionalist. They took him aside, and held him against a wall, squeezing his arms. 'If ever', they told him harshly, 'you insult our family again by doing a thing like that, we'll give you enough stick to finish you off.' They were very, very angry, and my father did not again dance with a woman in the village.

There were three formal situations in which boys and girls did manage to see something of each other. One was at church, another was at weddings, and a third was at 'the swings'. In the winter, people used to come together in high-roofed houses, and set up large swings, into which groups of boys or girls would climb in turn, and swing back and forth singing songs, while everyone watched. People said it was a chance to see others of the opposite sex, but there was no conversation between the sexes, and sometimes fights broke out between the young men over imagined or real insults. Of course, said my Uncle Pelekanos, 'There were ways of telling a girl with your eyes that you were interested in her.' He was reputed to have won his bride by simply announcing that any boy who married her would have to answer to him, and as he was immensely strong, and had successfully wrestled an ox to its knees, other suitors were obliged to retire. This story also gave a hint at another recent development which had occurred in the last two generations. Young men had acquired a right of veto, even of proposal. That is, instead of a father saying 'You're going to marry X's daughter', the young man could say, 'Father, would you agree to our asking for Y's daughter?' Or, more boldly yet, 'Father, I really don't want to marry Z's daughter, and respectfully hope you won't force me to.' Naturally, the poorer the parents the less they had to hold over a young man's head; young men often being as strong as their fathers, it would have been very hard for the latter to beat a son to the very steps of the church. For girls, the right of proposal had not arrived, and a veto was available only to the more privileged or pampered daughters.

The real sanction was less force than moral pressure. It would take a strong-minded youngster to stand out against the wishes of mother, father, and older married brothers and sisters, all insisting on the quality of the match. In village life, people rarely spoke of themselves as individuals in the existential sense. They saw themselves more as members of families.

There was one feature of the matchmaking system which at first seemed extraordinary, and this was the speed with which a newly engaged couple appeared to fall in love before my eyes. Couples were being 'matched' by their families, on the basis of a handful of qualities, and were usually comparative strangers to each other. A man expected his wife to be hard-working, faithful, a good mother and housekeeper; a wife expected her husband to be hard-working, a good provider, and a defender of the family and its interests in all public situations. That was, in local theory, enough to make good, solid, enduring marriages. People were emphatically *not* getting married because of grand passions, or of a meeting of true minds, or at the end of a quest for spiritual harmony. Yet, within a few days of the engagement, sometimes within an hour or two, the young people would give all the signs of having fallen in love. The boy would insist that he had to see his fiancée every day and she would share this insistence; the girl would be given to blushes and sighs, in both her betrothed's presence and absence; they would sit near to each other, holding hands, and pose for a formal photograph literally cheek-to-cheek.

There had, of course, always been a few luckless individuals who had fallen in love in spite of the matchmaking customs. Such things could be gleaned from popular songs and poems, and, indeed, stories about the old days in Argaki. Nevertheless, in the Greek villagers' opinion, to fall in love was something akin to being struck down by a disease, and was likely to lead to no good. 'Beauty cannot be eaten with a spoon', a young teacher friend of mine was told by his labourer father, after the son had fallen for a very beautiful but apparently indigent girl in Nicosia.

There was one story I particularly liked, about a gentle old man called Antonis, who fifty years earlier had been *muktar*, headman of the village. When he was young he had wanted to marry an Argaki beauty called (from her complexion) Kaisha, 'the apricot'. But she had been promised to another man, so he was obliged to marry someone else. Much later he became a widower, had children to be cared for, and was himself inclined to marry again. Now he had plenty of property, and Kaisha had a daughter, very like herself, of an age to marry. Antonis asked for her hand, and was given it. The middle-aged woman who told me this story clearly approved of its 'happy ending' and had no word to say against the girl's being married off to a man old enough to be her father.

One day a talkative, easy-going farmer, whose name I must not reveal, told me how, when he was single, he had wanted to marry a particular girl whom he really loved. His family was poor, and hers a cut or two above it, but he finally persuaded his father, against that man's better judgement, to ask for the girl's hand. Their suit was rejected, and he immediately married someone else, the usual village response to rejection being to get accepted elsewhere within twenty-four hours and announce it to everyone. 'Now I'm happily enough married today, but if I'm walking in the village and I meet that woman I wanted, even though it's twenty years ago, my heart still races as it did when I was twenty.' Few men were as outspoken as this, but from small hints, a sigh, a smile, a movement of the eyes to heaven, I was given to understand that many a mature man had felt such things when young.

People's memories were very long when it came to recalling who had asked for whose hand, and who had been passed over. There were even conventions about this. 'Two first cousins shouldn't both ask for the same girl in the same season', people told me. 'One should ask, and the other should wait to see, and only go later if the first one is refused.' Nor should anyone ever publicly refer to someone else's having been rejected. The full sensitivity of the whole matter was brought home to me by my complete failure to witness serious family discussions and negotiations over a match. When the winter season arrived a dozen of my best friends promised me that at the first hint of a match they would find me and involve me in the discussion. Night after night I sat disconsolately in the brightest coffee shop waiting to be called, but somehow, although they searched for me 'high and low', they could never find me at the crucial time. In the end in despair I tried to make a couple of matches myself, but inevitably these didn't come off. 'You need to be a bit of a crook, a con-man', people said to comfort me. They would readily tell me in detail about murders, thefts, their own debts and favours, but they kept me well back from first-hand contact with that most delicate matter, a match; and, given its importance in their lives and their right to privacy, I can hardly blame them.

Church spiritual and Church political (see Appendix 1, p. 192)

Everybody married in church. Even though there was a sizeable number of villagers – perhaps a third – who were communists, socialists, or called themselves 'modern' or 'progressive', and even though the men among them could be brought to say that they did not think God existed, that religion was largely superstition, that the Church owned far too much property and should care better for the poor, it was notable that no cases came to my knowledge of *anyone* – right, centre, or left – refusing to have his children baptised, to marry in church, or to have his old people buried by the priest.

It was well known that while many of the wives of the political leftists were usually willing to vote for the men their husbands suggested, unless (as had been the case in the presidential elections of December 1959) this involved voting against Archbishop Makarios, they found official atheism more difficult to accept than did their husbands. In fact, the latter also often looked uncomfortable when doubting God's existence, even when there was no fanatic traditionalist within earshot.

Most of the villagers, though, were unselfconscious yet serious about their religion, regarding its practice as 'natural'. They appeared unworried by dilemmas of faith and there was little reference to sin in daily conversation, although it was a lively enough idea with regard to serious matters. If prodded about belief, most villagers spoke as if God existed, and that was that, just as they knew that Nicosia existed.

Of course, there was one particular reason for the difficulty felt by the would-be secular rationalist in Cyprus. For nearly four hundred years there had been a sizeable Muslim Turkish minority in the island, at times conquerors, usually rulers, and lately fellow-citizens, pulling and tugging at the constitution and the division of patronage. The question, 'Are you a Christian?' was so easily confused in people's minds with that of 'Are you a Greek?' that it is doubtful if most of them ever distinguished the two, and it was therefore hard to answer in the negative. And for most people 'Christian' also meant 'orthodox'. The old ladies who asked me if *I* was a Christian knew little or nothing of Catholics and Protestants, and if I answered 'Yes' they assumed I was Orthodox. The Orthodox Church is nearly 2,000 years old, and regards Rome as its junior, although without the hostility that the Catholics felt to the Reformation and its progeny. It does not try very hard at conversion, as if its secure position among the Greeks and Slavs were enough, and indicated a 'chosen people'.

In spite of the leftists, therefore, the church was usually well attended on a Sunday morning. But although the service started at six in the morning most people would start coming in around eight o'clock, and it was only a few pious old folk who would be there for the full three hours. It was the same with fasting. There are well over one hundred days in the year when the Orthodox Christian is not supposed to eat meat, eggs, olive oil, and a number of other things, nor to drink alcohol. The two main fasts, at Christmas and Easter, each last well over a month, and if properly observed the person fasting is bound to lose weight and get quite weak if he is doing a hard day's work as well. But many of the middle-aged and younger men would not start fasting until five or ten days before Christmas or Easter. They would laugh, and say that they did heavy work; fasting was all right for the women and the old men. The women were generally more pious and punctilious, and most of them fasted more seriously, but there were a few who did not, and who shrugged and made rude remarks about the priests.

Argaki's church, Ayios Ioanis Prodromos. To the right someone has scrawled, 'Long Live the Three Bishops', prelates who rebelled against Makarios, and in 1973 declared that they had expelled him from his holy office. This was a political move in the campaign by Athens and EOKA B.

Village priests were usually married, and the celibate clerics were generally to be found in the monasteries. My father's father had been one of the Argaki priests; people said he had been well-liked as a man, but that he was not a very good priest – he was too fond of drinking and telling stories, and was not sufficiently devoted to pastoral care. Also, he could barely read and write. The priest when I was in Argaki was a fine-looking man from Kyra village, a few miles away, and he definitely had a calling. He had married the daughter of one of the wealthiest local farmers, so as well as working hard as a priest he had many acres to cultivate. He was often to be seen in his stovepipe hat and dark robe driving past the church on his tractor, and during the prelude to Easter he would be singing the liturgies for three hours every morning, and a couple of hours in the evening, as well as farming, all on a nearly empty stomach. In those weeks he used to look quite exhausted.

Like many Cypriot priests he was strongly identified with the nationalists of the political right wing; I can still recall my shock when on polling day in 1970 I saw that the organisers of the Progressive Party, a vehicle for right-wing men of EOKA (the armed Greek nationalist underground organisation), were using his house as their electoral headquarters. It was conveniently sited just across from the polling booth, in the primary school. It seemed odd to me that he could allow this. But just as the priest was also a farmer, and drove a tractor, so he was a political creature as well, with conservative–nationalist politics. Nor had the Cypriot Church ever pretended to be 'out of' politics or 'above' it. Indeed, how could they when throughout Byzantine history politicking had always been the life-blood of the Church's leaders, and when now the only rival nationalist leader to EOKA's Grivas was Archbishop Makarios himself, who, although he was never seen with a gun in his hands, could bring a hundred thousand people into Nicosia to hear him speak about the wish of Greek Cypriots for a political union with 'Mother' Greece. Who needs guns, if he has such power in his tongue?

There were many stories in Argaki about the fifty years of antagonism between the Church and the growing number of leftists in the village. My father had been the second man in the village to become a communist, in 1928 (and the twelfth on the island to join the Communist Party). After he had penned a few newspaper articles – one of which suggested that if the Church took Christ's teachings seriously, it would give out much of its land to the poor – he was called, in company with three other school-teachers, to a 'hearing' or trial organised at the Archbishopric. On the way he was pelted and insulted by some, and cheered by others, but when he arrived, he found his mother, the wife of the Argaki priest, on her knees before the Bishop, asking him to forgive her son, who 'didn't know what he was doing'. All four teachers then signed documents stating that they were Christians, and renouncing atheism. Bertrand Russell got to hear of this event, and wrote a piece in the *New Statesman* denouncing the 'medieval' trial which had taken place in a Crown Colony. The Church had got a law on to the colonial books saying that all teachers in Greek schools had to be practising Christians, and now it came in handy to discipline these young rebels. The other three seem to have taken it in their stride, but my father felt he had betrayed his ideals and the Party, and left the island within a few weeks, not to return for nearly forty years.

His nephew Tomas grew up hearing stories about him and about Haji

Matteos, the wealthy farmer much given to reading, who had introduced
him to leftist ideas, as well as about how the old men had been puzzled
that the two best-read men in the village should have become atheistic
leftists. Later Tomas, aged ten or twelve, was in Nicosia with his father
and saw a man being pelted with eggs and fruit. 'Why, father?', he asked.
'Because he is a *communist*', his father replied. 'And I thought to myself,
what a terrible thing it must be to be a communist, whatever *that* was, if
people were all so hostile to him.' Later, Tomas grew up to fight and
gamble and carry a knife or sometimes even a pistol, until he reformed,
and then too became a communist. His father, who was on the church-
warden's committee, was probably the man who supplied the Bishop with
a list of names of all the leftists in the village, so that when in about 1948
Tomas and his friends turned up to vote in the elections for the new
Archbishop, as they thought was their right, they found that they were
barred from the church, and their names struck off the electoral register –
appropriately in red ink, the colour of the highest ecclesiastical authority.

Unlike the previous generation, however, the leftists of the 1940s
retaliated. There is no collection or offertory in the Orthodox Church, so
worshippers, on entering the church, would normally pay out a few
copper *groschia* to buy a wax taper and light it later in the service. There
was a sidesman whose job it was to extinguish the tapers, which were then
melted down to make new ones and resold. The 'godless' leftists were still
churchgoers in those days and they now purchased their own tapers from
outside and brought them into the church, thus denying it a tiny source of
income. They saw this as an 'economic boycott'! Even more boldly, the
braver spirits among them refused to invite the priest to come and bless
the house in the annual ceremony of sanctification which drives away the
forces of darkness. Usually the priest would have been given a good meal
and a fee for this service.

Nevertheless, in comparison with the miniature civil war between the
rightists and leftists which was going on in some of the island's towns and
industries during the late 1940s this was fairly gentle stuff. For the most
part, people seemed to enjoy their religion, although it was clear that the
deeper Christian values were at odds with the cut-and-thrust of competitive, individualistic social life. For example, while lying was seen as
wrong, to lie in defence of the family was a virtue, as was sharp practice in
that same good cause. The family was so much the moral touchstone of
Greek life that when it came up against teachings which suggested loving
one's neighbour as oneself, then this part of Christianity had to be
mentally set aside. The Church, of course, smoothes over this rough spot
by giving great attention to the family, and suggesting that the earthly
family mirrors the Divine one. But clearly that myth has its origins in the

reverse situation: the Church has played up the Holy Family precisely because it cannot effectively combat the power of the earthly one, and 'family' is the most powerful metaphor we have for expressing love, commitment, and association.

As people grew older and saw their last children married off, they had more time and energy to take Christ's teaching increasingly seriously and without hypocrisy. One way this showed up was in their desire to visit the Holy Sepulchre in Jerusalem. This earned them the title 'Haji', for men, or 'Hajina' for women, meaning pilgrim, a title borrowed from the Arabic term for the Muslim Pilgrimage to Mecca. It became the one important last wish in an otherwise completed life. It seemed from the genealogies I took that it was more common to fulfil this wish in the recent past than it was in the present, but for this we will have to wait and see if the current generation of fifty-year-olds will make the Pilgrimage in ten years' time. Certainly it was the older people who were more interested in God, piety, and peace, and who, now they were facing the end of life, and might for the first time be faced with questions rather than unquestioned goals, were free at last to be concerned with such things.

At Easter, during the great midnight service, custom required that every person in the village come to church, and as the church was small and the village had grown, and since the long fast was coming to an end in an hour's time with a delicious meat soup, there was great excitement and a stronger sense of community than at any other time of the year, putting the commonplace and competitive weddings in the shade; every adult was supposed to look to see that all his close kinsmen were present, and to go to their houses and bring them in if they were not. In some parts of Greece every adult was supposed to embrace everyone in the village, but if this custom had once been observed in Argaki it was so no longer when I was there. But even without the physical embrace it was still a time of reconciliation and good will.

Watching the men and women kiss the ikons (males first, as in all else) it was easy to question the credulousness of village belief in painted pictures, vows and gifts to saints, visits to miraculous shrines, and the like. But people in the main seemed to enjoy their religion, to be untroubled by it, and comforted. They were hardly responsible for the political posture of the Church leaders, and the confusion of faith with nationalism.

Turks and Greeks

Argaki had been a nationally mixed village since before the British had arrived in 1878. The Greeks in Argaki believed that their ancestors had come as wage-labourers to what was, in effect, a Turkish village, before the middle of the nineteenth century. Certainly my own great-great grandfather (in the male line) had come as a wage-labourer about 1858. They believed that the incoming Greeks had worked hard, lived frugally, and either by buying land from their Turkish employers or by receiving it as gift in lieu of wages, had come to own most of the land, and to increase and multiply. This view so obviously fitted some of the Greeks' more general attitudes to the Turks that it might have been little more than a rationalisation of the 1968 *status quo*. They said the Turks had been 'lazy' and preferred leisure to manual work; but whether they held this view of the Turks before the latter started to lose control of their land-holdings is not known. From genealogies I found some instances of Turks having paid their Greek labourers in land gifts. I regret not having sought out the Turkish version of the village past, but in a moment the reader may come to see why I did not do so.

In Argaki relations between the Greeks and Turks had been generally peaceful, but there had been exceptions to this. The first happened (according to the old men) in the last days of Turkish rule, i.e. just before 1878, and occurred on the occasion of a Christian wedding. Some Turks came to the wedding, including one Turk from another village. He got drunk, and sat at the feast table commenting in a loud voice on the bride's beauty, and on how he would like to enjoy her. Such things are never done in the village – it was not even acceptable for one man in a coffee shop to say to another, 'What a lovely bit of stuff she is', if a local girl went by. Anyway, the Turk in his cups was far too outspoken, and three villagers came back for him later on, when no one was around. They struck him with the shaft of a cart, and he died. They buried him secretly, and the authorities never knew. Given the way things were in those days, and the other murders I heard of, this man was not killed *because he was a Turk* but because he had disgraced the bride's kinsmen. It was private, not intercommunal, violence.

The second exception occurred much later, about 1912. Since the 1821 War of Liberation Greece had fought a succession of wars with Turkey, and in the Balkan wars of 1912–13 Greek Cypriots had volunteered to go and fight for 'Mother Greece'; one man from the village, Tomas' grandfather, had done this, and had died. At this time a certain Katalanos, a mainland Greek who was a nationalist agitator, had been touring the island making provocative speeches. He came to the vicinity of Argaki (the villagers said he came to the village itself), and made an anti-Turkish speech, inspired by which three of the tougher young men of the village set fire to the Turkish coffee shop. For this the colonial government sent the three to prison for ten years each. Katalanos was eventually expelled from Cyprus, for his continued agitation, in 1921, the centenary of Greek independence from Ottoman rule (Hill 1952:535).

In 1891, according to official census data, there were 329 Christians and

116 Muslims in Argaki. By 1911, though, the Christians numbered 423 and the Muslims only 97. Subsequently, the Greek population continued to increase while that of the Turks declined, until by 1960 there were 1,219 Greeks and 72 Turks. Over this same period the national censuses do not show anything like this dramatic shift: they move from roughly 75% Greeks and 25% Turks in 1891, to 78% Greeks and 18% Turks in 1960. I have found no reason for the particularity of the Argaki situation, and can only surmise that, given the great predominance of Greeks in surrounding villages, Argaki Turks came increasingly to look elsewhere for their futures.

Richard Patrick, a Canadian political geographer, has made a detailed study (1976) of the number of mixed communities in Cyprus in the recent past. He showed that between 1891 and 1931 the number of mixed communities declined dramatically, from 346 to 252. The reader should note, however, that there was no significant bloodshed between Greek and Turk *in Cyprus* in this period. There may have been the odd personal dispute, leading to violence, just as there was *within* each community, but nothing more notable. However, in the early twentieth century, as was mentioned earlier, there were several major wars between the Greek and Turkish *nation-states*, of which the Balkan wars of 1912–13 and the 1922 Asia Minor campaign were the most important. The latter resulted in heavy losses of life on both sides, and led to a major population exchange. It is at least plausible to suppose that the two communities in Cyprus drew apart in response to the tensions between their so-called 'mother-lands', as nationalist rhetoric insisted on dubbing them.

There was one other, local, reason, however. In Ottoman times the mass of Greeks in Cyprus had been subordinated both in custom and law to the Turks, who were in government. The British, on their arrival in 1878, came in as the new rulers over the heads of both communities, and, administratively, placed the Greeks and the Turks on the same level. But this meant 'raising up' the Greeks, and 'pulling down' the Turks, to the great delight of one, and the discomfort of the other. The Greeks began a long political campaign for Enosis, 'Union with Greece', a form of nationalist agitation which accompanied their own increasing economic and political emancipation. The Cypriot Turks opposed this from the moment the British arrived, and became supporters of British rule in a way similar to the 'Loyalism' of the Ulster Protestants today. Both Turks and Protestants preferred to be governed by a third party to whom they pledged allegiance, rather than risk possible domination by majorities in a new state.

The first major intercommunal killings in Cyprus took place in 1958, when EOKA had been in arms for three years. Many Greek Cypriots believe that, prior to that time, 'Greeks and Turks lived together in Cyprus like brothers', but the Argaki data show that this misses out the occasional significant violence, and there is no reason to think Argaki was exceptional.

Britain granted independence to the colony in 1960. By December of 1963, tensions between the two communities had led to a constitutional crisis, and fresh fighting arose, which continued sporadically in 1964 and 1965. At this time a large number of Turkish Cypriots entered enclaves, which were protected by their fighting men, and of which there were a number dotted all over the island. Some Argaki Turks left for the enclaves, but the majority stayed in the village; this was done voluntarily, not under compulsion from the Greeks. A UN Peacekeeping Force reached the island in 1964, and did a good deal to damp down local conflicts as they broke out. But in 1967 Grivas, the commander of the Greek Cypriot forces in Cyprus and as bitterly anti-Turkish as he was anti-communist, sought to re-establish the authority of the Greek Cypriot government over a Turkish-enclaved village at Kophinnou, and, when the local Turks objected, ordered a massive attack. This provoked Turkey to the point of invasion, but American shuttle diplomacy forestalled it, by securing the removal from Cyprus both of Grivas himself and of some thousands of mainland Greek soldiers illegally present on the island.

In early 1968, as I returned to Argaki to start serious research, there were still road blocks all over the island, and from time to time hundreds of rounds of small arms fire would be exchanged (usually harmlessly) between the militiamen in the towns. The military dictators had come to power in Greece, and I could sense considerable anxiety about the influence of the junta, its supporters, and the more extreme EOKA nationalists. I decided not to draw attention either to my research or to the Argaki Turks. If the EOKA hawks thought I was especially interested in what the Turkish minority in Argaki was thinking, they might intimidate either them or me, and block my future work. So while I always kept my eyes and ears open for anything which concerned the Argaki Turks, I never intensively interviewed them, which explains why I am unable to present their views in any detail. My contact with them was mainly limited to those occasions when a UN patrol, usually a couple of Australian police sergeants, would turn up to make enquiries about the Turks and I would be asked by the Greeks to translate. I would explain to the police that the UN couldn't take my word for the satisfactory conditions of the Argaki Turks, and would lead them to the Turkish schoolteacher, a very tense, nervous young man who did not seem to speak much English and was not from Argaki. He was a 'spy', some of the villagers told me, there to report back to Denktash, at the time a prominent Turkish Cypriot leader, on the situation in Argaki. If that really was one of his duties, then it was little wonder he seemed anxious.

At this time the Argaki Turks were about fifty in number, mostly elderly, rather poor, with a few small children; their young people had gone off to the Turkish Cypriot enclaves and did not visit them. They seemed quiet, even subdued in the face of the 1,500 Greeks in the village who, in addition to their far greater numbers, were also much wealthier.

So no matter how pleasant most of their Greek neighbours may have been, the Argaki Turks must have felt at risk. Elsewhere in Cyprus in the mid 1960s there were fierce, murderous clashes between militants of the two groups. Such militants existed in Argaki. In 1965 a few roughnecks did a certain amount of damage to some Turkish property in the village before being brought under control by more thoughtful villagers. In that year too the Argaki Greeks formed a volunteer militia led by the EOKA men, and started to prepare for action against the Turkish village of Ghaziveran, some ten miles away. Some had talked of driving the Argaki Turks out of the village, and these latter, getting to hear of the preparations against Ghaziveran and fearing the worst, assembled, terrified, in the house of one of their leaders. My cousin Tomas, a leader of the Argaki communists, heard about this and insisted that Fedonis, the senior EOKA leader, guarantee the Argaki Turks their safety, which he did.[1] Fedonis had been a best man at Tomas' wedding, and baptised one of his children.

Some of the younger Argaki Greeks saw their involvement in the 'national struggle' in terms of patriotism, and they were itching to do their bit against Turkish 'insurgents'. Their leaders would not allow hostilities against the Argaki Turks, however, whom they defined as 'harmless', 'innocent', and 'fellow-villagers'. But just because wiser, more humane counsels had prevailed once, was that much of a guarantee for the future security of the Argaki Turks? The idea of 'Turkish–Greek relations' was inevitably an abstraction, embracing thousands of similar local situations, many of equal complexity, and of Janus-like ambiguity. Yet nation and state, politics and government were in the long run bound to swamp all such local circumstances, to define each individual's private attitudes, so that only saints and martyrs could rise above the full force of communal antagonisms.[2]

But beyond the hostilities there had been – and sometimes still were –

[1] About this time, a grandson of one of the three Greeks imprisoned for burning the Turkish coffee shop decided in his cups to emulate his grandfather, and fired the mosque in Argaki. Cousin Tomas and friends quickly doused the blaze. I did not learn of this incident until September 1980. For more detail on this period see Loizos 1975:140–50.

[2] Paul Stirling made this point in a review of *The Greek gift*, in *New Society* 1975:31 (648).

many other forms of contact between the two communities. Some involved small courtesies. My father remembered that when he was a boy, about 1915, his mother would send him up on to the flat roof of the mud-brick house, to turn over the *trachana*, chunks of wheaten paste drying in the sun which would in winter make a nourishing porridge. They had Turkish neighbours, and it was considered proper as he climbed up to shout out 'Cover yourselves', so that the women next door could put up their veils, and so avoid the shame of being seen by a man, particularly a Christian.

He told me how *his* father, the old priest Papa Loizos, had gone to market one day to sell some produce, returning after sunset. A few hundred yards outside the village, he had needed to relieve himself, so he went in among the olive trees, and undid his clothes. In the course of this, he placed his handkerchief, with the money he had received from the market, on a flat stone. Being absent-minded, he then forgot the handkerchief, and returned home. My grandmother asked him how much the day's takings had been and he went to take out the money, only to find it gone. A terrible clamour woke the whole house, but he soon remembered where he must have left it and sped off with a lantern to look. But he had not made a special note of the spot where he had stopped and all olive trees look alike at night by lantern light. He searched in all directions, without success. What a fool he'd been. What an idiot to let down his family in this way. Priest? He wasn't fit to be a village *donkey*. A man with seven children, to behave like a boy without a moustache – worse; not one of his sons would have been so foolish.

Depression filled the household, and although everyone resolved to go looking as soon as dawn came, it was a poor hope. And indeed, they looked and found nothing. Such activity of course caught the attention of the village, and was something at which folk were inclined to laugh. They always thought the priest a scatter-brained man, more interested in telling yarns in the coffee shops than in getting on with providing for his family. Now they were proved right.

My grandfather felt the rough edge of his wife's tongue that day, and had no defence except to beat his breast. But towards evening a miracle occurred. A Turk called Osman[1] came to the house, and said to my grandfather, 'Priest, what have you lost?' 'A handkerchief with money in it.' 'Here is your handkerchief and your money', said the Turk. He had been irrigating in the fields, had seen the priest enter the olive grove, but had been too discreet to approach a man answering the call of nature. When my grandfather had gone, something white had caught his eye, and he had found the handkerchief on the tree stump. Since his work took him

[1]   The village bonesetter for both humans and livestock.

far away from the village, he had only now come home. My grandfather blessed him for his honesty. 'And you are a Muslim, not even a Christian, but you return me my money. You could have kept it and no one would ever have known.' 'You are a good man with many children,' replied Osman, 'and I too am an honest man.'

Inevitably, there was the occasional sexual scandal between Greek and Turk. For example, there was a Greek man called Bambos who fancied himself both as a tough character and as a lady's man. For a while he had an Argaki Turkish girl as a mistress; since the affair was not stopped by her family the girl could not have had any very capable male relatives. (Whenever a girl was seduced by some big shot, it usually turned out she came from a small, poor, weak family.) Eventually Bambos' wife got to hear of the affair and was duly upset. She took counsel from an elderly female relative who told her, 'There is a saint who can cast people out. Perhaps this saint will grant your wish and send this girl packing. Go and pray to the saint.' She did as she was told, and sure enough, after a little while the Turkish girl left Argaki, and Bambos returned, for the moment, to a properly monogamous existence.

Then there was an uncle of mine who, while serving as a young policeman in one of the towns, fell in love with a bar-girl, as many a young man had done before him. This girl happened to be Turkish. Nevertheless, my uncle, still little more than a boy and in the full heat of passion, was determined to marry her. One of his friends, having failed to discourage him, said, 'OK, marry her by all means, but hadn't you better bring her home and introduce her to your mother *first* and get her blessing?' My uncle was naïve enough to consider this as helpful advice. In due course, his beloved came to Argaki to meet his mother, who was both forewarned and forearmed: she drove the girl out with a broomstick, railing the while at the enormity of a match between a fine Christian boy and a woman who was not only a harlot, but a *Muslim* harlot to boot. Before he had time to reflect my uncle was married off to a Greek woman more than a dozen years his senior.

Another example of how something might easily go wrong between Turks and Greeks arose one day in 1969 when a gentle, placid shopkeeper at the co-operative grocery called me in. Holding out a small tin imported from China, with a label in English, he said ' "Luncheon-meat", it's the same as bully-beef, isn't it?' 'Why?' I asked. 'Just to be sure', he said. 'Luncheon-meat is usually pork', I told him. 'Pork is like lamb?' 'No – pork is another word for pig-meat.' He turned rather white. 'All-Holy Virgin! I've been feeding the Muslims on pig-meat.' It seemed that the Turks liked this particular brand of tinned meat, which, like the Greeks, they fried as a quick midday snack. The shopkeeper's grasp of English was slender, and, not having seen the word 'pig' on the tins, he had assumed that all was well.

'What am I going to do now? I can't go on giving it to them, but I can't tell them, either.' We thought for a while. Finally, we hit on a solution. He would simply stop stocking it from the central warehouse, and would tell the Turks and Greeks alike that it was no longer available. And he would look harder at all tinned meat from now on.

Progress?

At first I used to sit in an Argaki coffee shop, aware that there were sometimes fifty conversations going on around me, any one of which might contain crucial insights into the village, but I could follow only one and imperfectly at that. The sheer impossibility of ever catching, still less recording, all the things that went on in the village sometimes threatened to overwhelm me in those early days, until I accepted that most of what was happening would escape me, as it must all observers. The answer was not to try to grasp the flux of facts, but to look for shapes, patterns, regularities.

Perhaps the most striking pattern, and the one I could most quickly grasp, involved the speed of recent changes, and the fact that the lives of the young were clearly going to be rather different from those of their parents and grandparents. My thoughts were at first strongly influenced by the contrasting appearances between the old – shabby, dark, sombre, silent – and the young. I would watch my younger cousins studiously mopping their costly tiled floors or cooking in their well-appointed kitchens, or grouped together in a close, sweaty circle of several hundred women, watching bride and groom shyly perform the dance at which they were to be hung with £1 and £5 notes by kin and friends. I would watch the tanned, dark-haired men noisily playing cards or telling stories in the coffee shops, or calling out to each other across the square, 'Hey! Come here, I want you', or racing their tractors to and from the fields, so proud and busy. And I would watch their demure daughters, and sons with heads shaved to fair moleskin texture, both sexes neatly dressed and healthy, with the big-eyed gentle stare of rural children trotting off to school early in the morning. They nearly all seemed to share two things – an apparent happiness, and a fairly intense preoccupation with life in the village.

The last hundred years of Argaki's history had led up to this, but there was a different story to be read in the faces of the middle-aged and elderly, particularly the poorer ones, a story of care and suffering. Some of the questions I'd brought with me from England (in addition to the technical ones I was studying) were about the nature of progress and the quality of rural life, and how a booming village in Cyprus compared with the urban industrial life of Britain and America and Europe. In the end the answers did not lend themselves to a very straightforward reckoning.

The village now supported more people than it had done before, on better diets and in generally more comfortable circumstances. More land was being farmed than before, more productively and more profitably. People expected to live longer than their grandparents, and very few babies or their mothers would die as the outcome of pregnancy. Few people had been forced into migration; the poorest seemed to have left a generation before because they could not live decently in the village. More recently, the poorer migrants expected to return, buy land, and take a more dignified place in the village. All along a few people had left because they felt cramped by Argaki. But now people of both sexes could read and write, travel easily all over the island and abroad, and expect to have a much greater say in whom they married than had their parents or grandparents. Though women were still notably very much in the hands of fathers, brothers, and husbands, they were living markedly more adventurous lives than the old ladies who told me how they had hidden themselves the first time their fiancés came to see them. Some of my women cousins had been to university in Greece, and one, Eleni, had a senior position in the Ministry of Education, and hob-nobbed with government ministers.

There was also now a new class forming in the village, chiefly composed of the teachers and civil servants, who felt they had been profoundly changed by their education, and were not willing to sit in the coffee shops drinking brandy and eating clay-baked goat meat with their fingers. They complained of the farmers, labourers, and truck-drivers, the gambling, the swearing, and the spitting of their kinsmen, and wanted to form their own exclusive social club for more 'serious' leisure activities; but the people they excluded would have been their own fathers and brothers.

A poor family could pay to educate a child by the month or the quarter, and this was much easier than slowly saving up the lump sums needed to buy land. Access to education appeared to offer better life chances to the poorer villagers; there was only so much land, and if you bought the piece I wanted, then I had lost it. Rich families could own a great deal more land than they needed for a simple life, and they could pay for expensive educations, but they could not accumulate empty places in the secondary schools. Even though the unemployed graduate had begun to appear in Cyprus by 1970, education still seemed to offer hope of an escape from the narrowness of poverty.

But there was another less attractive side to education, and this was the sense of superiority it gave to the people who obtained it, implied by the Greek word *morphosis*, which hints at a change in form, if not in essence. It seemed to result in a downgrading of the many skills possessed by peasant households. Villagers insisted that they were *just* villagers, and the word they used sounded both on their lips and those of the townspeople like 'yokel' does on ours. 'We don't know *anything*', people said; but they obviously all knew a very great deal. The history books suggested that this sort of feeling had been present in Greek culture since the first city-states had produced an urban literate elite, but it was now being brought home to the village very forcefully. In the 1960s blood had nearly been shed over whether the village was to have a 'Graduates' Club', whether a new measure of success was to be crystallised in a village institution.

The younger people seemed to me, and to themselves, a good deal less mistrustful, competitive, and quarrelsome than did their grandparents, and for this they tended to credit higher education. 'Our minds are broader. We understand things better', they said. But it was by no means certain that their education in itself was responsible, for they had lived, in the main, much safer, better-fed, and more rewarding lives than those who had been young in the depression of the 1930s, or earlier. Besides, not all the youngsters were so well-disposed to the world: some had taken to going out at night with machine-guns, to overthrow President Makarios. The economic boom had super-charged most people's aspirations, and many youngsters were deeply dissatisfied with their personal lot.

The greater influence of the market economy and of government brought new goods and services, for which the villagers became willing consumers, but rarely were they able to control either the supplies or the prices. Motor vehicles, petrol, spare parts, olive oil, flour, clothes were all purchased. The civil service offered new careers, but occasionally a villager whose face or politics were wrong could get his promotion blocked, or find himself posted to some far away place to cool off. Thus politics occasionally made itself felt and people's lives were hedged about with fears and factors they could not control.

Pondering these new dependencies, one had to remember that in the old days there was even less security or freedom of action. My father remembered seeing a poor man on his knees to a richer farmer who had lent him money against his land and was now foreclosing. 'Your family, the Raftides, terrorised the village', one old man told me, remembering how his brother had been murdered in a brawl by one of my father's cousins, and the killer never brought to justice, even though the whole village knew his name. He was still walking around free in my time there, wearing black for a son of his own who had himself been murdered. But there was a difference in how these deaths had occurred. My uncle (as I called him in Argaki) had killed a man in a private brawl, the strong against the weak, a big family against a small one, and this kind of violence had been brought slowly (though never completely) under control by the colonial government; security of person and property had definitely been increasing, slowly, in the last fifty years. But my uncle's son, for whose life and death there were two sharply contrasting accounts (see Loizos 1975:241–7), had been involved in the political world beyond the village. He had been an EOKA militant, had killed British soldiers with a shotgun, and had become the henchman of Sampson, a Greek Cypriot political activist. His private motives had become entwined in public matters, and in a new kind of political violence which was something more than the heat-of-the-moment enmities of village families. Once, village men had fought over local things – land, women, family honour – and had known more or less what they were doing and why. Since the organised politics of ideas had come to the village, some of the villagers had started to fight over less coherent interests and beliefs, and, sometimes, with encouragement from men in Nicosia, Athens, Ankara, Washington, and Moscow. This was to be a bigger game, a deadly serious game, and one for very high stakes.

Chapter 3

PORTENTS

1973

The first weeks of my 1966 visit provided a hint of the political differences that existed in the family, and so in the village too. One night soon after I arrived, another 'feast' was in progress, and Pakis was interpreting, as usual: 'Your Uncle Pelekanos, O, he is a *big* communist, and so is your cousin Tomas, whose hair is turning white. Yes, and there are others: that man, Dimitris, the husband of our cousin Merope, and this man on your left, Ttoolis, a lorry driver, he too...'

Pakis was now asked to explain in Greek what he had been telling me, upon which there was some laughter. 'Ask him what *he* is', I was told by Tomas. I duly asked. 'I am a progressive man, but democratic socialist, *not* communist. I am with Tito, Nasser the not-aligned bloc, smaller countries.' 'O Pakis ine pseftis' (Pakis is a liar), said Uncle Pelekanos, with a grin. 'Eh-ee-vah' (to our health) and we all chinked our glasses with each other. Everyone had a good laugh over Pakis' account of himself. It was then explained that some of the other men around the table, such as Uncle Pipis and Uncle Tchiangos, were men 'of the right' – nationalists, 'reactionaries'. Everyone seemed relaxed and we soon moved on to something else.

I was soon to have a lesson in Argaki's politics which left me looking pretty silly, but like so much else about learning the ways of the village it proved instructive precisely because after my gaffe everyone took the trouble to explain things to me. I was invited one evening to eat in the house of a man called Polyviou, who was a friend and drinking companion of several of my cousins, and whose younger brother was a son-in-law of one of my uncles. It was a pleasant evening; we had been eating well, and were getting down to the serious drinking. Conversation had started up between my cousin Tomas and myself, translated by Pakis, as on several previous evenings. It was a kind of game in which I attacked the 'communist' position, and Tomas attacked and required that I defend the 'capitalist' position. I had found that once one of these exchanges started it was hard to stop it, since not only would the others be determined to have the last word, but, having had it, would then *demand* that I reply to it! For some reason I had entered sufficiently into the spirit of the matter to feel that simply to concede a point and call a halt was somehow disappointing, a refusal to give of one's best. It was all light-hearted enough, and Pakis would greet each exchange with comments like 'Ah, now here is an interesting point. Your Uncle Pelekanos says, why is it that the Americans have their spy stations here in Cyprus, if they do not wish to extend the power of NATO?' 'I don't know', I would reply. 'Perhaps they simply wish to keep track of what the cunning Russians are doing.' Pakis would answer, 'Oh, very good, Petro. Let us see what Pelekanos can say to that!'

This particular evening we got onto the subject of the 1956 Hungarian Uprising, which in English liberal circles was considered pretty fair evidence that the Russians were not in any simple sense defenders of the weak. I expressed this view, and Tomas predictably replied both that the USSR had to defend her frontiers against the West, and that the uprising had been started by American *agent provocateurs*.

> *PL:* But there had already been much criticism of the regime from Hungarian intellectuals before the uprising. It was not popular. The Petofi circle and other groups had reform programmes.
>
> *Tomas:* But the Russians were invited to help the Hungarian comrades put down the foreign-inspired uprising.
>
> *PL:* But Imré Nagy was a genuinely popular leader, and the Russians deposed him and put in his place Rakosi, who was very *unpopular*. Then they killed Nagy.
>
> *Tomas:* The *Russians* killed Nagy? But look, if we are going to have a serious political discussion, and you as an educated man must realise this, then we must have a proper respect for the *facts*. Everyone knows, cousin, that the *Americans* killed Nagy.

I could scarcely believe my ears. The murder of Nagy was one of the nastier mopping-up operations by the Soviets, according to well-informed and impartial sources. The claim of Tomas to believe that the Americans were the killers was upsetting. There was a snake in my new-found Eden, and I was too tired and too unused to the local brandy to face this with equanimity. The conversation grew somewhat heated, and I was taking the whole thing much too seriously. What was particularly disturbing was that Tomas (whom I already liked a great deal) showed no signs of modifying his position. Indeed, he was now claiming that everyone also knew that Lyndon Johnson had been the man responsible for the death of Kennedy.

Tomas Diakourtis, b. 1923, Argaki; m. 1952 Argyrou Varella (see p. 178). One of the first men in Argaki to support the Communist Party, in the days when such an act required great personal courage. He struggled to build up the retail co-operative shop in the village, in the teeth of merchant opposition, and has served as its secretary, as well as occupying key posts on most Argaki committees. Has visited the USSR on a delegation and is a leader respected even by most of his political opponents. First cousin to the author. (Disguised as 'Sklyros' in *The Greek gift*.)

I got to my feet, insisting that our arguments were getting us nowhere, I was tired, and would they excuse me but I felt like going home. I knew dimly that it wasn't the right way to handle things, but it was too late to contemplate an alternative. Everyone was getting up, and faces were now very serious indeed.

'Petro, please, do not be foolish', Pakis was murmuring, gripping my arm tightly to make sure I didn't make good my threat to leave. 'We are all relatives and friends here. There is nothing disagreement. Misunderstanding only. We change the subject . . . we do not have arguments about politics. Is joking matter. Not serious.' I still didn't really understand what was wrong, and went on huffing and puffing about how Tomas should have more respect for the truth; but of course Pakis wasn't going to translate this sort of inflammatory comment. I tried to stick to my wish to go home, but more and more of the people present were leaning forward, and restraining me. Polyviou, the host, had worked on a British base and was now remembering his English:

> Petro, listen! This man Tomas may be a bloody fucking communist, and I, nationalist. I drink with him one hundred times. One hundred times we discuss politics. He say, I fuck your leaders and I fuck your Enosis. I say to him, I fuck your Khrushchev, I fuck your Soviet Union. But we don't never get angry for this. Argaki is the best village in Cyprus. Communists, nationalists, they good friends, go every night to *taverna* together, and drink too much cognac. They say what they like but they never make for angry. And you are guest in my house. If you go now, I am sorry man, you do not like my friendship. Tomas is my friend, you are my friend. You leave from Tomas in my house, is like you leave from me.

It began to dawn on me that I would have to eat my words, since feelings were strong, and here, clearly, was something I didn't understand. I had stumbled on something a little more serious than a question of my bad table manners.

For the rest of the evening I had to endure a lecture on how I should keep my head, and understand that political discussion was non-serious, and that friends and relatives ought never to take politics so seriously that it harmed their good relations.

This could have been meant to imply that politics were not something local people were at all interested in, but this was not the case – men read political newspapers with great attention, and debated issues with some vigour, and many women read papers in their houses. In fact, the reason why the villagers insisted on not taking politics within the village so seriously that relationships were damaged was precisely because this was an ever-present danger. They did not tell me in 1966 that they had just gone through a major incident, which had nearly broken all the rules they were so busily impressing on me.

In 1965 a newly formed group of enthusiastic socialists (quite separate from the communists) had been meeting in a house, when they realised that outside was a group of right-wingers, listening to them. Angry words were exchanged, since it was claimed that the rightists had guns under their coats, to be used if needed, and had told the socialists that they were to have no more meetings. The village was in uproar, which was made worse when a small item appeared in a newspaper putting the right-wingers in a poor light, and suggesting that they were also anti-Makarios into the bargain. Now there were more threats, more tension. All sorts of people tried to mediate, including political figures from Nicosia, a local MP, the village priest, and some of the educated people. Eventually a form of words was found to establish an uneasy peace, but it meant that for at least a year there were twenty or thirty very angry, nervous men in Argaki who avoided 'the other side' in the coffee shops and wouldn't speak to them (see Loizos 1975:150–8).

The danger did not need to be spelled out to the villagers. If one hothead had fired one bullet, and taken one life, there could have been retaliation, and costly escalations. People who were neighbours, kinsmen, schoolfellows, could have been deeply and permanently estranged. Of course, a private quarrel could also produce some of the same results, but what alarmed villagers was the organised nature of politics, its use of groups of ever-increasing size, so that more and more people, including outsiders, could be brought in to continue the dirty work. A private quarrel could be sealed off, between the two individuals or their immediate families. But political factions were corporate vengeance groups, and harm to one person meant the solidary involvement of many, many others.

With these things in mind, the ways the villagers had developed of coping with political differences were founded on two things – the fear of civil war in the village, and of being beaten or killed by enemies, and the preference for a quiet village where if everyone somehow kept the scope of political competition in very narrow and strict limits, they could all get on with the serious business common to all – that of earning a living, and seeing the children honourably married off. Every time they told me that this village, Argaki, was a place where certain things did not happen, they meant 'where we will do our utmost to see they *do not* happen.' They were controlling themselves, and me, by repeating their home-made rules of village political life. Of course, people only keep on intoning the rules if there is a real fear of their being broken. It was clearly something of a balancing act.

The Argaki Turks, as was explained earlier, were few and quiet, so there was no active issue between them and the village Greeks. But throughout Cyprus (including Argaki) two sets of divisions existed among Greek Cypriots. First, and of longest standing, there was the antagonism between the left and the right. The right insisted that the leftists were atheists, without a drop of patriotic blood in their veins and ready to sell out Hellenism whenever the USSR dictated. The leftists responded by calling those on the right fascists, using pseudo-patriotism to mask their true interests, i.e. the exploitation of the poor, the weak, and the working masses by the few, the rich, and capitalism. They described rightists as cat's-paws of the imperialist countries (the USA and the UK) and 'tools of NATO'. Naturally, many Cypriots, and many Argaki people in particular, refused to take up a position under either of these labels.

The second major cleavage was between those who were for or against Archbishop Makarios as elected President of Cyprus. Makarios had been the chief political leader of the Greeks in their anti-colonial struggle against British rule. His military associate was General Grivas, a passionate Greek nationalist, and an extreme conservative in politics. He had created EOKA, the Greek Cypriot underground movement, but had differed seriously with Makarios on tactics and timing on several occasions during the revolt against the British. He never forgave Makarios for accepting the 1960 Constitution, by which Britain gave Cyprus its independence, because Enosis was ruled out by it. Most Greek Cypriots liked and admired the Archbishop, but the EOKA fighters soon split into a minority who followed Grivas, and a majority who followed other EOKA commanders in supporting Makarios.

The Archbishop remained popular until the end of the 1960s, but the basis of his support changed: while more right-wing nationalists went over to the opposing Grivas faction, the leftists who had previously had doubts about Makarios began increasingly to see him as a committed democrat and started to give him firmer support. This support only further angered the ultra-conservative Grivas, who came to see Makarios as 'soft on communism', in addition to his other alleged disabilities.

These two antagonisms existed simultaneously; at their extreme they contained the same people but within each were other people who changed alliances depending on the issue. These were the moderate conservatives. They would appear alongside left-wingers in mass demonstrations of support for President Makarios, but in another context (for example in their attitude to NATO) they would side with the Grivas conservatives, against the socialists and communists.

One legacy of EOKA was that after independence, when the fight against the British army was over, young men all over the island had developed a tendency to admire the carrying of arms, and to assume a style of swaggering bravado. Fresh from schools which had promoted a passionate commitment to Greek nationalism, the young came to see the ex-EOKA fighters as men to be revered, and imitated. Argaki had produced a number of EOKA militants, one of whom was nicknamed Gigas, 'the Giant'.[1] He had a large number of relatives, and was popular

---

[1] In *The Greek gift* (pp. 241–85) Gigas is called 'Levendis'.

in the village. In 1963 he was shot to death in the city of Famagusta in obscure circumstances, and the man who killed him was finally acquitted for lack of evidence. In Argaki, his relatives blamed the Minister of the Interior for this acquittal, and began to look on the government with bitterness.

Gigas had been a comrade-in-arms and drinking companion of a famous EOKA commander, Nikos Sampson, who owned and edited a sensational tabloid newspaper called *Machi*, meaning 'battle'. *Machi* featured Sampson weeping at the graveside of Gigas, crying out, 'My brother', as well as articles suggesting official complicity in Gigas' death, although sufficiently obscurely to avoid a libel suit.

Seven years later, Sampson formed the Progressive Party, and as its leader contested the 1970 elections to the Legislative Assembly. He was elected but his party did poorly. During his campaign he had spoken publicly of the murder of Gigas and in Argaki his party obtained dramatically stronger support than it did nationally. To many Argaki villagers the young men who supported Sampson seemed like a collection of ill-informed, uncouth rowdies, and they were not taken very seriously at the time. But they were not simply hooligans, and, as I shall shortly explain, their prominence expressed not just their sympathy for the dead Gigas but certain structural tensions in Greece and Cyprus.

Since 1967 Greece had been ruled by an ultra-conservative military dictatorship, which had few friends among Greek Cypriots, nearly half of whom voted for one of the two left-wing parties. The Athens junta imprisoned and tortured some of its opponents, and conducted a fierce ideological onslaught on socialists, liberals, and other democrats, whom it lumped together as 'communists'. The Greek dictators had no love for President Makarios since he was democratically elected and popular, and seemed tolerant towards communists, treating them in the main as if their Marxist ideas and their admiration for the USSR did not make them any the less respectable Greek Cypriot citizens. Makarios' massive electoral support relied on a substantial communist component, so it was hardly surprising that he did not snub the left, but for this kind of pragmatism the junta had neither understanding nor time.

In the early 1970s relations between the junta and Makarios became increasingly embittered. The Constitution allowed Greece to maintain 950 soldiers in Cyprus, and these officers were charged with the training of young Greek Cypriots who had to do two years of compulsory military service. During this time these officers did their best to indoctrinate the young Cypriots with the junta's ideas, and kept a list of any conservatives who were particularly hostile to the Makarios government. They also made friends with disaffected EOKA militants, older men with

combat experience. Finally, they started clandestinely to distribute
weapons, uniforms, and remuneration to those they enrolled in a new
underground movement formed in 1972, which became known as EOKA
B, to imply a continuity with the original EOKA. Greek Cypriots such as
General Grivas and EOKA veterans were its leaders, but Athenian army
officers were its paymasters and partners in insurgency. But now, instead
of a struggle against the British colonial presence the struggle was against
'the enemy within', those 'false' Greeks who were 'betraying' the national
cause by going soft on Turks, soft on reds, and all out for themselves. The
new EOKA wanted an immediate union with Greece, whatever the cost,
and did not believe that there might be a danger that Turkey would
oppose this by force. They tended to argue that on the battlefield a single
Greek was worth five or six Turks. Had they read Turkish they would
have known that Turkish extremists did the same sums – in reverse.[1]

In Argaki EOKA B sought to recruit some of the young men who had
devotedly worked for Sampson in 1970. These tended to come from the
less prosperous families, but a few of them were well off. Many villagers
insisted that they were among the intellectually less gifted of their
generation, and argued that in other places at other times they might
simply have been labelled 'juvenile delinquents'. But they were not
juveniles – they were men in their twenties and thirties.[2] People were
irritated by them and, because of the latent threat of violence, came
increasingly to be afraid of them.

The common factor which rallied these young men, who refused to join
any left group, was their restlessness and frustration; their one paramount
grievance was the exaggerated importance of the English language in
Cypriot life. These youngsters were often unemployed; they had finished
Gymnasium, even attended a Greek university which had raised their
aspirations, but although in local eyes they formed an intelligentsia, they
had little prospect of success. In school they had been made to devote
most of their time to Greek language, literature, and history, particularly
that part which involved the 'heroic' nationalist struggles against the
Turks, 1821–1922, and the English, 1955–9. The classroom walls were
usually covered with tinted photos of EOKA heroes, a 'hero' being a *dead*
fighter. Very little time was spent on the *English* language, so Argaki
school-leavers (like those throughout Cyprus) found that while they could
go to a Greek University straight away, they would not get into an English
or American one without double or treble the annual expense, and at least

---

[1] I am grateful to Paul Stirling for the information on Turkish nationalist
arithmetic.
[2] See Markides 1977 for a valuable comparison of age and social composition of
EOKA and EOKA B.

two extra years of study. Only a few elite children, who had attended an urban English-language school, could avoid this delay.

But if they went to Greece, and came back to the island after five years of old-fashioned and inadequate instruction, they could expect only fairly lowly government jobs. The higher reaches of administration, law, medicine, the police, and business tended to require real proficiency in English. In the civil service there were formal examinations in English to be passed. One Argaki police sergeant could not pass the next level of English exam and restlessly complained about this for years. The EOKA B people tried on several occasions – in vain – to use this as a reason for his joining them. A large proportion of EOKA B members were discontented policemen, and in Argaki there were several of these.

After all the years of talk about Enosis, and of nationalist propaganda instead of technical education being disseminated in the schools, the dominance of English *had* to be politically divisive. People who knew only Greek argued that they were being penalised for this. To the Argaki youngsters it seemed that Cyprus, a 'Greek island', was a place where a Greek education 'counted for nothing'. National leaders made speeches about their commitment to Hellenism, but gave the plum jobs to people with *English* qualifications; indeed the English word 'qualifications' directly passed into Cypriot Greek. National betrayal! Corruption on high! So sang the right-wing press, and the EOKA B followers in village coffee shops nodded sagely.

The way they felt was brought home to me (in both senses) by an Argaki boy called Kyriakos. He had just been to the British High Commission in Nicosia to get a visa for a trip to the UK. At best an indifferent student, he was applying now to go for higher education, although those who knew were sure that this would mean only a token three hours a day in a London language crammer (which might have paid off if he had had any talent for languages) and then, more to the point, twelve hours as a waiter or dish-washer in a Soho kebab joint. The High Commission, not without experience of these matters, saw through the plan and turned him down. On returning to Argaki Kyriakos soon had a crowd of nearly fifty persons around him, and he was shouting loudly:

> They wouldn't give it to me! They told me to go away! And do you know why? Because it's the *Turks* who are running the place. The man who took my form was a *Turk*. It's still Ottoman rule, that's what it is. And he *refused* me, a stinking dog of a Turk. You see how the British really *love* the Turks, and let them run their embassy.

The faulty logic, the racially motivated assumptions, the need for a scapegoat when something went wrong, were all typical of extreme nationalist thinking. He did not really know who had taken the key decision in his own case. He had simply *assumed* that it was the Turkish Cypriot he had dealt with, and that the decision had been partial, a low blow against a Greek patriot. His anger flowed out in curses. Later, when he was revealed as an EOKA B supporter, it surprised no one.

One thing that gave an impetus to EOKA B was the economic boom that affected Argaki and the Morphou region, as well as most of Cyprus. From Independence on, despite the hostilities with the Turks, the Greek Cypriot economy took off, and on all sides many people were getting appreciably wealthier; their children were better educated and were reaching further up the status ladder. People came to *expect* rapid improvement, and those for whom this did not happen were faced with two explanations: either they themselves were less capable than many others, or someone was blocking them – the Turks, the British, the traitorous reds – *someone*, and perhaps all three in alliance. This was the way the EOKA B supporters argued.

At first Argaki people were worried enough, but tended to dismiss EOKA B activities as high-spirited, if misguided, pranks. There was a sense in which the young men seemed to treat as a kind of game the putting on of masks and uniforms, going out at night to frighten people, or shoot up a police station. After all, Makarios and the government did not at first hand out heavy prison sentences. The Archbishop, who had come to power as an ardent Greek nationalist himself, was said to regard the EOKA B people as misguided idealists, and was unwilling to get tough with them; besides, had they been given exemplary sentences, their younger brothers would very probably have joined the nearest EOKA B unit straightaway in retaliation. This had been the experience of the British with the first EOKA groups.

However, in the early 1970s when the government started recruiting special police to deal with EOKA B, and their interrogations got brutal and the sentences less mild, the game became rougher and dirtier. And even if one stood aside from the violent encounters between the Specials and EOKA B, regarding them as matters between 'professionals' with their eyes open, it was still clear to everyone that from 1972 the political situation was deteriorating rapidly. The priesthood was split into pro- and anti-Makarios factions, which led to brawls in the churches both in Cyprus and as far away as London. There were quarrels in coffee shops, intimidations, and killings.

Argaki villagers were not insulated from these conflicts. At some time around 1972 there arose a factional struggle over the post of *muktar*, during which the far right succeeded in ousting the elderly incumbent and putting in an aggressive young candidate of their own. They were said to

The main square in Argaki, with pre-election slogans.

have got a Greek general who shared their political views to bring
pressure on the relevant Cypriot minister to achieve this. The same
pressure group started up an openly political club in the village, telling
those courageous enough to criticise this that a club which promoted
Hellenism was 'non-political'. This was particularly offensive since they
and their predecessors had twice in earlier years prevented the formation
of a club for educated men, on the grounds that it would be 'political'.

During this period the Argaki EOKA B unit swelled, and although
most of its exploits remained obscure there is reliable evidence that on at
least one occasion some twenty of them set out with their guns for an
assault on a near-by police station. They were observed by a socialist
militant who followed them. At the last minute they called off their attack,
but the socialist did not see fit to report their foray either to the police or to
his party leadership, on the characteristic grounds that it would embar-
rass and upset the whole village, that some of the would-be assailants
were his relatives, and so forth.

The crisis and the hatred between pro- and anti-Makarios groups led to
retaliatory violence, some of which went beyond measure, while some, as
in the following incident, was quite outside the law. There was an Argaki
man called Mattsoukas, who had been active in the first EOKA, and had

become a political client to the powerful Minister of the Interior.[1] The
Minister was later involved in a plot (which narrowly failed) to assassin-
ate Makarios, and soon after this was shot to death. His bereaved client
Mattsoukas, who owned a petrol station on the road from Argaki to
Nicosia, now became a bitter critic of President Makarios, and was said to
remark to his customers: 'Makarios is a bum-boy.' One night a number of
masked men beat Mattsoukas up so badly that he spent many months in
hospital, and in Argaki people said, 'They've ruined him – he's nothing
but a wreck.' I heard no one suggest that his punishment had fitted his
'crime'.

EOKA B divided Cypriot society, and divided kinsmen. Much later,
when the insurgency had done its worst, the fathers and uncles of the men
who had been involved in it again tried to excuse them by saying 'They
didn't know what they were doing. The mainland Greek army officers put
them up to it and led them on, and our boys were paid to do those things.'
This was all true enough, but did not explain why most young Cypriots
did *not* join the movement. They, too, had to do their military service in an
army led by extreme right-wing officers, they too had their frustrations;
but they did not sign up, for £20 or £30 a month, to overthrow their
elected government. Nevertheless, there was one sense in which the
insurgents did *not* know what they were doing. They had neither the
political experience nor the imagination to see where their actions would
lead, or where they themselves were being led.

In 1973, from the safety of London, I was reading up Cypriot history and
writing up my Argaki research data, not fully appreciating the turn that
events were taking, even though the London Cypriots talked constantly of
them. I found that after the intensity of field research in the village, in
order to make any sense of the long-term developments in the island, I
needed to stand back from the rush of day-to-day events. My return to
British life had left me emotionally rather detached from Cypriot politics,
since my reading of the island's history made it seem unrelievedly
depressing, a story of lost opportunities for accommodation with the
British and the Turkish Cypriots. There was no Cypriot political party
with which I could identify. The familiar and thoroughly British thought
came to me that whatever the Greeks were good at, politics was not one of
their strengths, fifth-century Athens notwithstanding. They were good
enough conversationalists, but when it came to running governments it
was Hobson's choice between the military dictatorship in Greece and
Makarios, who was democratic to the Greeks but, at best, aristocratic to
the Turks. If only he would stop winning diplomatic victories and offer

[1] In *The Greek gift* (pp. 258, 286) Mattsoukas is called 'K. Karas'.

the Turkish Cypriot 'rebels' an attractive, conciliatory compromise. The island could be a paradise, the Greeks were prospering, and one strong conciliatory gesture from them might draw the Turks back into the republic. Ah, said my wiser friends, but EOKA B would destroy such a gesture, if not Makarios himself, in five minutes. Well, then, I replied, why the hell doesn't he crack down on them? I was bored and disgusted by politics because, arrogantly and naïvely, I thought I knew better. Only much later did I come to see the complex cross-pressures that Makarios had been facing (see Loizos 1976). On the morning of 15 July 1974, I was breakfasting in London when the phone rang and a cousin visiting the city said through her tears: 'They've killed Makarios.' 'Who have?' 'The soldiers – the mainland Greeks, and those EOKA B people.' For the next few hours the radio bulletins contained reports of heavy fighting throughout the island, and of tanks attacking the Presidential Palace. In the afternoon I went to the Cyprus High Commission to find thousands of London Cypriots, good-naturedly ignored by the police, jamming the streets. Eventually we heard the official announcement that Makarios had escaped alive, which broke the tension and brought emotional relief to all. I knew then that however British I was and however aloof I had kept myself from Cypriot party politics, I was also emotionally extremely attached to the islanders, and involved in their fortunes, whether I wished to be or not.

Part II

WAR

Chapter 4

COUP D'ÉTAT
July 1974[1]

Early on that same morning when people in Argaki, and all over Cyprus, turned on their radios, they heard martial music, followed by an announcement that President Makarios was dead, that a 'revolution' was under way, that the military were in command and that a curfew had been imposed. For some, a small minority of EOKA B activists, this meant that five years of intermittent insurrection were about to be rewarded.

For the men of the *coup*, the first crucial act was to make sure that the socialist militants, and other core followers of Makarios, were arrested or, at the very least, disarmed. So, the orders of the day were the curfew, road blocks, and the arrest of potential resisters for interrogation. If the Argaki pattern was typical, one of the ground-rules seems to have been that arrests and searches in one village were made by EOKA B men from neighbouring villages, of whom, in the case of Argaki, Philia and Masari were the prominent ones. Meanwhile, key Argaki EOKA B supporters were making arrests in *other* villages.

The communists and socialists had been caught off guard – that, after all, is axiomatic of a *coup d'état*. One of the communist leaders in Argaki received a phone call from Polyviou, a member of an armed group supporting Makarios, who said, 'Bring the leftists down to Morphou, so we can demonstrate.' He thought for a bit, but since he had received no order from the party, he refused. Although individual communists seem to have fought alongside other Makarios supporters, the party did not appear to have mounted any mass resistance. To start with, they had no guns, whereas the socialist militants had some, apparently as part of a semi-official agreement with Makarios under which many of them had enrolled as special constables. The Argaki socialist group had some

[1] The events described in this and the next two chapters were recounted to me in 1974. See pp. ix–x, 188–94, for further details. I was not in Cyprus in 1974.

machine-guns but as we shall shortly see they did not manage to use them.

We must infer that those first days were marked by great tension and anxiety, each political activist maintaining a restless surveillance of certain others, to ascertain if enemies were about to make hostile moves, and if it were to be a time of killing. The villagers soon saw who favoured the *coup* from the way they behaved. Some started openly carrying machine-guns 'to support the new government' or publicly expressed their satisfaction with the way things had turned out by what they said in the coffee shops. EOKA B supporters made themselves available to the army for the task of rounding up possible opponents and disarming them. Some men, including at least one who had married into the village, went to enroll as policeman, to replace those police whom Sampson's henchmen were dismissing or would dismiss. But, as we shall see, there were also certain important gestures, acts of communication across party lines, which played their own small part in shaping the reactions of Argaki people, although they were powerless to influence events in the larger arena.

One of the keenest EOKA B supporters in Argaki was a man called Kajis (a pseudonym) who in his youth had been mixed up in a gang war which had arisen when certain men near Limassol had invented a Cypriot variant of the Mafia's protection racket. In 1968 Kajis had boasted to me that a few years earlier, when Greek and Turkish irregulars had been fighting, he had shot a Turkish shepherd; he spoke as proudly of this as an English schoolboy might have done about scoring a goal in an 'away' match. In recent years, he had been passionately in favour of the Greek junta and Enosis. His close friend Gigas had been murdered in 1963 and the suspect acquitted (see p. 55), which had probably pushed Kajis further into his oppositional outlook.

As spring turned to summer in 1974, Kajis knew that the *coup* was about to happen, and was given orders to stand by. But he did not know the precise date, until 15 July:

> Monday I was sleeping, and a fellow came and said 'Get up – the Revolution is on.' I got up, took the car and went to the cache. Out came the automatics. I'd got six machine guns, and I put them in the car and drove off to the coffee shop, leaving the guns in the car outside. We waited and listened to the radio, different stations. I heard Makarios was dead, so I went off to Morphou. That afternoon, when Sampson had been sworn in, I went straight off to Nicosia. I embraced Sampson, took some weapons, fifteen new ones, put them in the car and went on duty under our senior man at Morphou. I took a police car and some of our lads to Morphou, and we were given orders to start arresting people. We

were to co-operate with the army, which had taken command in
Morphou, to arrest the supporters of Lyssarides [the socialist leader].
Just them, not the communists. To pick up anyone with weapons,
whoever we knew about, and anyone we *suspected* had guns, and bring
them in. An order came to arrest some people from Argaki, and I said to
them, 'You must not take any of the Argaki people, OK? OK!'

We followers of Grivas, the men who wanted Union, the EOKA B
men, we knew where *everyone* stood. This one is left-wing; so-and-so is
with Makarios; that one's with Azinas, a nationalist. We had a file on
everyone and the goods on everyone. We had it all written down, which
groupings people were with and whether they had guns or not.

In the week following the *coup*, Kajis came into his own, and the way he
described the events made this clear. He was from a family which had
once been wealthy, but his father, a figure of ridicule in the village, had
squandered a fortune. Kajis may have never enjoyed as much power and
importance as he did for the six days of the *coup*. There are two themes in
his account, just below the surface. One is the banality of having
overthrown the legal government of the republic, revealed in his casual
throw-away 'all in a day's work' delivery. The other is his wish to be seen
as a man who was ready to get his fellow-villagers out of any political
trouble.

This was further demonstrated by Kajis' account of how, during the
first days of the *coup*, he went drinking with two 'best men' from his
wedding. One of them, my cousin Tomas, was a communist, as the reader
now knows. The other, Andrikos, had once been in the original EOKA
and was a former drinking-companion of Sampson, although in recent
years he had taken a government post, and had stopped murmuring
against the establishment.[1] Yet it is only superficially surprising that these
two men would sit drinking with Kajis, even so soon after the *coup*. Their
parties were formally opposed, but it had been long the practice in Argaki
for friendships to be maintained across such obstacles, and for drinking
together, in public, to be a way of expressing this intention. The act was a
piece of political ceremonial, which communicated the belief that village
friendships could override and outlast national antagonisms; this probably helped reduce tension and anxiety on all sides.

At this meeting Andrikos asked Kajis to take him to see Sampson. Kajis
replied that he knew what Andrikos wanted – the release of a man called
Pipis, a socialist sympathiser who had been arrested because of a personal
quarrel with an EOKA B supporter in his office. He was not regarded as a
man likely to bear arms. Pipis was a first cousin of Tomas, and married to

[1] For a fuller account of Andrikos' political career see Gellner and Waterbury 1977:
124–6.

Andrikos' sister. He was also a godsibling of Kajis'. Kajis assured the other two men that he would get Pipis released. I was able to confirm that Pipis was arrested, and released after a few hours, but cannot be sure how great a role Kajis played in this. He had every motive to do his best, given the strength of the relevant relationships; but he also had every reason to tell me a story which put him in a very good light, in the hope that it might get back to the men involved, who might then help him in *his* hour of need.

Kajis had his own version of 'professional ethics', which emerged in another episode. He claimed to have intervened on behalf of a pro-government militant called Christos (a pseudonym) who was being held in the Morphou army camp, and who had once protected him from arrest by the special reserves. This man was thought to be the head of a small armed group, and he himself told me that when he was arrested and marched through the streets of Morphou some of the EOKA B supporters were delighted to have caught a 'big fish'. Kajis continued:

> As I came back to the Morphou camp with a load of guns, Christos called out to me: 'Hey, *koumparé*, I handed out guns to some people, and I'll give you a piece of paper with all their names on, and you go and get them.' 'Right, *koumparé*, I said to him, 'You know we're friends. I'm not forcing you. You can't say I forced you. You're giving me this paper off your own bat, right? Then I'll go and pick the guns up.' He gave me this little scrap of paper with nine names on it.
>
> Anyway, off we went and arrested all nine of them. Eight of the nine handed over the guns straightaway, and so we didn't take them in. If you handed over, you didn't have to go inside. Some Czech automatics and two Martinis. One man had nothing. Said he was in Christos' group but hadn't been given a gun. 'But look, we've got your name down here, written down. Now you'll be for it. Right, it's inside for you.' He got knocked about a bit, I dunno, there was a bit of blood running, we put him in the car and took him inside. I'd got this police Landrover, and he was inside when we got back to the camp. Christos called out to me. 'Hey, *koumparé*, he called, 'I didn't give Andreas a gun, I forgot to tell you. I wrote it down but I never took him one.' I said to him, 'Lucky you told me, he'd have got hurt when he went inside. There'd have been consequences. You telling me you'd given him one and him saying he hadn't. He'd have been hurt.'

The point of his recounting this episode was undoubtedly to show that he felt that innocent men should not be beaten up, even in a military *coup*; there was even a note of apology for the amount of rough treatment Kajis himself had handed this particular man 'in ignorance'. Kajis continued:

> The thing that surprised me was about Gallos [a pseudonym] from our village. I had no idea he was in a group, getting mixed up in secret

organisations. But the list said that fifteen days before the *coup* he'd been seen in Platres, at the house of the socialist leader, Lyssarides. Really strange. I said to a friend, 'We said we wouldn't pick up anyone from Argaki, so I'd better go and get him by myself.' I went to the village and found Gallos sitting in the coffee shop. 'Come over here, brother-in-law',[1] I said to him. Some of his relatives were there. I said to them, 'I'm taking him somewhere and then I'll bring him back again. Don't give it a moment's thought.' We got in the car and set off.

'Well, brother-in-law, I never thought you'd be the sort of man to join Lyssarides' group.' 'You know how it is', he said, 'Crystallos Tirkas kept going on at me [to join the socialists], and me, well, I'm not really with them. Bring me a piece of paper and I'll sign it, sign that I'm with Grivas.' I said to him, 'We don't want you to do that, we simply want you to be a fighter for Greece and Enosis. Look here, you've got a gun, give it to me, and you won't have to go inside. I'll take you to your house, and that'll be the end of it. Nothing will happen to you. We don't knock people about. We just want to get in the illegal weapons so that the army can take them over. Your group leader told me he'd given you a gun.' He started crying, 'Brother-in-law, he *didn't* give me one. Crystallos had six guns and he showed us how they work, but he hung on to them. I never saw a gun again, and never laid a finger on one.' I took him inside, but of course nothing happened to him. I took him and showed him to the captain. 'He didn't have anything', I told him. 'He's with us', I said, and I sent him back to the village.

Kajis also told me of another attempt he had made to get an Argaki man released, his old drinking-companion Patroklos, who had reputedly joined the pro-Makarios forces as an undercover special constable, and was therefore a sworn enemy of EOKA B. Kajis went to the central prison where Patroklos had been detained, but found it under the charge of a mainland Greek officer whom he didn't know, and who absolutely refused to release the prisoner. Kajis tried very hard to persuade the officer that he himself had enrolled Patroklos in EOKA B as a double agent, so that he really should be released. But he got nowhere with this argument, which was in any case quite untrue. Kajis said he ran the risk of being shot for his efforts, and he was anxious for it to be known how hard he had tried, for later Patroklos, who was released through the agency of another EOKA man, complained that Kajis hadn't really bothered himself, and had failed to reciprocate past favours, which was a very serious charge in the moral economy of the village.

If Kajis' account of these attempts to protect his Argaki friends is to be believed, it reveals him as amateurish in his failure to see that the

---

[1] The Greek word was *sympethere*, which is used in Cyprus more widely than 'brother-in-law', and can be glossed as 'affine'. Also, unlike the English term used here, it is used as a term of address.

bush-league subversive game that he and his EOKA B friends had been playing in the Morphou region was transferred by the *coup* to a metropolitan stadium. The men now making and enforcing the rules were ultra-serious, ultra-conservative professional army officers, from Greece. They were not prepared to make special exceptions for local drinking-companions. The game was now a deadly one, and its name was civil war.

Much later, an Argaki teacher sympathetic to the EOKA B militants explained his subsequent disillusion with the anarchic conduct of this period, which included assaults, robberies, and attacks on Turkish property. 'In a proper *coup* none of this would have happened. In Greece in 1967, no one lost a copper coin.' A 'proper' *coup* . . .

For a few villagers, perhaps 100 out of the 1,500, the *coup* was a 'joyous day', the start of a 'revolution', the end of a 'tyranny'. One can only reflect how words can be twisted into many gnarled shapes. Most villagers did not share these reactions to the *coup*, and felt deep hostility to it, but although a few were to find themselves caught up in resistance, most did not. The curfew confined them to their houses, and although battles took place at points of strategic importance in the island, villages were not the usual sites for confrontations since their immediate control was of minor importance only. Few villagers, even socialist militants, expressed much regret at having missed a chance to resist, although some men, like Tomas, were retrospectively angry that the government had not trained and armed them for such an emergency.

A number of socialists and other supporters of Makarios from Argaki were arrested, but without bloodshed. Crystallos Tirkas, the Argaki socialist leader, had been made to hand over his cache of machine guns, and the outstanding shotguns and pistols in the village hardly posed an immediate threat to the Greek army. There were other minor incidents that occurred in the village during the week of the *coup*, trivial when compared with what happened elsewhere, but which stuck like splinters in the memories of the villagers in their later bitterness. For instance, Vassilis, a communist, complained to me that a young EOKA B man had fired a few rounds in the air deliberately to intimidate him. Another had been standing, gun in hand, outside his house, and when Vassilis' wife had come out on to her balcony to see what was happening, had told her to go indoors again. 'If she had been pro-EOKA, he'd have come upstairs for a coffee', Vassilis said.

Andrikos (see p. 67) was known locally to be an active supporter of Azinas, himself staunchly pro-Makarios. Accordingly, a squad of soldiers, supported by several EOKA B militants from a village near Argaki, came to his house and demanded that he hand over his weapons. He gave them a pistol. He knew at least one of the EOKA B men well. 'He was an old friend whom I'd helped many times', Andrikos told me. The use of EOKA men *from a neighbouring village* was characteristic of how the local EOKA people wanted to do business – people in Argaki did not want to make these arrests themselves if they could avoid it, but at the same time, they had to be done by men with good local knowledge.[1]

Andreas H. N. Toumbas, b. 1946, Argaki; one of ten children, supported with difficulty by a fireman father and labouring mother. Andreas had an unskilled job in a box factory, but then entered the police force, which would have been harder to do had his family been left-wing. He married an Argaki girl who had a dowry-house and a 0·7 hectare orchard, and enjoyed a secure, comfortable life, but well down on the village wealth ladder.

I received a number of different retrospective accounts of how the *coup* actually occurred. One young villager, Andreas Toumbas, was on duty as a police guard at the Archbishopric, when it started:

---

[1] There were exceptions, of course. My cousin Loizos Pipis, a socialist school teacher, was arrested by the *muktar* of Argaki (a known EOKA sympathiser) and six soldiers. He was taken to the army camp in Morphou, interrogated without violence, and released after two hours.

I was at the Archbishopric, on 15 July 1974, guarding the President of
the Cyprus Republic, Archbishop Makarios. That day the Archbishop
was away at Troodos, and we knew that he would come from the
mountains to the Presidential Palace to carry out his presidential
business, as he usually did. I was on duty from 5:45 a.m. At about 8 a.m.
we heard the first shots and we knew that a *coup* was on. We took up
positions at the Archbishopric. We hadn't expected a *coup* at this time.
If, for instance, it had been the day the Archbishop told the mainland
Greek army officers to leave Cyprus, we would have expected it. We
would have been in better order and the *coup* would not have happened.

So, at 8:00 a.m. we heard the first shots and took up our positions. At
8:30 we heard more shooting, and they said the military are doing
exercises. We had a radio link to HQ, and to all the other police stations,
and we heard over the radio that there was definitely a *coup* going on. We
started securing our position, to defend the Archbishopric, without the
soldiers noticing. About midday, army units started letting us have it
from long range. We were pinned down, and we couldn't see who was
shooting at us. We could only see the heavy gun which was firing at us.
Well, then we took our bazookas and other weapons, and went down
into the street, towards the flat rooftops, to repulse the *coup*. But we
couldn't take on the army properly, and they pinned us down until 8:00
in the evening. Earlier in the day we heard the Archbishop over the radio
from Paphos. He told us not to surrender and to fight on, and that he
would send reinforcements from Paphos. We held out until 8:30 that
evening but, when we saw the soldiers around the iron gates of the
Archbishopric, moving to surround us, we put up a white flag, a white
handkerchief it was, on a bit of a stick. We put it up in the air to show
them we wanted peace.

Because it was night-time we shone a torch on the bit of cloth, for the
soldiers to see, that they should stop shooting. But they didn't stop. We
got their commander on the radio, at HQ, and he told us he would
arrange for the shooting to stop. But it still didn't. We said, 'they're out
to kill the lot of us', so me and another fellow decided to come out with
our hands up. That's what we did, and luckily, they stopped. We said,
'We surrender', and they said, 'Everybody out of there'. Then they all
came out, the soldiers surrounded us, and the officer told them to stop
shooting as we'd given in.

They had us all outside, hands on our heads and they searched us.
They told us to stay there, and, after twenty minutes, we asked them for
water because we were tired and thirsty. The officer said 'OK, have a
drink', and then we asked for cigarettes and they gave us those too, and
we had a sit-down while we waited to see where they would send us.

Then they made us sing the National Anthem, and shout, 'Long live
Sampson!' The threat of their guns forced us to say what they wanted.

After midnight army vehicles came and took us to the central prison.
There was a captain there, and as we got out of the lorry, one at a time,

he kicked us. As we went into the cells he told us to take our clothes off from the waist up. We took off our clothes, and were half naked.

They dealt with us one at a time, hitting us. As we were being dealt with, a captain came up and asked us, one at a time, our names and where we were from. When my turn came I told him who I was and that I was from Argaki, Morphou, and he said to me, 'I know you.' He said 'What are you up to? Your brothers were with us but yet you, where did you get *your* crazy ideas from?' He was trying to say that my brother, Kyriakos, sympathised with EOKA B, but not me. So he gave me a kick and pulled my hair, just as he did with the others, and went on down the line.

Later they took four of us and put us in a cell at the central prison. We were so tired and hungry that as soon as we got inside we fell asleep until morning. In the morning I was hungry and asked for something to eat but they didn't give us anything till four o'clock that Tuesday afternoon, and then just a *koulouri* [biscuit]. There had been forty-five of us at the Archbishopric, and all the police stations gave in before we did. Our post was the last to fall. Most of the people with me were in civilian clothes and so they were able to escape, but I was in police uniform and couldn't escape because I was afraid I'd get shot and killed, you see.

Another young villager had become a member of the Tactical Reserve Police, which had been specially recruited to deal with the EOKA B insurrections of recent years. He told me how during the *coup* his unit had been involved in the fighting, and how a man firing a Browning machine-gun had been wounded. Their commander called out to my informant, 'Hey, do you know how to use it?', to which he replied, 'Not me, sir. All I know how to do is cook!' In fact, he knew perfectly well how to fire the gun, but when he told me this story, he did so without the least embarrassment, rather with a certain pride at his own quickness of wits.

His unit, about 150 men, finally surrendered, after their commander had been captured and told them over the two-way radio to give in. First they were made to lie on the ground, but he was not afraid, because there were so many of them. Then he was taken to prison, where he saw an Argaki boy, an EOKA B supporter, to whom he said 'Hallo – what's going on?' 'Huh! You didn't want to know me before, did you?', replied the boy, and cold-shouldered him. Later he saw another Argaki EOKA B sympathiser, who was a warder, and who said to him curtly, 'You're lucky to be alive.' Inside the prison he saw several other Argaki boys who were either prison officers who supported the *coup*, or EOKA B volunteers, who were helping them. He was twice beaten up. The second time was by men who before the *coup* had been imprisoned as EOKA B suspects, and had now been released to help their comrades. They formed a double line, and beat him and other pro-Makarios supporters now in their hands.

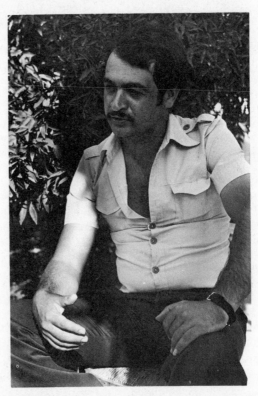

Christos Kaourmas, b. 1954, Argaki; unmarried, the second son of Eleni
Kaourmas (see p. 209). After completing secondary school and his
military service, Christos was employed as a prison officer in Nicosia.
During the invasion he was taken prisoner by Turkish soldiers and, with
many others, taken through the main towns of central Turkey in a
victory procession (see Appendix 3, p. 211).

Christos Kaourmas, an officer who had worked in the prison for several
years, was quiet and usually kept out of politics:

> On Monday 15 July, the *coup*. By chance some of my workmates came to
> the village and said to me, 'Let's go to work because they've been in
> touch with us from the prison and told us to come on duty.' So we set out
> in the afternoon. When we got to Yerolakkos, the police station had not
> yet been captured by the putschists. The police stopped us. There were
> lots of people there, civilians with guns to help the police. They stopped
> us. At first they thought we were Sampson's people, setting out with the
> idea of helping him in Nicosia, so they set about us really ferociously,
> and fired bursts over our heads, to make us tell them the truth. They
> locked us up in the police station for about an hour, and then they let us

go back to our villages, because Nicosia had fallen to the *coup*. If we'd
gone on ahead they might have killed us. So we went home.

Tuesday morning I woke up, and listened to the radio. It told all the
police and security forces to go to work. So I set off too. There were a lot
of checkpoints on the way to the capital. As soon as I got to the prison I
saw that all my workmates had been put under lock and key. They
locked me up too. Later, a few EOKA B blokes showed up who knew
who I am and who I'm not. They knew that I'd never been mixed up in
armed groups, political parties, or situations of any kind. They called to
me to come out and start work. So about ten o'clock this is what
happened. They let most of the warders out, except for ten or fifteen
who'd been [politically] involved in the situation. At the same time as
this was happening they were bringing into the prisons lots of Makarios'
people. They kept them with their hands up with the Greek Army
officers standing by.

There was an officer there who was really decent. We don't have to
condemn the putschists all the time, [by saying] that they did this and
they did that. In this one situation I saw a second lieutenant in the
reserves (they'd called up all the conscripts) who had got something
personal against one of the Makarios men, and as soon as he saw him
brought inside he started assaulting him, but the Greek officer in charge
wouldn't let him and struck him, saying 'That isn't right, it isn't humane
behaviour.' You see it's always been the rule in the prison that whoever
is the government of the day, the prison laws are observed. And there
was relative order in the prison during the week of the *coup*. They were
bringing in men who had been knocked about, and wounded men too,
but as soon as they got inside the prison gates, they all calmed down, and
no one suffered a thing while inside.

That Tuesday I got sick and went off to the hospital, where it was
quite a different matter. I saw a bloke there who'd been a prisoner
charged with a homosexual offence. He was a reserve officer and as soon
as the radio announcement about calling up the reserve came through
this man was put in charge of the Danish hospital, which later became
notorious. He gave orders that the wounded supporters of Makarios
should be left unattended and priority should be given to the soldiers
and pro-Grivas people. There were lots more with the same view. Once,
by chance, some policemen brought one of their mates into a ward
occupied by soldiers, and this officer cursed the policemen, wounded and
all, for intruding. The soldiers always had to have priority. It was like
that for four or five days. He was half-crazy, but he was
second-in-command. A vile man.

The Friday afternoon we heard that an invasion was imminent.
Rumours started to get around – they'd landed at Famagusta, in
Kyrenia, and there was general chaos. I got up, to leave the hospital; I
said to the doctor, 'Doctor, I'm off.' It was complete chaos in there,
bedlam, not the slightest order. He said to me, 'Off you go then.'

I went off to the prison. I found a fellow-villager, Kyriakos, there [a senior warder]. I asked him if he was going to the village, would he take me in his car? Since I was sick and couldn't stay. The doctor had given me sick leave. Kyriakos said, 'I can't go to the village now. Anyway, there's all kinds of trouble afoot. And if anything happens to you on the way, they'd put the blame on me. OK? OK. Stay here and go tomorrow evening.' So I stayed.

About quarter to five that morning some of my workmates were coming off duty, and came into the room where I was sleeping. One had a radio in his hands and he turned it on and found Bayrak, the Turkish-Cypriot propaganda station. It was giving out that the Turks were on their way to liberate Cyprus. As soon as they'd woken me with this, I heard the planes start bombing Eldyk, the Greek Army HQ, across the road.

The transport planes started bringing the [Turkish] parachutists in and they started jumping. The [EOKA B] men in control started giving out weapons immediately, arms which had been stored in the prison, to the warders they knew were with them. They were giving out guns until 7 a.m. and still not a single order came through. The prisoners were still locked up, and they didn't let them out. There must have been 2,000 or 3,000 in the cells, when normally they would have been 650.

About seven o'clock the order came through to let the prisoners out. We opened up and for a moment you could see the corridors and streets filling up with men who didn't know whether they were laughing or crying. The planes were bombing us and the parachutists were coming down, and pretty soon they started letting us have it with mortars. I was pinned down – I couldn't even put my head out. That's how it was to be till Monday. No bread. No water. Nobody had any taste for combat. You waited there saying, here comes a shell which will land in the midst of us and that'll be that. That's how it was for three days.

During the six days between the start of the *coup* and the Turkish invasion, men loyal to President Makarios continued to put up a resistance. A few police units, some armed socialist militants, and some communists who found weapons fought on with rifles and machine-guns, which were all they had to use against tanks and artillery. As with Hungary in 1956, and Chile in 1973, they were crushed in spite of their bravery. It is conceivable that a rapid mass mobilisation of armed civilians might have deterred even professional soldiers equipped with heavy weapons – such a mobilisation is said to have sustained the elected Bolivian government in November 1978.

The invasion by Turkey stopped the miniature civil war between the Greeks in Cyprus, and so it is impossible to say how long it would have gone on, and how many lives would have been lost in it. If the putschists had succeeded in destroying organised resistance quickly, there would undoubtedly have been torture and executions for many months afterwards. There were many old scores to be settled, and the fighting of that first week had created many new ones. In the area between Paphos and Limassol, where there was strong resistance, the men of the *coup* are said to have buried some of Makarios' supporters alive, and to have put out the eyes of others.

There is one terrible image of what might have happened in Cyprus, which comes down to us from a much earlier period in Greek history. Thucydides describes the outbreak of the Peloponnesian War, in the year 431 BC. It started in the city-state of Corcyra, the present-day island of Corfu, or *Kerkira*, as it is called in modern Greek.

...the Corcyrans continued to massacre those of their own citizens they considered to be their enemies. Their victims were accused of conspiring to overthrow the democracy, but in fact men were often killed on grounds of personal hatred or else by their debtors because of the money that they owed. There was death in every shape and form.

And as usually happens in such situations people went to every extreme and beyond it. There were fathers who killed their sons; men were dragged from the temples or butchered on the very altars; and some were actually walled up in the temple of Dionysios and died there ... To fit in with the change of events, words, too, had to change their usual meanings. What used to be described as a thoughtless act of aggression was now regarded as the courage one would expect to find in a party member; to think of the future and to wait was merely another way of saying one was a coward; any idea of moderation was just an attempt to disguise one's unmanly character; ability to understand a question from all sides meant that one was totally unfitted for action. Fanatical enthusiasm was the mark of a real man, and to plot against an enemy behind his back was perfectly legitimate self-defence. Anyone who held violent opinions could always be trusted, and anyone who objected to them became suspect.[1]

From this, at least, most of the Greek Cypriots were spared. But the cost was very high: the invasion of Cyprus by Turkey, and the loss of many people and much territory in war.

---

[1] Quoted in Mackenzie 1975: 123–4. The translation is by Rex Warner.

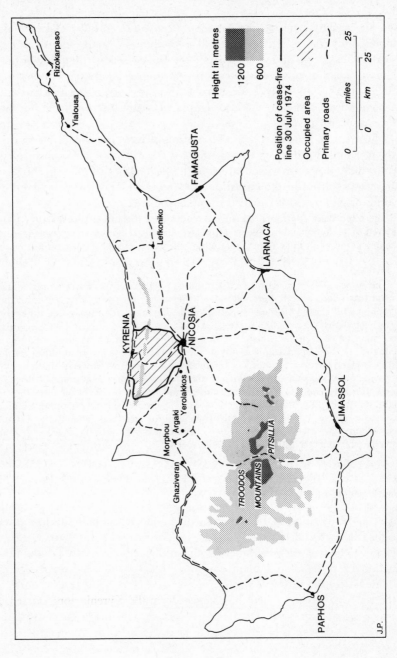

Position of the Turkish occupation forces; 30 July 1974.

Chapter 5

WAR
July–August 1974

The first phase of the Turkish invasion lasted from 20 to 30 July. The Greeks, dazed and disorganised by the coup, nevertheless managed to confine the Turkish forces to a fairly small space, and when the cease-fire came, had some cause for pride. In mid August there were negotiations, in Geneva, at which Turkey proposed major changes in the constitutional relations between the island's two communities, a much greater geographical separation of Turks from Greeks, and a weaker central government than had been agreed in 1960. The Greeks made counter-proposals, but the Turks' reply, in effect, was, 'Take it or leave it.' The Greeks asked for forty-eight hours to reconsider the Turkish proposals, but this was refused. The conference broke up at 3:00 a.m. on 14 August, and at 4:30 a.m. Turkey restarted military operations, the 'second round', as it came to be called.

This 'second round' was a rout for the Greek Cypriots. They had no aircraft, and no significant armour with which to repulse Turkish tank advances, supported by bombing and strafing planes. In three days the Turks had captured 38% of the island, including Argaki, which lay within a mile or two of their most forward position.

During the first round of fighting, the Argaki people were mostly spectators, listening to the rather garbled and suspect bulletins from their radios. They had decided during the week of the *coup* that the radio was no longer to be trusted. A number of young villagers were either doing their national service, or were members of the reserve, and they were called up immediately the invasion started, so village involvement in the course of the war was intense. Then the refugees from the Kyrenia zone started to reach the villages, and Argaki people heard eyewitness accounts of the shooting of unarmed civilians and of rape. Some of the Argaki EOKA B contingent went off to attack the Turkish village of Ghaziveran, an account of which is given by one of them later in this chapter.

The period from 20 July to 20 August was marked by confusion; the

79

villagers of Argaki, and the Cypriots in general, experienced the seizure of power by a small, irrational, and unpopular group, who nearly killed President Makarios, both a popular elected leader and the head of the Church. Then the British, believed by many Cypriots to be 'enemies' of Makarios, saved his life with a magic helicopter, and he departed, first to Britain and then to the USA. For a few days it looked as if that country, in the person of Dr Kissinger, would recognise Sampson's puppet regime, but, soon after the Turkish invasion, Sampson stepped down and was replaced by Clerides, who in Makarios' absence was the legitimate acting President of Cyprus. At this time, too, the military junta in Greece collapsed, and former Prime Minister Karamanlis came to power. Then, the Geneva conference was followed by a huge expansion of Turkish conquest, while both super-powers stood quietly by. Perhaps, people said, there really was a plan cooked up in Athens, Ankara, and Washington for a 'NATO solution', which, if known, could explain all these weird happenings. How *else* could the world be turned upside down so swiftly and disastrously? It had to be 'the Plan'.

'It wasn't in the Plan', 'It was all foreseen in the Plan', became common phrases on many lips. 'The Plan' could explain why the Kyrenia artillery batteries had failed to stop the Turkish assault craft; why Greek soldiers, always said in school to be worth five to ten Turks, could be so easily defeated; why Turkey had thanked the USA for her 'understanding' and why the USA had failed to stop the invasion. Perhaps the USSR was also in the Plan, for after years of huffing and puffing she had done nothing concrete to stop Turkey either, which left the Greek Cypriot communists especially bewildered.

After the war people said bitterly, 'We were fighting the Turkish army in Kyrenia, while in Limassol people were still going to the beach for a dip.' Certainly the invasion did not affect everyone in the same way, or at the same time. But people far removed from the firing were still very frightened. In Argaki, a young girl called Androulla Batsallou, who had just left secondary school, had got into the habit of keeping a diary, a quite unusual thing for village people to do. She wrote it in the rather stiff, formal style which her teachers had told her was 'good Greek'. The two themes which emerge are her terror and how, during lulls, her life resumed its normal pattern.

20 July: Day: Saturday. First day of war.
Attack by the Turks against the Greeks. A day of fear and terror. This day, Saturday, I got up to hear my mother say to me 'My All-Holy Virgin, listen to those bombs.' Then I got up immediately and ran to the radio. My knees became weak when I heard it say that the Turks had turned upon the Greeks without any warning. From moment to moment the war was growing in intensity, and the

Androulla Batsallou, b. *c.* 1955, Argaki; single, from a small and not
well-off family. She completed gymnasium. Her habit of keeping a diary,
which she kept up throughout the events of 1974, was known to a
number of villagers, who were impressed by it.

bombs and smoke struck the hearts of all of us. The radio continually called on the
army to tear the heartless enemy to pieces. In a little while there was an
announcement in the village that all the infants should be baptised, and so all who
had unbaptised ones rushed to do this. Seeing all this I didn't want anything to
eat, and I stayed all day on the sofa, listening to the radio. In the evening I lay
down on my bed together with my mother and we listened all night to the radio
announcements.

Second day of war: 21 July. Day: Sunday.
Today, Sunday, we listened terrified to the noises of the war. We got up in the
morning and when I was dressed I went with Rita to church. Everyone was
unhappy and weeping and praying. After the Divine Liturgy I kissed the ikon and
went home. Every now and then I heard the aeroplanes going high overhead and
my heart raced. At half-past nine they started flying so low that I thought I would
lose my wits from fear. When I went to shut the door I saw a plane flying very low,
and it turned suddenly and out came very black smoke. I ran and hid under the
bed with my sister. All the time I thought we were going to be bombed. My heart
was going to burst when I heard the village being bombed. Not knowing what I
was doing I took down the All-Holy Mother's ikon and clasped it to my breast as I
lay beneath the bed. When this was over we got out and went to see a friend in her
unfinished house, because it had two storeys and so we were less fearful. As soon
as I got there I felt a bit braver because we talked and forgot it all a little. In the

afternoon, some friends joined us there, and so I stayed the night there. We made up beds and laid down on the ground. Because the house was unfinished and there were pebbles on the ground, I ached all over my body. In another room were quite a lot of soldiers staying, not locals. They were guarding us, and because of this I was not as scared as before. At dawn we heard a lot of artillery and I trembled with fear.

22 July: Third day of war. Monday.
Monday, today, I heard a lot of artillery and was very scared. I got up at 5:30 and had no appetite for food, none of us did. We kept hearing planes going over and so we went and hid in the bathroom. When they had gone we came out again, and so on. I sat and talked with the soldiers who were on guard at 4:00 the radio announced that the National Guard had given orders to stop fighting the war, and so we became a little less afraid. A little earlier they had announced that there had been an artillery barrage in Famagusta and that twenty tourists had been killed at a hotel, as well as a child whose family was unknown. A local woman had left her child with her husband in Famagusta and as soon as she heard this she started wailing because she thought it must be her child. Later the radio announced that the Greeks were victorious, having brought down nineteen Turkish planes and taken lots of Turkish villages. We were glad to hear this and since the danger was over went back to our homes. The first thing I did was to have a bath and lie down. But when evening came there was more artillery fire and I was scared. I went and lay down at my neighbour Panayotta's and we kept the radio on all night. But there were no announcements, only songs.

'I sat and talked with the soldiers who were on guard.' They were not locals. Normally, she probably would not have found herself in a situation where she was sitting and talking with young unmarried men who were neither relatives nor neighbours. Her grandmother at the same age would have left the room if a strange man had entered it.

23 July: Fourth day of war. Tuesday.
Today, Tuesday I woke up at Panayotta's, since that was where I had slept the night before, and went home. I started the housework and when I had finished it I had a bath and sat and did my lace work. After lunch at noon I lay down for a bit on my bed and in the afternoon I got up and went for a little while to Heleni. I sat and worked my lace, with the soldiers for company, and we talked about the war. In the evening we fixed them some food and after the meal I went home. Heleni and I were in the company of Doros, a soldier from Famagusta, and at 8:15 we left the house taking blankets for the soldiers to lie down on. At 9:15 we saw the news on television and then went to sleep.

24 July: Fifth day of the war. Wednesday.
Today, Wednesday, when I woke up I did my housework and after bathing and dressing I went and invited the soldiers to come and eat. Then I went back home and got the food ready, with my sister helping. At 12:30 my mother went and brought them over and we looked after them really nicely. After the meal we sat and talked and then they went off. Off to the coffee shop. But I saw one of them going off by himself, so I called to him to come and join us. He came and sat with us, with me and Heleni and her family, and we chatted. Later we played halma [a board game, like draughts]. Later on my mother set things up for him so he could have a bath. And then we played halma again. And while we were together, we got

on well, he and I. When it was almost evening a neighbour came with £20 which she owed us. Later in the evening after the meal we sat and chatted and when we'd had enough we went to sleep.

26 July: Seventh day of the war. Friday.
Friday, today I was woken up at 3:00 in the morning by artillery firing. I was terrified and started trembling. I trembled so much that my teeth chattered. At last I rested for a little while then got up with no appetite and started my housework. When it was finished I lay down on my bed and stayed there till 3:00 p.m. This was the only day so far when I couldn't eat a thing. I got up, dressed and did some lace work. But a friend came so I set the lace aside and we chatted. Then we went for a stroll and while we were outside Doros came by with another fellow and they said they had been up at Masari village. Later we went out for a bit and then I went back to my own place for a while. A neighbour called me over to her house but no sooner had I gone when I saw Doros with some other fellow going to my house. So I went home. We sat and chatted for a bit, playing halma, and later they left. And after the television news I went to sleep.

28 July: Ninth day of the war. Sunday.
Sunday, today I got up and started my housework trying not to make a noise because Doros and another soldier were asleep. I wanted to go to church but because there were soldiers to be looked after I didn't go. When they woke up I gave them their breakfast and they went off. Then I mopped the house and lay down on my bed. After a bit my cousin came with her kids, and they wanted to stay with me, but she went off. At noon we ate ravioli, then I lay down and slept. When I woke up I heard that the Hare's son had died of his war wounds, and I was very sad.

The daily movements described in Androulla's diary, and her caring for the soldiers, were suddenly interrupted. For her the war had been a series of frightening sounds, radio bulletins, and the occasional aeroplane flying low over the village. But the death of a village boy, whom she had known all her young life, brought the war home in a new way. Her diary had recorded her being frightened on every page, but not 'sad' until now.

The diary is a little misleading, because Androulla's responses were inevitably personal, and rather restricted, confined by the life and narrow experiences of a young girl in the village. There are so many other things which might have found their way into her pages: had she a brother at the front, for example, the diary would have been full of her anxieties on his behalf. One villager told me how his son had been at the Kyrenia front, and the boy's mother would not or could not eat, from worry. The father, however, wanted a meal, and this led to cross words, almost to blows, between him and his wife. 'I took it one way and she took it another', he told me.

'I heard that the Hare's son had died of his war wounds.' By the time Androulla heard this, everyone in the village must have known that the young man was in hospital. His father, nicknamed 'the Hare', was a shy man, who served on one of the village's two co-operative shops. He was well liked, with no enemies. Word went round the village: 'Have you heard? The Hare's boy has been wounded. Andronikos. Badly. Three bullets through his chest.' In the last chapter, we heard from the young prison officer, Christos Kaourmas, about how he was caught up in the *coup* against his will. He here tells us something about the Hare's son, Andronikos, which the Hare himself probably did not know, or at least, would not believe:

> The Hare's son got hit on the Saturday [20 July 1974], and I heard about it the next day, and got there in an hour, to the hospital. His fellow-villagers and friends simply *had* to go straightaway, as soon as we heard. He was still alive then and was able to speak: he had his wits all right. He was afraid he might die, but naturally he didn't say anything to us at the time like, 'I'm dying.' Later on I heard from other villagers who went later in the week, from Tuesday through to Friday (he died on that Sunday); he was saying to *them*, 'Look, lads, I know I'm dying.' And he was very bitter about one thing. He'd got hold of the idea that it was our lads who had shot him from behind, of course without meaning to. You see, they were told to advance to attack a Turkish strongpoint and they would be given covering fire, and it was while they were doing this that he got three bullets from our own side; they went in the back and out of his chest, the doctors said. He himself realised this, for he said, 'If I was going because of the Turks I wouldn't be that bothered, but it's from our own side that I'm going.' He said it to his friends, and he said it to his family, too.
>
> There is another explanation of this which I had too, but I can't be sure if it is true or not: Andronikos was in fact with another lad, who was in one of the socialist armed groups, and during the *coup* this lad had killed an EOKA B fellow. The friends of the EOKA man were there that Saturday morning [the first day of the Turkish invasion] and one said to the other, 'Hey, there's the one who shot our mate. Let him have it.' But Andronikos got it, *instead of* the man by his side it was meant for. He told me the name of the man it was meant for, afterwards, because he knew that it was two EOKA blokes who were meant to be giving them cover.[1] But as I said, I don't know if he was right about all this, or not.
>
> Anyway, Andronikos told his friends that he'd caught it from our own side, and sick as he was, knocked about, it put him into a psychological state, it undermined his morale so he had no will to live. But this detail about how he died, well, people around here aren't saying much about it, so that his relatives won't be upset. Because *they* didn't believe him when he told them he'd caught it from our boys. His father says, 'my son was killed by the Turks', and he gets a little comfort from the idea that at

---

[1] Once the Turkish invasion started, the fighting between Greek groups stopped, and, as in this incident, opposed groups sometimes had to face the Turks side by side.

least his son went and fought the Turks and that they killed him in war. The father doesn't know that there is some reason for thinking it was from our side. He would be even more cast down if he understood. At least he has that one comfort, of thinking his son died in the war. Imagine how the man will feel if he knows the other story.

Vassos G. Melachrinou, b. 1931, Argaki; m. 1954, Eleni Spirou (b. 1935, Argaki). Each received 0·7 hectares at marriage, not enough to raise three children. Vassos worked as a tailor in the village. He was in constant pain from his kidneys, in spite of a series of operations. In 1975, as a refugee, he did tailoring work at very cheap rates, and was furious when a civil servant classified him as an 'entrepreneur', thus cutting off his refugee cash allowance. His reaction was shared by many refugees when faced with such decisions.

The Hare has a brother, Vassos, a tailor, whose son Spiros was badly wounded in the fighting, and was expected to die. The Hare and Vassos were both poor men, unaggressive, and quietly left-wing in their views. It was one of the more savage ironies of the *coup* and the war that their two families, while in no way responsible for the events which overwhelmed them, were to suffer so much, to give so much blood, while most EOKA sympathisers escaped unharmed. Vassos here explains how he came to hear that his son had been wounded, and the aftermath:

Two Argaki soldiers met President Makarios, as a result of their war wounds and bravery. At the extreme left is Mikailis Loizou Sotirou, his face scarred by napalm burns, and behind him to the immediate left of Makarios, is Spiros Vassou Melachrinou. Spiros endured twenty-six operations to his face.

The Hare's boy took eight days to die. My boy was shot on the Wednesday [24 July] but it was Friday [26 July] before he got to hospital. The Hare was at the hospital to see his son, and found his nephew, my boy, there too, and he came and told me on the Saturday morning [27 July]. I went to Nicosia and saw him. He was at death's door, and there seemed no chance of his surviving: there were six rubber tubes in him. On the Monday [29 July] I sent my wife. I said to her, it isn't too bad, and I left her there, and she stayed continually for a month at his bedside until they took him abroad. Right now he is in Athens for treatment. They are cutting bits of his bones and taking skin from one place and putting it back somewhere else.

The boy gave his mother three pound notes, all blood-stained, he had on him when they shot him. As soon as he came to his senses in the hospital he said to his mum, take this to my dad to look after, and if I get well I'll keep this money as a souvenir. But when we fled from the Turks, it got left behind in Argaki. We left at two in the morning, and I forgot the money in a cupboard, where I had the Cashmir I was tailoring and ten pairs of pants cut, ready for sewing. That money stayed in an old diary I used to write the measurements in.

Why did he want to hang on to the money, you ask? As a comfort. As a souvenir. When he grows old and reaches fifty or maybe seventy he'll say to his kids, see this money? I had it on me when we were fighting the Turks. You see, he should have died, but he survived . . .

The doctors had given him up. They said if his soul had been in some other part of his body it would have left him. My boy said to me, the Turks themselves, the ones who came up and shot me, if they saw me now they wouldn't believe it was me. And he himself hadn't believed he'd live. He'd been shot on the Wednesday and our boys found him on the Friday. When he saw our soldiers, later on, he put his hands up, thinking if they were Turks, they'd shoot him and put him out of his misery. His blood froze solid from the cold, and he'd lost so much of it they had to give him twenty-six bottles.

Spiros' father was also able to give me another version of what happened to his son, the 'official' version written by Spiros himself, as a report to his commanding officer:

Private Melachrinou, Spiros, Argaki, Morphou.
Infantry Driver, 65B 26/7/74.

I was driver for the Commander of Kythrea sector. On Wednesday, 24/7/74, he told me to take him to Koutsoventis to see one of our platoons and I took him. We reached Koutsoventis at 7:00 p.m. We found the platoon, and lieutenant-colonel Bottas, Giorgios, gave orders to the front line and told them their battle positions. On the far side of Koutsoventis is Sykhari village, which was under Turkish occupation. We finished our task and got ready to return to Kythrea, when they told us that a patrol of 15 men was to proceed to Sykhari, in retreat. The commander then ordered me to take him to see the patrol. I took him and we found the patrol on a hill. I was chatting with the soldiers from this platoon when someone shouted out that three buses were coming down from Sykhari to Koutsoventis. We took up battle positions and got ready to open fire on the buses but the commander stopped us saying that they were our own side.

We didn't open up and the buses came forward. That was our fatal, pre-ordained mistake. Had we opened fire on them when we had our weapons trained on them and they were without cover, not one of them would have got out. We sent two soldiers to see who they were, and they killed them before our eyes. We opened fire at 9:00 a.m. and the Turks, between 150 and 200 in number, started to encircle us.

We gave battle for five hours. Many Turks were killed because they don't know how to fight.

About 2:00 p.m. . . . [document illegible] a second lieutenant in the reserves, Petrou, who was in charge of the patrol, gave the order to withdraw. We numbered off and we were five men alive, with Petrou wounded. We now decided to retreat since we had not the slightest hope of being relieved. We retreated and the Turks kept up their attack continuously with concentrated artillery fire. Then one more of our comrades was killed, and only four of us were left.

At 2:15 I received my first Turkish bullet, in the throat. The bullet was a dumdum, and it burst as soon as it hit me, with the result that my throat was torn and my lips and jaws were hanging loosely. I dropped my gun and held my throat with both hands. One of my jaws was completely smashed. One of my comrades, as soon as he saw me like this threw down his gun and started weeping. I made a sign to him to tell him to go and leave me. I sat down and waited to die. Ten minutes went by, and with great surprise I realised that I could move and that I was breathing through my open throat. I moved on and caught up with Petrou and the others, two of whom were now wounded. But while I was catching them up I received another five bullets from the Turks, two in my feet and three in my hands. All four of us threw ourselves down under a tree and waited. We heard voices and saw the Turks approaching. I now lay down on my back so that my open throat would show, and pretended to be dead. Two Turks came up to us and one killed Petrou and then went off. The other came up to me, and with his pistol shot me in the area of the heart. This was the seventh bullet that I received from the Turks. When the Turks had gone, the three of us who had survived went on, and one of them found a water-bottle. They had a drink, and gave me a turn. I took the bottle, drew the water into my mouth, and then I saw from the corner of my eye the water pouring out of my throat onto the ground . . . I took off my vest and threw it away because it had become so red with blood. Meanwhile night had fallen, so we went to sleep there among the thorns and rocks. That night I came close to freezing. Thursday at dawn we started off again but without really knowing where we were going. We dragged ourselves up the mountains all day till dusk. We went to sleep just like the night before. Friday came. About noon, because I couldn't speak, I wrote on a piece of paper to tell my friends that we should get out to get help. They didn't agree, saying there were Turks around. I knew very well that if I stayed there I would die because I had lost so much blood, and I decided to get out. I reached a dirt-road, and I was exhausted. I went on about two hundred metres, and saw some soldiers up on a hill. I didn't know if they

were Turks or our own boys but I went on fearlessly. They saw me and
called out. I didn't understand what they said, so I put my hands up.
They came up to me and told me they were from the 361st Infantry. I
showed them my identity card and they took me up the hill. They took
me on a donkey to a village, and from there in a car to Nicosia, at 4:00
p.m. on Friday.
ends

signed   Melachrinou, Spiros.

The wounded Spiros and the dead Andronikos were first cousins and thus
were closely connected, in village kinship terms. But there is another
connection between their two situations. The dead boy's comrades, a
group of young men who had grown up together with a strong sense of a
bond between them as well as of a gap between them and their parents'
generation, wished to hide from the Hare and his family the possibility
that his son had not been killed by the enemy. The wounded Spiros gave
bloodstained bank-notes to his mother for safe keeping. The connection
between these events is that for Greeks of all ages it is a compelling idea to
give one's life or life's blood in battle for one's native land (*dhia tin
patridha*): *pro patria mori*, as the Roman poet Horace asserted. The idea of
self-sacrifice for one's nation in war has elsewhere a power which it may
be hard to imagine for readers who have matured in the thirty-five-year-
long peace of Northern Europe.

So far the events of this chapter belong to the category of 'normal
warfare', if such a thing exists. But what now follows is a little different,
and part of a kind of warfare – politely called 'irregular' – which most of
us would prefer not to contemplate. In English writing about the several
centuries of conflict between Greeks and Turks, the term 'irregulars' has a
slightly sinister resonance, because it has come to be associated with the
indiscriminate killing of civilians. But this is something not unknown in
regular armies, so the distinction is hardly clear cut.

In the last chapter, the EOKA B militant called Kajis described how
during the six days of the *coup* he and his fellows dominated Argaki. Here
he describes how when the six days of the *coup* were followed on Saturday
20 July by the Turkish invasion, he went off to join the attack on the
Turkish village of Ghaziveran,[1] about twelve miles from Argaki and
nowhere near the Kyrenia invasion area:

> Saturday morning at 8:00 a.m. Akis Karanis woke me up saying, 'Wake
> up, Makarios has sent the Turks to us.' I was still asleep, half-drunk, no,
> *really* drunk, and awfully tired. I'd been four or five days without sleep, I
> don't know, I hardly knew what was going on. I said to my *koumparos*

---

[1] For mention of earlier hostilities against this village, see p. 43.

Akis, 'What's up?' 'Makarios has sent us the Turks and they're attacking in Kyrenia.' I got up, grabbed the guns, got out, took a Landrover and got moving. The fighting-groups were getting together here and there, and a battle was starting at Ghaziveran, so that's where we went.

We took up defensive positions in the first houses. A Vickers gun broke down and we sent it back to be fixed. When we got it back, we let fly . . . *takka toukkou takka toukkou* . . .

Meanwhile Ghaziveran was *silent*. The captain wanted us to set fire to some houses, so we did. We chucked petrol on them, and set light to four or five of the first houses. Their *muktar* called out from inside, 'All right. We surrender.' The shooting stopped and they surrendered. As soon as they did so, our battalion commander Photis, a friend of mine, went into the phone-box to relay that the Ghaziveran people had given in. When he'd got through, he came out of the box and someone in a house gave him a bullet *here*, in the forehead. He never said 'mother'. Then someone else got hit. Bullet through the head. Who's bought it? An Argaki boy.

When *he* got shot I just went berserk, like a rabid dog. I burst into a house. There were six or seven people inside and a child. I swung the machine-gun and mowed them down. All seven. Afterwards I noticed the child. What harm had it done, you ask? It was *Turkish*. They'd shot my fellow-villager, they'd shot my captain, so I'd shot them. I had a row with an officer from Nicosia, one of our people, and we nearly killed each other, about why I'd shot them. I said to him, '*Why* did I shoot them? I'll tell you. Because it's *war*. Now, it has to be done *in cold blood*, you understand? You have to keep your nerve.' Anyway, we took Ghaziveran, they surrendered, we put their young men into a prison-camp near the secondary school. Dawn came and the planes started. *Takka toukkou*, they bombed Ghaziveran, hit the school and killed a Turkish woman, one or two got killed or wounded, and some others. Our people didn't get wounded. The Turks got wounded from bombs from their own side. How come the Turks bombed Ghaziveran? If they knew our army had gone in, all right, but how come they bombed the school with their women in it? And, as a matter of fact, their soldiers were all there too.[1]

Kajis did not stop there, but went off to the Kyrenia front to fight the Turkish army. His account was full of descriptions of the noises of different weapons being fired and shells exploding, and of narrow escapes. Later, in the second phase of the war, he was in Limassol, in recent years

---

[1]   An official Turkish letter to the UN by Rauf Denktash listed an 'act of massacre' in this village, in the following words: 'The indiscriminate shooting into a school compound where women had gathered (at G[h]aziveran) and killing six women, one at the verge of giving birth' (Turkish Cypriot Human Rights Committee 1979:36–7). It looks as if elements of Kajis' account were intended to disguise a rather less 'justifiable' atrocity.

an EOKA town, and now more than ever so, since the men of the *coup* sought a possible stronghold, in case they should suffer reprisals. It was in Limassol that he heard that Argaki had been taken by the Turkish army, and his response, so he told me, was to go and shoot an elderly Turkish woman. 'And I'd have got one of their *hojas* [a Turkish Muslim cleric] too, if a UN bugger hadn't stopped me.' Let no one say the UN peace forces can do no good in a war, for there are always numbers of men like Kajis – wandering about, killing promiscuously. I would prefer to believe that the killings were merely Kajis' fantasies (which in itself would be bad enough), but that would be at odds with everything Kajis ever said in the past, and with the fact that both his friends and his enemies warned me early on that he was a killer.

Kajis and his actions were exceptional, but even one Kajis in every village could clearly do a great deal of damage to Greek–Turkish relations; several such men on each side of a mixed village could create enough suffering to destroy any residual trust which might exist in thousands of people around them. Fortunately, there were others who behaved in a very different way. I was given the following account by an Argaki boy, my nephew Hambos Michaelides, who told me of his friendship with a Turkish Cypriot, a relationship which survived both the war and the deeds of men like Kajis. In 1974 Hambos was doing his military service and was posted to the 'Green Line' in Nicosia. This area was so named in 1964 when a British mediator used a green crayon to mark on a map the road which divided the Greek and Turkish cease-fire positions.

> Before the war, on the Green Line we talked a lot with the Turks, very often, and we were friends with them, there was no bad blood between us. We knew each other's names and everything, and we chatted all day when we were on sentry duty. The Turkish positions were about twenty metres away from ours. Before the war we were allowed to go as far as the road itself, the Green Line; we were on one side of the road, they were on the other. That was as close as we were allowed to go. To break the monotony we found nothing better to do than to talk to each other. The Turks knew Greek, because they were Cypriot Turks. So we used to talk with them and knew them all by name.
>
> Before the war I'd known all the Turkish soldiers opposite me by name, and where they were all from. I was very great friends with one Turk from Polis Chrysochous village, whose name was Tourchien. We used to walk out together, down into Nicosia for a couple of hours. Just that. He told me all about his family, his dad, what he planned to do later on, all that sort of thing.

The soldiers on both sides were brought meals from time to time, and Hambos started offering Tourchien a little of whatever the Greek Cypriot soldiers had just received. At first Tourchien had been reluctant to be seen

Hambos S. Michaelides, b. 1953, Argaki; youngest of five brothers; their father, Sophronis, brother of Parthenis (see p. 152), was a prosperous farmer and produce merchant, who taught himself English and Russian in order to read literary classics. His sons, however, preferred farming and commerce.

accepting food, but had taken to meeting Hambos in an alleyway, out of sight. After the *coup d'état*, the district, Kaimakli, became a centre of socialist resistance, and since the National Guard dared not venture into the area, Hambos and his comrades did not receive their normal meals. With only a tin of marmalade between five young men, as the hours went by they started to get rather hungry. Hambos then gave Tourchien money to buy quantities of *halloumi*-cheese, water-melons and bread for the hungry Greeks, from the Turkish sector. Thus three days passed. Hambos continued:

> When the first round of the war finished, Tourchien came looking for me, by my watchtower. He came and called out to the soldiers to see how I was. They told him I'd been slightly wounded and that they'd taken me back to the company's base. Later when I went to another watchtower in the second round, he came along one night at three, and called out. He called my name, and I got up, even though it was three a.m., and answered him, and we asked after each other. 'I'm all right',

he said. He said he'd be there the next day, and we'd talk again, when it was daytime. He really wanted to know how I was.

Later, after the war, there were shortages in the Turkish zone, and they'd give us money to buy things for them. Cigarettes usually. They weren't allowed to buy fags at first, and they tried to give us fags from Turkey in exchange, which they themselves couldn't get used to. Then they wanted brandy, which they couldn't get on their side. We always put the prices up a bit, to make a bit for ourselves as business on the side. Milk for the children, anything that wasn't in good supply over there.

Hambos was twenty in 1974. When the first major killings between Greeks and Turks started, in 1958, he was four. He can have had little real contact with Turkish Cypriots, except for a few elderly people in Argaki. At school he was exposed by Greek nationalist teachers, and by many of the newspapers, to a daily stress on the alleged hostility, unreliability, and antagonism of Turkish Cypriots, a poor prognosis for trust or friendship. Twenty years of such conditions should have produced an entire generation of youngsters who would not be able to live with those of the other community, even if there was a settlement, but Hambos' father, a self-educated man with leftish ideas, had never accepted the Greek nationalist view that the Turks were to blame for everything, and this had influenced his son.

When people live through a dramatic event, they end up with stories they want to tell about it which seem intensely meaningful to them, but which may strike outsiders as bizarre, or even pointless. Perhaps this is why younger generations are so easily bored by the war stories of their elders. An Argaki villager called Yannis Xenofondos was in the reserves, married, a father, and past thirty when he was called to active service. He told me that while he had been under fire, his one thought had been to stop his motor-cycle getting strafed. He kept moving it, but the planes kept coming back. To me, other details were far more interesting – such as how he and his comrades saw their defeat as having been produced by a high-level 'betrayal' (a theme which also occurred in the 1922 Asia Minor rout of the Greek army by the Turks, when Greek generals were tried and executed for 'treason'):

> There we were, thirsty and hungry. Since the betrayal had been so completely thorough, we couldn't find food or water. There wasn't a Greek army officer anywhere to tell you what to do or what not to do.

Yannis was a strong socialist, completely out of sympathy with the Greek army officers who were nearly all supporters of the Greek military dictatorship, to which he was opposed. The disorganisation in the army must have been extreme, and morale poor, since men were being commanded by officers who had just overthrown their popular, elected government, drawn them into a one-sided war with Turkey, and were still trying to enforce 'military discipline'. This hostility certainly came out in Yannis' account:

> There were ten of us. At midday we got about an hour's rest from the planes. About 1:30 they started on us again, and we stayed pinned down till dark . . . All night the machine guns drove us mad. Then this colonel started: we had a colonel who was half crazy, he really didn't know what was going on, but his head was full of ideas about military conduct. A real idiot. 'Colonel, sir, colonel sir, let's get out of it', we said. 'No one is leaving', he said, drawing his pistol, 'No one' . . . Not long after that, he took off by himself!

After many more adventures, Yannis and his comrades joined up with other retreating, disorganised, hungry, thirsty men, withdrawing until they were clear of the Turkish advance. But after a night's sleep in safety at Kykko Monastery, he found himself in trouble again. The colonel who had disappeared during the rout, now re-appeared:

> In the morning, the colonel says, 'Back to the camp.' 'Hey, brother', we said to him, 'It's hardly time for that, with the Turks and all . . .' 'We're going to camp', he says, and goodness knows what else. 'If anyone runs off, I'll shoot him, I'll do this and that . . .' We said to him, 'Why did you get out when *you* could have been fighting? Last night why didn't you stay with us? Why didn't you stay and tell us how to fight a war, we who haven't any idea of how to do it?' Like me, I went as a soldier in '63, and did one year. Of that year, two months were training, and now I pass for a soldier. What use is a man of 30 who had two months' training in '63?

Nevertheless, Yannis was, however unwillingly and, in his own eyes, amateurishly, a soldier. He nearly got killed, he nearly got captured, and he was wounded when he burned his hands moving ammunition boxes away from a napalm fire. But other men, sometimes civilians, got drawn into the war in less predictable ways. During a lull, Andreas Hassapis, a cook who lived in Argaki, went to find his son, a soldier on the Green Line in Nicosia, to give him some cigarettes and pocket money. He had the misfortune to take a wrong turning, near no-man's land.

> I went down to Bairaktaris and went to the trade union medical clinic, next to where the Turks are, that is, and just opposite our guard-posts. It was a truce that Thursday, 25 July, note, and while I was looking for my boy, the Turks were observing me. I didn't find any of our people to ask what was going on. Well, in any case, as soon as the Turks saw me they said, 'Where are you going?' I was about to turn right around and go back to the clinic, but they would have thrown me to the ground. I put my hands up straightaway. They grabbed hold of me, and took me away. We went to the guard-house and they say to me, 'What are you looking for?' I say to them, 'I've got a kid who's a painter here and I've

come to see him.' Well, one of them says to me, 'In '63 they killed my seventeen-year-old, so why should we let you go? You're 45, you're not that old.' I say to him, 'What wrong have I done, *koumparé*, I've got five kids, what wrong have I done you? I came here for other reasons. I wasn't carrying a gun, I'd got my cigarettes only, and a bit of cash I'd brought for the lad.' Well, that's what we were saying when a Turkish Cypriot officer came along, and said to me in Greek, 'Where are you from?' and I say, 'From Argaki, why should I lie to you?' He says, 'I have a colleague who was a fellow student of mine, from Argaki, he's a certain Andrikos who works in the Land Registry Office. He had a surname', he says. I say to him, 'Pipis'. That is, he was trying to catch me out to see if I really was from Argaki. 'Now I'm sure, and I really believe you are from Argaki', he says to me. 'No one will do anything to you', he says to me. 'Get in the car and I'll take you to the United Nations', he says.

Hassapis was unlucky to walk without knowing it into Turkish hands, but was fortunate not to have been shot on the spot by the man who had lost a son in 1963. When he was questioned about where he was from, he was lucky again, because it was chance that his interrogator knew someone from Argaki, someone who could serve as a test of his bona fides. The value of knowing whom one had caught was two-fold. First, the Turkish army would undoubtedly want to know if *Greece* had started committing troops to the Cypriot war, since, if they did do so, a counter-attack on Turkey through Thrace or elsewhere would be probable. Secondly, the Turkish Cypriots would have feared that their fellows still in Greek-held areas might be held as hostages, and a man from Argaki, where there was a small Turkish population, might be especially valuable in exchange for Argaki Turks.

The patchwork nature of the dispersal of the two ethnic groups throughout the island made many combatants think in terms of hostages, and counter-hostages. Hassapis was interrogated on the Turkish side of the Green Line, in Nicosia; opposite, on the Greek side, was Hambos, the young Argaki conscript who, a few pages back, described his friendship with a Turkish soldier. Some Turks shouted across to him, asking if he knew a sergeant called Hassapis? 'Why?' he countered. They produced the older Hassapis. 'We've got his father', they explained. Hambos was now very anxious, in case the son, the younger Hassapis, should find out that his father was a prisoner, and be driven to 'do something foolish' during the truce, such as open fire on the Turks. Fearing for his friend's sanity, he told his commanding officer what had happened; the latter then contacted various members of the Hassapis family, and made sure that the son was swiftly transferred away from the Green Line before anyone could tell him of his father's fate. Hassapis senior again takes up the story:

They put us inside a car. But instead of taking us to the UN at Mitseri,
we went to the Saray Hotel. If we'd gone elsewhere, to the military
prison, we would have got beaten up. At the Saray they again
interrogated me – 'What were you looking for?' – and when they started
they took our watches, our money, anything we had. The sergeant said
to me, 'Don't worry about either your watches or your money', he said,
'as soon as you leave you'll be given it all back'. We were there four days.
Four days . . . The Sunday at 5:30 a Turkish warder said to me, 'You're
going to be released in a quarter of an hour.' I said to him, 'I hope so.'
But it seemed that later came another order from Ankara that the
prisoners should go abroad to Adana in Turkey, and some of the men
who were already in a truck on their way to being released were stopped,
and put back. At 8 [o'clock] I saw that they were hurrying them along
three at a time from the prison they were in; they were tying their hands
behind their backs like this, and covering their eyes, and I say to the old
man from Yerolakkos I'd palled up with, 'It's Turkey we're headed for.'
He says to me, 'You're crazy!' I say to him, 'Straight to Turkey, that's
where we're going.' They put us all in a bus and off we went to Kyrenia.
Turkey it was!

Hassapis was not the only Argaki man to be taken prisoner to Turkey,
there were several others, and later we shall hear from one of them about
the experience (see Appendix 3, p. 211). Following each of the two periods
of fighting, there was a time when many villagers were desperate for news
of their soldier sons. After the second round, the soldiers in turn were
equally anxious for news of their parents and other relatives, for they
knew that the front had come close to Argaki, and later they learned that
the village had fallen to the Turks. The most crucial thing which any
fellow-villager could do for any other was to give news of the condition
and whereabouts of kinsfolk. Yannis, the soldier we last heard from in
dispute with his commanding officer about going back to camp, lost his
argument, and had to wait some days for news:

September the 4th they let me go. Where's my family? My father-in-law?
I didn't know which way to turn to find them. I knew the village had
been taken, because we knew where the Turks had advanced. I knew my
brother-in-law Andrikos had taken them off in his car. Then I found a
fellow-villager, Christakis Pelavas. 'Look,' he said, 'your father-in-law is
in Kato Amiandos village, but I don't know if your wife and kids are
there too. You go up there and he'll tell you where they are.' I found a
car, I was ashamed to get in it because of my clothes, khaki army
trousers, all stained and torn, shoes in shreds, almost barefoot, shirt all
ripped. We drove along through the forest; it had burned, scorched trees
everywhere. A black ruin, black everywhere. Hungry. Thirsty. Finally
we got to Amiandos. I found my father-in-law. He said, 'Maroulla is in
Livadthia, with my *koumparos* and the kids are all right.' So I went to

Livadthia and found them. I borrowed some clothes, had a bath and
stepped out to the coffee shop.

The person who was perhaps hit harder by the war more than anyone
else was the village priest, Papa Loizos. On 20 July, when the Turkish
invasion started, he was coming out of the church when a villager asked
him to baptise his child. The priest then decided to baptise all the
newborn children, some twenty in all, since he feared that if they died
unbaptised they would not share in eternal life. So he arranged the
ceremony, carefully separating the boy babies from the girls, so that
should they survive there would be no bar to subsequent marriages
between them – for Orthodoxy teaches that baptism creates blood
relations, and had these babies been baptised 'at the same font' they
would have been as brothers and sisters.

The priest stayed in the village until the war came very close:

> After the first round of the invasion I did my best to keep our people
> calm, and tried not to think about the mountains we could see burning
> before our eyes.[1] I went on with my work, both the work of my fields and
> the work of my faith. Until 15 August I performed the liturgies; but by
> the morning of that day most of the village had gone, so I thought it good
> that I too leave, along with my father-in-law, the only other person to
> have stayed.
>
> I could not go to get my parents (who were in another village, closer to
> the front) because of the aeroplanes, the aeroplanes which were
> overhead, which would have killed me. When the Turks came on 16
> August they entered our village. My mother was cut off, in her house,
> with an old woman called Mattra.[2] On the 18th the Turks arrived at my
> mother's house and she thought it good to close her door so as to stop
> them coming in. The Turks started shooting from outside and my
> mother fell dead. My father at this moment was watching from another
> room, from the *sospito* (as we say in Cypriot dialect), the inner room.
> Well, finally, when the Turks had gone, my father said to old Mattra,
> 'I'm going to Argaki to bring my son so we can bury her.' He went to
> Argaki, as I learned from my fellow-villagers who were then cut off and
> who today are free. He went to Argaki but I do not know what happened
> to him, if he turned back or where he went, or if they shot him on the
> way. He just disappeared. I have taken steps to find him through the
> Red Cross, not once only but eight and ten times, but there has been no
> answer. You understand, I simply do not know what happened to him.
> If he remained unburied or if the Turks buried him, I do not know.
>
> When my father left the old woman Mattra, he said to her, 'Wait for
> me – I'll be back soon.' She stayed there for the rest of the day, but when

[1] The Turkish invasion resulted in serious forest fires in many parts of the island.
[2] A pseudonym.

Papa Loizos, b. 1923, Kyra village; m. 1949, Maria HajiZenonou (b.
1930, Argaki). His family was the richest in Kyra, while Maria's was one
of the richest in Argaki. He received 6·3 hectares of Kyra land, and she
got 2·8 hectares in Argaki. In 1959 he decided on the priesthood, and ten
years later his ministry and 2,000 citrus trees made him one of the
busiest men in the region. He wore his priestly habit even on his tractor.
He was said to be ultra-conservative in politics, but he himself
maintained that this was largely a result of his bishop's stance.

the old man didn't come back she left and went to her own house, where
she stayed inside for three days. Three days she stayed indoors. As we
heard later, she had neither food to eat nor water to drink. My
brother-in-law heard this from the old woman herself. She had a bucket
of water she'd been washing clothes in, which had not yet been thrown
away, and she drank that water. After three days the Turks came and
raped her. That old woman is ninety years old. It is shameful to say this,
but that is what happened; she herself told my brother-in-law. Of course
I didn't see this happen myself. But you know they raped women from
our village. They raped [an old woman] from our village, as I heard. It
grieves me to tell you these things.

So with that in mind I am *glad* that they shot my mother when they
did, so that such a thing did not happen to her. *I think God should pour
boiling water on them.* But I know I should not say such things.

I see my parents as Christian martyrs. They died the death of martyrs
for their religion and for their native land.

Chapter 6

FLIGHT

August 1974

The *coup d'état* had started on 15 July 1974, and was followed by a week of fighting between Greeks. On 20 July Turkey invaded Cyprus, and on the same day the UN Security Council called for an immediate cease-fire. Three days of fierce fighting between Greeks and Turks ensued, and on 23 July the Security Council renewed its call for a cease-fire, although sporadic fighting continued until 27 July.

There was then a period without fighting, while two rounds of negotiations took place in Geneva between Turkey and Greece, with Britain in the chair. The second round of negotiations were broken off by Turkey on 14 August, and she started a new advance within two hours of leaving the conference-chamber.

The Argaki villagers soon found that the Turkish advance was going to affect them. At first they could see the signs of fighting in such distant villages as Myrtou, towards the Kyrenia range, but, hour by hour on 14 and 15 August, the Turkish line advanced towards Morphou and Argaki. Some people left the village on the 14th, others on the 15th. The village was bombed several times, and Turkish planes were bombing the surrounding district continuously.

Although this was one of the most alarming and dangerous periods in their lives, the villagers did not in retrospect describe their actual departure from Argaki in very dramatic terms. Their accounts were rather low-keyed, and they did not embellish the moment of severance, which they had only slowly come to see as highly significant. Here is the event as seen through the diary of Androulla Batsallou:

14 August – the aeroplanes are attacking Cyprus again. Wednesday, today, at dawn I woke from my sleep to hear planes going over. I was really scared and started trembling. I turned on the radio and it said that the Turks were again attacking us, so I took my sister and we went to our neighbour, Panayotta's house, because it was of mud brick. Later still, we went to another house, and at six we took whatever we could, put it all in a car and started to leave the village. Just as we were leaving, HajiVassilis and his family stopped us on the road and so they

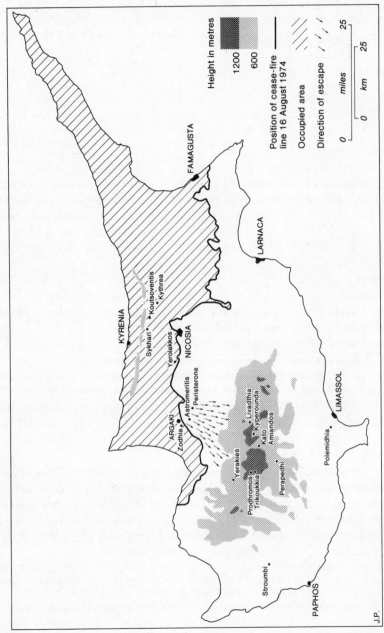

Turkish positions on 20 August 1974. The arrows show the main escape routes taken from Argaki.

came with us. We couldn't find any petrol and we went on until it ran out. On the
road we found some soldiers and they gave us petrol and bread. We went on as far
as Trikoukkia, because HajiVassilis knew a house we could stay in, up there.
When we arrived we found quite a lot of our villagers, and this cheered us up a lot.
There was the Hare, with his family, and others. We settled down, where we
could, in the various rooms. Some inside and some outside, and we rested until
finally we joined in a small prayer.

Vassos, the tailor, was worrying about his boy, the soldier who had
been shot seven times by the Turks. He also felt that the war was coming
closer, so he sought solace by drinking with an old friend:

> On Monday [12 August] the police came to the coffee shops at seven in
> the evening and told us to close up, turn out the lights, and go home –
> I'm talking about the second round of the invasion. My wife was at the
> hospital with our lad, by his bedside day and night. So at 7 there I was
> by myself with the other kids, one eighteen and one sixteen. I said to
> them, 'Off to bed now, and out with the light.' I know what my friend
> Venjamin likes and I found him and said: 'Hey, at home I've got a bottle
> of English whisky – let's go and drink it so the Turks don't get it. For the
> way things are looking they're coming here too', I told him. So we went
> and drank that whisky Monday night.
>   So the second round started finally on Wednesday. At 2:30 I was
> asleep alone, with the kids in their beds asleep. Then we got up and left
> in a bus I'd never seen before. I didn't even know the driver. We got into
> the bus, and we had no idea where he was taking us. In fact he took us to
> Kyperounda, and it took from 2:30 till dawn to get there.
>   My wife was at the hospital with our kid and so she didn't know we'd
> left the village. Later they took the boy from Nicosia Hospital to Lanitis
> Secondary School, and my wife with him, and we didn't know they were
> there. The Wednesday I'd reckoned I'd go to Nicosia to see the boy. But
> Wednesday the planes came, we went to Kyperounda and they put us in
> the cinema, a hundred people, in the cellar of the cinema.

Another man who gave a rather plain account of his departure was
Pantelis, a salesman in one of the Argaki co-operative's two general stores.
A quiet, usually modest, man, he nevertheless wanted to make it clear
that he had stuck to his job longer than many a lesser man might have
done:

> I was a soldier in the reserves at the time, but the co-operative
> committee in Argaki asked for six days' leave for me to work in the
> village shop, and the Ministry gave me this, so I was back in the village
> from 13 August until 15 August. I worked for those three days, serving
> everyone, because the girls who used to work in our other shop had left
> the village two days earlier. The village had almost emptied in those last
> two days, and I stayed to serve those few who remained, with just the

main things – cigarettes, essential foods. I was one of the last to leave the village.

I was with Ttoolis Polyviou, and there were five or six more families. We got in his truck about nine o'clock at night. Your cousin Tomas was there, and he'd put his brother-in-law, Sophronis in [since he was bedridden], and his family and three or four other families, until the truck was full up.

Tomas took the co-operative's van, and he followed us. That night we got to Kyperounda. About ten persons had stayed behind in the village, the ones who remained enclaved, and some soldiers also stayed, up by the water tank.

We got to Kyperounda and that night we slept in the cinema. There were a lot of people there, so the next day I sent my wife and the kids with my dad to Perapedhi village.

The only things I took with us from the village were a radio and two suits and a good bed-cover. Two suits, one radio, one coverlet and a

Takis Dionysiou, b. 1935, Argaki; m. 1959 Eleni Danil (b. 1937, Argaki); three children. He brought 1·7 hectares and she 1·1 hectares to the marriage; her family built the dowry-house. By 1969 they had 980 citrus trees, and owned a tractor which he used to plough for others, on an hourly basis. He was then an energetic middle-sized farmer, intent on getting more land; about a fifth of the village farmers had larger holdings than he.

torch, because there was a black-out on at the time, and when the kids used to get up in the night we needed the torch. O, and my wife took her gold, and some clothes for the child who was four months old. Gold sovereigns, bracelets and crosses.

This man's account was rather typical, both in its simplicity and in the fact that he took relatively little with him out of the village. Every time people recalled the day of their flight, they were forced to remind themselves of what they later came to see as errors of judgement. Mostly, they made the spur-of-the-moment decision to leave virtually empty-handed, which later, in their penury, they bitterly regretted. Small wonder, then, that they tended not to dwell upon the last hours in the village.

In contrast, the recollections of Takis Dionysiou, a successful farmer, were vivid, detailed, and unusual:

It was Thursday [15 August] the day we left Argaki. The evening before I started to irrigate my field, an all-night stint. My old father-in-law was in the orchard with me, because we had melon-beds in among the trees, three or four plots, and he was sleeping out to keep an eye on them so they wouldn't get pinched. So I stayed irrigating all night. When dawn came, we got up from a nap and heard the aeroplanes start bombing from about two miles away. They were coming over and having a go at the box factory in Zodhia, and they were passing right over our heads, some very low, some high up. We took cover. I had the car there as well. Then the sun came up and I went on watering the field, that is, I finished it off till the field had drunk enough. I said to the old man, 'I'm going. What am I going to do here all day? When it's night time I'll come and pick you up. I'll go and see what's going on.' But when I said that, I didn't expect that we'd be leaving Argaki.[1]

To get to the village I took some tarpaulin and covered the whole of the top of the car with it, leaving just a big enough space in front of the wheel for me to see to drive, because the planes were everywhere. As soon as one passed over, another one was coming in behind it. [So, stopping and starting, under this rough camouflage] I reached Argaki. When I got there I was very, very tired from having been irrigating all night. The aeroplanes were going over continuously, and sometimes machine-gunning the village, but I lay down and I slept. I was asleep until sunset. I was very anxious, but where could we go? I instructed the kids not to go outdoors. The house was made of *klithari*-bricks, mud and straw, so I told them to get against the solid walls. The walls were thick,

---

[1] The point of this remark is that when Takis finally left Argaki, the old man was not with him. Later, Takis describes his search for him, and his mother-in-law. On the general problem of old people in 'disasters' see Appendix 2, p. 201, and the paper by Friedsam (1962) cited there.

if they machine-gunned. Not like this one. You remember going to my house, it had an inner-room. Well I put them in there and kept an eye on them so they wouldn't go outside. Outside the house, in the village, some people were hiding in the concrete irrigation channels, others were . . . well it was *pandemonium* in a few words . . .

I awoke from my sleep and was about to go to the coffee shop when my wife said 'Most people are leaving, what should *we* do?' I said 'It's nothing. Stay here with the kids. We've got the car, and if need be we can leave in it.' I ate and went to the coffee shop. It was between 8 a.m. and 8:30 when I got there. My neighbour Parthenis started leaving with his daughters. He took them to Yerakies village [in the Troodos mountains]. My wife sent me a message with the littlest kid, to say come home because she wanted me. I'd just got to the coffee shop and heard what they were saying, that the Turks were going to get all of us, and all sorts of things, so I stayed there. My wife got anxious and came after me right to the coffee shop![1] She said 'We've *got* to go.' 'All right, you go on home and I'll follow.' We went home. We took just a few things, a suitcase with a few children's clothes, and a jacket since we were going to the mountains, that is, a jacket each for the kids, and we set off with nothing but that case. We set out and got to Yerakies. O, I forgot. There was some meat in the fridge, eight or nine pounds in weight and we took *that* with us too. And a loaf, you know, whatever was handy. I don't know if you know the road? The one that goes up to Kykko Monastery? We got to Yerakies and it was so full there wasn't even a place to park! We went to a house, a poor man's house, and he took us in. He had forty people in his house. Our fellow-villagers were all together in one room. Parthenis, who had a mother-in-law from Yerakies, was there. You know, we're neighbours. We stayed in his in-laws' house. That night we handed our meat out and the woman of the house took it and she fed us. Not just us. Parthenis had brought two or three sacks of potatoes, and they peeled two sacksfull. All of us, people from Zodia village as well, people from other villages, we all ate.

In the morning we got up. We couldn't all stay in that one house. I went with Parthenis to find another house. He has six or eight people in his family. The man whose house we'd slept in actually got cross with us, asking why were we leaving, did we think he couldn't look after us? We said to him, 'It's difficult, forty people can't stay in one room.' It *was* difficult. The poor man had given his rooms to everyone and he himself had slept outside [in the cold of the mountains]. We found a house and we went and slept in it. We got up the second day of being up there, and went outdoors on a terrace, and we could see the place down in the plains, flat lands, where the aeroplanes had been constantly bombing the villages on the Thursday. I said to Parthenis, 'Whatever the risks, we *must* leave here and go down to our village tonight and bring out what we

---

[1]   An unusual breach of normal female conduct.

can, for we won't be going back again.' Everyone had left by now. You
see, when we were down in Argaki we'd heard what the Turks had done
before [during the July invasion], how they'd dishonoured women,
raped, murdered, and we believed, that is, I at least believed, that we
would *not* go back to live in Argaki. Because they'd been *bombing* our
village. When they bomb a village and everyone leaves . . . [that's it]. I
reckoned we *had* to go to Argaki and take what we could lay hands on.
And that is what we did.

Takis set off down the mountain with his next-door neighbour from
Argaki, Parthenis, a substantial farmer who had left a lot of valuable farm
equipment behind. Takis was sure that the Turks would not enter Argaki
at night, even though the Greek soldiers were in full retreat, because he
had learned in his own military training that this was too risky. It was late
and dark when they got back to Argaki. Takis found his younger brother
and asked him to drive Takis' tractor out, but his brother had already
arranged with a friend to do this. The friend was busy filling Takis' trailer
up with his own goats. Takis needed the trailer, but the friend already had
the goats loaded. Takis told the story as if the matter was settled calmly,
when the friend suggested they find another trailer, which they did, but it
seems probable that some hot words were exchanged at the time.

Takis described the evacuation as if it had been rather easy – complete
silence, complete darkness, and men entering houses to ransack them!

> It was as if we were thieving from out of our own houses. In ten minutes
> I'd loaded all the clothes from the wardrobe. I put a sheet on the floor,
> put all the clothes on it, made a bundle and tied it up. I thought I took
> all the clothes out of the wardrobe. Just my bad luck though, one jacket
> stayed behind, and it had all my receipts in it, from the carrots, the
> oranges – if I had those now it would really make a difference, for up till
> now I haven't been able to draw any money out of the co-operative.
>
> I filled my waggon up with anything I could put in it – *halloumi*-cheese,
> tomato-paste, any kind of food I found. I left the fridge, the gas cooker
> too, but I took the TV and I took . . . well, I filled that waggon till it
> couldn't take any more. I called to Parthenis, and the two of us set out
> together. We set out at 1:00 a.m.
>
> You know what a tractor's like when it's going up a mountain road.
> We had them going flat-out up to Yerakies. We parked them on one side
> of the road. I could see that Parthenis wanted to go back and get his car
> – you know, he still had two vehicles back in the village. He says to me,
> 'I'm really sad about that car.' I say to him, 'OK. Let's go back *again*.'
> He says, 'It's a bit difficult, after all, what are you going to bring out?'
> 'Me? I'm going to get my fridge, if I can, and maybe the gas cooker.' 'All
> right', he says. We set off.
>
> But I've remembered something which I won't forget. On the way a
> partridge ran into the car. Parthenis said to me 'We hit that partridge.'

Pavlos and Panayotta Petrou ('Mourtas' and 'Mourtena'); he was born in 1907, she in 1909, in Argaki. They were a farming family, well liked in the village, with children and grandchildren.

[Partridges are a great delicacy in Cyprus.] I said, 'Go on, go on and leave it.' He said, 'What, leave it there?' So we stopped and walked about for a few seconds, but the seconds were ticking by, and no matter how much we looked we couldn't find the partridge. So we started off and got to the village. It was about 2:30. We went fast, and when we got inside the village it was dead quiet. Everyone who wanted to go had gone. I forgot to say this before. The first time we went back I went looking for my father-in-law and mother-in-law. The old man should have come back from the melon-bed and he remained cut off [see Appendix 2, p. 201]. The second time we went back I looked for the old lady and couldn't find her in the house. Neither one nor the other.[1]

I helped Parthenis, whose son Mikailis had some dowry things, and he had the girl's dowry things too, so we filled one car up with sheets, all kinds of clothing. His other car we filled up with glassware, his daughter's dowry things again, and some potatoes. Foodstuffs. I didn't say anything to Parthenis about the fridge or anything, and the only things I took from the second trip were some hoes, blades of a machine cultivator, and a spare tyre for the tractor, worth altogether about £35.

---

[1]   When I recorded this interview, in late 1975, Takis had his wife's parents living with him. As the reader will appreciate by the end of this chapter, the issue was too sensitive to probe.

The reason I didn't get the fridge was that it was very dark, the fridge was very heavy, and I'd have had to call Parthenis to help me. It wasn't logical to waste time. I found some food instead, and I didn't get the fridge.

A small number of elderly people – about thirty in all – remained in the village when everyone else had left. As we have seen, some got left behind by accident in the confusions of last-minute departures, but others chose not to go, refusing to believe that there was any real danger. One such man was old Mourtas, whose wife Mourtena described to me how their son had come and called to them to leave the village with him, but the old man would not go: 'Where do you think you're going? You'll really leave your homes like this?', he said.

A little later she could see planes bombing the near-by villages, and asked her husband again, 'Well, old man, what about it now?' 'Oh, the Turks won't get us', he replied. 'No fear. They won't take our village. No, they'll head further west, up the coast.'

So she went off to feed the goats, her own and her daughter's and a neighbour's. But now the planes started to bomb Argaki itself, and a bomb – she called it a 'bottle' – fell just where she had been standing a few moments before. She ran home, to find her husband going to bed unwell, and refusing to eat. The raid had resulted in a fire, which she helped six other elderly villagers to put out, since they feared the whole neighbourhood would burn. It was high summer, and since the older houses had wooden beams, and were surrounded by thornbush fences, in the dry heat they would have burned readily. In her own words:

> Some of us took the hosepipe and fixed it on the tap; some were rushing about elsewhere. I was holding the hose and spraying it everywhere, and others were using buckets. Finally we put it out and went off.

Now another old man arrived, saying that a Landrover with four armed Turkish soldiers had just entered the village square. Two old men who heard this were determined to escape immediately. Mourtena went home and told her husband what had happened. They were both so utterly terrified that, quite empty-handed, they stole out into the orange grove with four other old people. When night fell, Mourtena crept back to the village for food and blankets, and they then spent the night out in the fields. At dawn some of the others decided to escape from the area, but Mourtena's husband was quite infirm, so the couple could not go with them. At this point she hid some money she had brought with her among some reeds.

> I said to my old man, 'Now come and eat, have a bit of the melon and a bit of *halloumi*-cheese.' 'You've gone mad. It's only dawn. You're going on about eating melons *this early*?', he said. [Melons are normally eaten

only when it is hot.] I said, 'Eat a bit of melon, now that it's morning.'
But he wouldn't. Old Tomas made a sign to me: 'Turks are coming', he
said. A Landrover appeared, and then another one, from over where a
field was being watered, and the Turks thronged the field. If I told you
there were a thousand . . . there were *more*. They filled up the field, all of
it. They got out and started going on in Turkish, then they went off. Off
they went. My old man was tired. We'd wandered into one field and
found it watered and muddy. The old man said, 'I'm going to sit here,
and I don't care what happens to me.' He sat down, I sat next to him,
then we heard shots and they were almost on top of us. 'What are we to
do, old man? The Turks'll have us', I said to him.

The old man was really unhappy. 'What *can* we do?', he said. 'If
they're going to get us, they're going to get us. That's it.' Three Turks
arrived, two as tall as *this*, and armed, armed like you can't imagine, they
were carrying heavy weapons, they had bayonets. They had bullets *here*.
They had something else *there*. Well, they *arrived*.

My old man said, 'Hallo there, lads. I can see you're having a hard
time of it, just like us.' The unarmed one was a [Turkish-Cypriot]
fellow-villager of ours. He explained to the others that we two were
looking after our melon-beds.

One of the soldiers said, 'Gel otour' ('Come and sit down'). Then he
said, 'Gel otour butarafta' ('Come and sit on this side!'). Then he said,
'Hellim ketir ekmek' ('Give us bread and *halloumi*-cheese').

I said to him, 'Here's your bread, here's your *halloumi*, here's olives,
grapes, anything you like. Take whatever you want to eat – cucumbers
and tomatoes – go ahead', I told him.

They took what they wanted and then started asking us lots and lots of
questions. Could we understand Turkish? We did know a bit, but we
said we didn't, just to be on the safe side. Then the soldiers asked what
two old people were up to out in the fields?

'Our goat ran off, and we came looking for it, and then the old man got
tired so we sat down here.'

'Why did you two old people sit down just here?'

'Oh my, I don't understand what you're saying to us. We've got our
melon-beds here, and that's why we came here.'

If we hadn't been right there in the melon-beds, they might have shot
us. They'd have said, 'What are you up to [hiding] in the trees?' At last
they went on their own sweet way, without another word.

Later, Mourtena decided to go back to the reed patch to retrieve the
money she had hidden but, when she got there, she found that Turkish
soldiers were resting very close to it. Nevertheless, she stole up, shoes in
hand, and took it away. Then, very slowly, she took her husband through
the orange groves towards the western edge of the village lands, to a small
chapel called Ayios Andronikos, much loved by the village women. When
they got there they lit some candles, made the act of submission, and said

prayers, and went to sleep in the chapel. When they awoke in the morning, they could see Turkish soldiers looting the nearest village houses, so they went away into the orchards.

Later, they found themselves surrounded by Turkish soldiers on both sides, so they hid. Later still, the old woman went back to the little church and found it in a mess; she lit the candles, filled up the oil lamps, kissed the ikon and left. They spent the next three days in a near-by orange grove. For five days they ate nothing but three oranges, which had stayed on the trees after the harvest. They got very thirsty, but eventually she found water. At last they crossed the lines at Peristerona village, from which they were taken by truck to the Limassol side of the island. They had been nine days and nights on the move, hiding from the Turks, and during that time they had travelled only three miles.

These two old people escaped, but there were some thirty who did not. For various reasons, and in various circumstances, they stayed in Argaki. Some of them saw one local Turkish woman greet the conquering soldiers as liberators. At one point, a number of them were put under guard in a single house. Hungry and thirsty, they asked a passing Turkish fellow-villager to get them something to eat, and later he threw them a couple of tins of bully-beef, looted from the co-operative shop.

I found it difficult to get detailed accounts of the experiences of those who stayed, or were caught, behind Turkish lines. Elsewhere in the island, the war was accompanied by sexual assaults by Turkish soldiers on persons of both sexes and varied ages. This meant that concerning any person who had been in Turkish hands there was always an unspoken question: had he or she been assaulted? In Mediterranean cultures, to have suffered any form of sexual assault is deeply humiliating. The victim feels defiled, violated in a most shaming way. Furthermore, in the 'honour' societies of the Mediterranean, to rape any member of an enemy group is, in a sense, to score at the expense of the group as a whole;[1] as a belligerent Cypriot might say, 'I fuck your mother, and your daughter, and your *whole clan*.' I did not want to add to anyone's sufferings by asking them whether or not it had happened to them, and this extended to my dealings with their close relatives.

This said, the reader can now be introduced to the experience of two elderly Argaki men, as recorded by them in statements to the police, which I examined at Nicosia Police Headquarters.

> I'm from Argaki, Morphou, but now I'm staying in Plaka as a refugee. At the beginning of the second round of the invasion, my children left Argaki to get away from the Turks. They asked me to leave with them,

---

[1]   I am indebted to Paul Stirling for this point. See also Amir 1971.

but I wanted to stay in the village. On 16 August, when the Turks came into Argaki, there were about thirty of us remaining in all, men of my age and younger, women and elderly men. When the Turks came into the village I stayed at home alone. That same day they started to search all the houses.

When they got to my house they called out to me to open the door for them so they could search. I opened the door to them, and they came in and searched. They found a shotgun belonging to my son-in-law, and they took it and left. The next day they came and searched again, and took from me a watch, a ring, and two pounds I had in my pocket.

On 25 August the first Turks left, and others came to the village to replace them. This same day, Matteos [a pseudonym], a fellow-villager, came to my house, so we could keep each other company.

And on the same day still, a Turkish soldier came to the house and searched us. He found ten shillings on me, which Matteos had given me to keep in my pocket. He took the ten shillings and then he searched the whole house, for money. When he'd looked and found none, he came back to us . . .

The old man then described the indignities to which he and his comrade were forced to submit, at gunpoint.

After Matteos and I had suffered this humiliation, we decided to escape. Twice we tried, and twice the Turks caught us. Once when they caught us they asked us why we wanted to get away, and Matteos told them what that particular Turk had done to us. Then they told Matteos that they would take him to a doctor to be examined . . .

After a perfunctory examination the doctor told the old Greek that there was 'nothing wrong with him'. Subsequently the old people in Argaki were all brought together in two houses, presumably to prevent a repetition of the event. A little later, they were all removed to Morphou, near by, and, after an interval, released to the Greek side. The statement ends with signature, date, and the witness of a police constable.

So much is left out of that police statement: bewilderment, fear, disgust, shame, the changes in the victim's perceptions of time passing, and so on. Nor does the statement give much clue as to the motives of the assailant, for, although we know that the victims felt humiliated, was that the main reason for the act?

It is idle to speculate further. In war, after all, men feel free to do things they would be ashamed of doing in their home towns or villages for fear of discovery and punishment. They are free in two different senses: first, the disorganisation of war zones permits private acts of violence, and secondly things may be done to enemies which will be shrugged off by one's own people. 'It was war. They were enemies.' That at least was the justification offered by Kajis (p. 90) for his murder of seven Turkish Cypriots.[1]

---

[1] The reader who seeks further detail on acts of rape and murder by Turkish soldiers may consult the Council of Europe's report, *Cyprus versus Turkey* (1976). To learn of Greek Cypriot violence against Turkish Cypriots, consult the Turkish Cypriot Human Rights Committee's *Human Rights in Cyprus* (1979).

To mention these two documents in the same paragraph is not to suggest that they are similar in accuracy or authority. However, because there definitely have been significant numbers of barbarities committed by Greek Cypriots (usually of extreme right–nationalist persuasion) against their Turkish Cypriot fellow-citizens, and because Greek Cypriot official sources are silent about these, the reader may benefit from this additional reference.

Another useful Turkish Cypriot source is Volkan 1979.

Part III

DIASPORA

Chapter 7

REFUGEES

August 1974–April 1975

International developments

It was only after many conversations with the refugees that I could begin to induce any pattern in their experiences. The chief theme to emerge from the first eight months of their severance from their village was their realisation – which came to some quickly, some slowly – that their return to Argaki would be at best problematic, and was at worst distant, if it ever were to happen at all.

One after another of them told me that they left the village thinking they were only going to be away for a few days, thus taking little more than food and clothes. Most went up into the villages of the Troodos mountains, in the opposite direction from the Turkish advance. Mountains are easier to defend than the plains, and in Greek history they are the traditional 'free' areas of national resistance; but the Argaki people were thinking mostly of immediate safety, not long-term issues. Those mountain villages which were used to house summer tourists were now swollen by ten and twenty times their normal populations, and people slept where they could – in cinemas, schools, courtyards. Large numbers were simply received into private homes – at worst the host family would move into one of the two rooms and the guests would crowd into the other. Then the waiting began.

During September 1974 official Cyprus started to sort things out; the civil servants were British in their professionalism and the national emergency brought out the best in them. They were soon organising tent camps, particularly for those people from the Kyrenia and Famagusta regions who had not found mountain refuges, and they gave everyone refugee identity cards, relief food, clothes, and small cash allowances. The Argaki people, however, did not go into the tent camps of the plains. They either stayed in the mountains or, if they had close relatives in Nicosia or Limassol who had a little space, they moved in with them for a while. They were to become spectators in the propaganda and diplomatic struggle which continued after the cease-fire. For the next four months the events they heard about on the radio and read of in the newspapers only added to their uncertainty.

The first spectacle to be played before them involved the discovery of fresh atrocities: each side produced evidence – such as the uncovering of mass graves before assembled correspondents – that the combatants on the other side had killed civilians in cold blood; and among the Greeks fresh details began to circulate of the assaults upon girls and women of all ages by Turkish soldiers.

Then there were newspaper accounts, poignant in the extreme for the Argaki villagers, of the Turkish army (like so many armies) systematically looting Greek homes, and sending back to the mainland boats crammed with the fruits of the Greek Cypriot boom years – cars, tractors, televisions, refrigerators, washing-machines, and the like.

Several Argaki men had been taken prisoner, and they joined the hundreds of other Greek Cypriots who were conducted, often in harrowing conditions, through the towns of central Turkey in a victory procession which resembled a Roman triumph. They sometimes feared that they would be lynched by excited mobs (see Appendix 3). Meanwhile their families in Cyprus were often desperate for news, not knowing if their menfolk were dead on the battlefield, wounded, or alive and well. Parents waiting for news had only to hear of a soldier who had been in the same unit as their son, and they would find him to extract from him every detail of where and when their boy had last been seen. These episodes were commonplace. It was also common for a family to refuse to believe that several witnesses had seen their boy killed.

Yet another public drama, which had most serious implications for Greek Cypriots generally, and for their refugees in particular, was the gradual migration of the Turkish Cypriots to the north. They went for varied reasons: after the mass graves had been uncovered, some believed that they would be safer with the Turkish Army standing between them and the still-armed EOKA B zealots; others, particularly those who were poor, may have been further attracted by promises of Greek property. Since everyone knew that the Morphou region, for example, contained the most well-appointed modern houses and profitable citrus groves, and that its former residents were living as refugees in the south, it followed that there must be empty property there for the asking. Furthermore those who were reluctant to move north were almost certainly subject to threats from Turkish-Cypriot nationalists, and told that they would be regarded as traitors to the national cause and breakers of ethnic solidarity if they did not move. The migration did not take place overnight. It was a slow process, occurring throughout the early months of 1975. The Turks, after all, were about to become refugees in the same sense as were the Greeks of Argaki, but whereas the Argaki villagers had fled from an advancing army, and were mostly empty-handed, the Turkish Cypriots had more time for reflection and to settle their affairs, however disadvantageously. Generally they were leaving less because of a definite threat than because of the previous twenty-year history of strained relations and sporadic killings, and because in the north they faced a future uncertain, yet promising.

The departure of the Turks to the north was politically and structurally the most important consequence of the invasion and partition of the island. It was strongly reminiscent of the 1922 population exchange between Greece and Turkey, the partition of India in 1947, and many other similar subsequent events, all apparently irreversible. Concerned about the outcome of the negotiations between the protagonists, the eyes of the refugees were firmly fixed on the various international diplomatic manoeuvres, reports of which filled the newspapers. The drama of these negotiations was the one which most strongly impressed most of those to whom I talked in April 1975. But the pattern of events following the war proved to be a series of false dawns, and these were to continue throughout 1975, as the reader can quickly appreciate. On 25 August 1974, not ten days after the cease-fire declared by Turkey (when she had taken 38% of the island), Haluk Ulman, the foreign policy adviser to Turkish Premier Ecevit, said that Turkey would insist on retaining a minimum of 28% of the territory of Cyprus. Had Turkey given up Famagusta, its satellites, and the populous Morphou area as well, the majority of the Greek Cypriot refugees could then have returned to their homes. On 30 August the UN Security Council unanimously supported a resolution calling on the Greek and Turkish Cypriots to resume direct negotiations and to work with the UN to solve the refugee problem. On 16 September the first exchange of war prisoners took place. Optimists argued that surely this was a step towards other mutually advantageous exchanges. On 23 September the US Secretary of State, Dr Kissinger, told the UN that 'the United States is prepared to play an even more active role than in the past in helping the parties find a solution to the centuries-old problem of Cyprus.' Perhaps this meant that the US would persuade the Turks to withdraw?

In April 1975, the Argaki refugees said to me, 'What do you think? We'll go back, won't we', with a smile, expecting either simple confirmation or the reply, 'O, we'll go back. The question is, when?' Spirits rose and fell with every headline. The same man, in a half-hour conversation, would first set out with complete conviction all the reasons why the UN, the Great Powers, and the hard-headed interests of all parties would dictate a rapid settlement of the Cyprus problem, which would be based on all the refugees going home; or perhaps not the Kyrenia people, since Turkey might need a small zone of special security, the closest point to her own coastline. Then, when some new and indigestible fact was put before him, or he put it before himself, the whole argument would be reversed. Everything could be interpreted in exactly the opposite way: Turkey would not yield an inch – when had she ever given up anything? The USA had now got what she wanted – a partitioned Cyprus. Russia? Expect nothing. Sophisticated men were capable of reversing their views several times a day.

In July 1974, President Makarios had escaped in a British helicopter from the Sampson *coup*; but for the next four months he did not set foot in Cyprus, and his absence allowed expectations to arise in many Cypriots that when he did return, the situation would somehow miraculously be put right. Such feelings were encouraged by those of his supporters who wrote, neatly and in very large white-painted lettering, the Greek word 'Erchetai' ('He is coming') on many a prominent wall, and on the side of at least one mountain. Everywhere, his name was written like a protective charm, the graphic equivalent of an incantation. If messianic hopes and millenarian dreams were arising, however, they were rapidly dashed, for when Makarios returned on 7 December 1974 the Turkish Army did not budge an inch. A huge crowd of his admirers went to Limassol to greet him, and in the confusion and tension of the day Elias Pelavas, an Argaki bus-driver, a harmless, popular man in his sixties, was shot dead by a jumpy EOKA B gunman. Limassol had been an EOKA B strong-hold, and many of them may have feared that with so many of Makarios' supporters filling the city they might face spontaneous retribution. The weakness of Clerides' interim government was clearly demonstrated by the fact that EOKA B supporters were still openly carrying guns, even after all the damage they had done to their own people.

There were two other political landmarks in the first eight months after the war. First, the US Congress imposed an embargo on the supply of arms to Turkey, arguing that Turkey had used its American weapons quite illegally when it invaded Cyprus. The embargo was introduced against the advice of Dr Kissinger, who argued that this act, far from extracting concessions from Turkey, would harden her negotiating position. The other event that aroused refugee hopes was a UN-sponsored meeting between Greek and Turkish leaders in April 1975, but this produced no important results.

Realisation

Such, then, were the major political events which framed and indeed shaped the Argaki refugees' views of their immediate situation. But before any of these occurred, the Argakides had to go through the experience of their first days as refugees, even though they did not yet seriously see themselves as such nor absorb the implications of the term. We can get a hint of what this was like from Argaki's youthful diarist, Androulla Batsallou:

15 August

Refugees in Trikoukkia. Thursday, today. We woke up this morning in Trikoukkia because we had taken refuge from the Turks. The kids' noise woke us up. We straightened out our clothes, and then we went outside and started looking at the high mountains and beautiful views. Then we drank some tea and I went for a walk with Heleni and then we returned to our refuge.

We sat here and sat there until noon, then I went with Heleni and Klykou to church near by and we lit candles, and sat on the bench there, under a large tree. In the afternoon some children came carrying a dog, so we started talking to them. Soon their grandma came and took them off with her. In the evening we had a light snack and went to bed.

16 August

Today is Friday. I got up this morning, and straightened out my clothes, which had been spread out everywhere. Then I had a glass of milk, and went with Klykou to the church of the All-Holy Virgin. We sat under the large tree, talking. After a bit, a man came with some fruit and brought us some, and we ate it. After a bit quite a few young people had gathered there, and were sitting with us.

When we returned to our house, our *refuge*, three soldiers, co-villagers, came and told us that the Turks had taken our village. The women began to wail, and my eyes filled with tears.

Later we ate a little. I went for a walk with Heleni to Prodhromos to buy bread and other things we needed. There wasn't any bread so we waited till it came. While we were waiting, my neighbour Androulla arrived, and another co-villager, Kouvarena, and we were glad to see them. At last the bread came, and everyone rushed to get at it. Real *pandemonium* broke out, and some people ended up without any bread. I managed to get a loaf, but Heleni didn't. At last we got back to the house. We all sat and talked. Sometimes we cried and sometimes we laughed. At last we went to sleep.

18 August

Sunday, today. When I woke up, I ate something, dressed and went to Prodhromos with Klykou. Seeing other people we managed to forget our sorry state for a bit and had quite a pleasant time. We sat at a café and had soft drinks, then went up to the hotel to see my co-villager Prezou with her daughters. But we didn't know the way and mindful of our honour we didn't get as far as the hotel. We strolled about and saw other people we knew, and we all went to the children's garden. Walking downhill, I lost my balance and hurt my foot. Then, Louiza with us, we went to the hotel, found Prezou and had a real talk. We set out for the house below, and the rains caught us, and we were late. We got home, ate, rested and then went back to Prodhromos, and Maria Xyda came with us. We had a really good time, laughing and joking. At last we went back to the house. I sat and taught the children for a while. At last I went to sleep.

Although the first word after '15 August' is 'refugees', it does not appear again in these three days, and there is no hint of that state becoming permanent; she weeps when Argati is captured, but soon after she is quite light-hearted – 'We had a really good time, laughing and joking.' Within a month this young woman's mood turned to bitterness as she came to understand the realities of her situation:

17 September

Yet another page filled up, as refugees in Prodhromos. Lord God, when will that blessed day come when I shall write in capital letters, 'return to my village, to my ancestral home'? As I fill each page, I say, this is the last day we'll be refugees. Tomorrow we'll go home again ... [text unclear]. Perhaps tomorrow we'll go home again and then joy and laughter will bring colour to our lips, which for days have been lifeless by reason of the assault by the ungodly people who have driven us from our homes, and who from day to day take the lives of so many of our brothers and sisters. Today I read in the newspaper that the Turks raped 13- and 14-year old virgin girls who in the end could not endure it and simply died. Another day, I read worse, and the next day, worse again. My God, how can you put up with so much evil? Why do you not hurl fire to burn these unbelievers, all of them, every one?
We do not forget our hopes, and our only hope is in you, my God. We are waiting, waiting. That blessed day will sometime come and we are all waiting for it.

It took less than a month for the seriousness of the situation to take hold of her; she was not, after all, the head of a family, and had not been encouraged to reflect much on the public world of politics. But within this short time arose an obsessive anxiety about the future – 'Yet another day ... tomorrow ... waiting, waiting ... that blessed day'. The very urgency of the appeal suggests a fear, although not stated as a conscious thought, that perhaps she will *not* go home. Most of the refugees, though, and the women in particular, probably did not permit conscious expression, still less serious consideration, of that thought for the first six months of diaspora.

No one event seems to have been the cause of most people's stopping to think of themselves as *temporary* evacuees, away from their homes for days or, at most, a few weeks, until the Turks might agree to let them return. I suspect that it was the repeated use of the word 'refugee' itself by the mass media, politicians, and the wider society, which slowly began to make them consider the implications of semi-permanent homelessness and destitution. It was clear that for some time many people resented the word. One villager recalled seeing a child take a fig from a tree, and hearing a local shout, 'These damned refugees, barefoot gypsies that they are, will eat us out of house and home.' He got very angry and replied to this man, 'Before you say things like that, you should know that in our village, a single house site was worth more than *your whole community*.' He added, to me, 'No one here who hasn't been a refugee understands what it means to be one. They really look down on us.' Another man told me, 'They call us "refugees" as if we were gypsies. I've lost God knows how many thousand pounds' worth of property, and in a village which has fifty apple trees to its name, *they* label *me* "refugee".'

Someone else described how he felt strange living on the food given him by the government's relief programme: 'The Government gives me five tins of bully-beef. But I'm not used to being fed by *others*. I was the one who was always feeding other people.' One of my wealthier relatives, a resident of Nicosia, did not experience homelessness, but first fully understood the loss of her Argaki house and orchards when she realised she would have to *buy* oranges for the first time in her life. 'We, who gave so many away to other people ...' A group of Argaki women described how they preferred the company of other refugees, feeling uneasy with women who still had their own homes. They disliked having the word 'refugee' used about them, repeating its familiar association with 'gypsies', adding that the local women accused them of eating meat every day. A few minutes after telling me this, one of them teased a three-year-old by saying, 'Hey, you little *refugee*, you,' while another added, 'Refugees are nicer people.' They thus reminded me that when words offend it is often not through the words themselves, but the context in which they are used. American blacks may call each other 'nigger' but whites must not use this term. When the Argaki women felt ill at ease with the locals, it was not over the literal word 'refugee', but what the word said to them about their new position in the world, particularly about their position in relation to those other women.

Encouragement

While people were still gradually and painfully taking in their new situation, its more serious implications were being strenuously denied, particularly by those men who saw it their duty, as family-heads, to do so. This was explained to me by Dionysios, formerly an Argaki farmer with a comfortable holding:

> Just after we fled from the village I got sick. My throat dried right out, *here*, and I felt terrible. I went to the doctor, and he said, 'It's laryngitis,

Dionysios Photiou, b. 1912, Argaki; m. 1932 Panayotta (b. 1914), who came to live in his house and bore him six children. He had received 1·1 hectares at marriage, she 2·5 hectares, but later they bought a further 4·6 hectares. Five of their children were married in Argaki in 1969; at this time Dionysios said, 'I've got four fridges and two TVs – my children's, so why should *I* buy such things?' Takis Dionysiou (see p. 102) is his son.

pharyngitis', I don't know what he said. I went to the doctor and he gave me some medicine and I got better. Then a few days later, same thing again. Back to the doctor. Me, who was never sick in my life.

I think it was from the pining and the upset that I went down with this. My throat dried out and it was some sort of pharyngitic thing, the doctor said. My throat hurt *here*. Pharingolic?

I said to myself in that first week, we'll soon be back in our village. I said to the family in August, 'By November 1st we'll be back.' When November 8th had passed I said to them, 'We'll go soon. By Easter we'll be back!' And I really expected we *would* be back. Then Easter came, and I still have the hope that we will. I do not lose hope.

How will we get back? I can't say. I *think* we will go. They say we *will* go. I have a presentiment, and I have courage and I've encouraged my wife to believe we'll go back, and that she shouldn't grieve. I've given all my family this *encouragement* and they are awaiting our return. And now, even now, I'm not losing my courage. You must have hope, courage. If you have no courage you can't enjoy life. When you have courage, you buy the lottery ticket saying, maybe I'll win this time, and you have that hope.

But at least we didn't lose a child or grandchild in the war. All my relatives are all right.

I know about those government schemes for getting 'restarted'. I don't want work now. The government people said they would give me a card and put my name down for any work I wanted to do. As they've done for everyone, that is. What do you want to do, sir? they asked me. What sort of occupation would you care for?, they asked. I said to them, I don't want to do a thing. [See Appendix 2, p. 199]

After getting together so many possessions and losing the lot, now I don't want to do anything, I told them. I'm an old man now. In two years' time I start my pension, what work should I turn to? Really, where would I be going? After all the property I built up, can I think of doing that *again*? Let the youngsters do it, who have children to rear up. They can do it. I've married off my children and seen them set up properly. I'm not going to start farming, or anything else, again. Of course, I'll pick up the odd day's wages where I can, do some half-arsed job if it comes my way, so that my old woman and I can get on OK.

How have I coped? I'm *not* pining. I start to pine but then I cast it out of myself. I manage to do that. I give courage to my loved ones, and I cast the grief out of my heart. Listen to what I'm telling you: you lie down at night and fall to thinking, ah, there I was in the village, I had such a lot and now the Turks have taken all that away from me. You go over what you had and what you've lost: well, you can't get to sleep at night easily. But if you lie down and say 'Come Christ and the All-Holy Mother' and you cross yourself, turn to your pillow and say your prayers, then sleep comes, you go to sleep easily. You wouldn't go to sleep if you started thinking, I had a sweetheart once, but now look at the wife I've got, I lost everything I had ...

You understand? 'Agnati?' That's Turkish. It means, You understand?

Other men repeated these sorts of things in discussions – how, in spite of their fears, they had told their wives and children over the weeks and months that they *would* go back to the village, and, implicitly, how as men, and heads of families, they had had to master their fears and griefs, to give courage to those they regarded as weaker than themselves. Many insisted they were not disposed to start up a new enterprise, or to hunt for a job. In April 1975 many of them proposed to 'wait and see'.

Degrees of deprivation

Initially, the villagers as refugees were all reduced to a similar state, and all shared certain basic losses. It was some months before social differentiation became a concern again, but eventually they became anxious to distinguish different degrees of loss and vulnerability. There were many unfavourable comments made about those who still had a lot going for them – a job, piece of land, a house somewhere – and who yet complained about being refugees. I was upset to hear one of my close relatives bitterly denouncing another on precisely these grounds; but I could see her point. If they were both 'refugees', they weren't refugees *in the same sense*. One had lost her *only* home. The other, a Nicosia resident, had lost the home she grew up in (now her weekend retreat) and a fortune in orange trees. But she still had her home in the city, a good salary and her social position.

It might be thought that those with fewest possessions might be least affected by the loss of them, and there may be some truth in the comforting view that the poor have a robust adaptability which sees them through hard times (see Appendix 2). Some left-wing Argaki labourers

Giorgios Kalloirkou, b. 1926; m. 1949 Revecca Pipi (b. 1930); four children. At marriage he received 2·4 hectares, she 2·5 hectares. By 1969 they had planted 1,550 citrus trees, and were among the richest farming families in Argaki. Giorgios was linked by marriage to a rather active conservative kin faction, but by temperament he was a quiet, private man, who avoided politics, and was fully occupied with his land.

suggested this to me one day as I shared their lunch. They were working as road-menders, a job none of them had done before the war, and when I asked them how they felt about it they said, with smiles, 'We're poor and we've always been used to having nothing and hard work.' But nobody else sought to make light of their situation in this way, and the poorer women gave me the impression of being more distressed than most. For even the poorest Argaki families had owned their own houses, however modestly appointed, and the village had been just as much home to them as to others; perhaps even more so since their lack of means to travel kept them more constantly within its confines. The poor seemed highly vulnerable, and their women particularly so (see pp. 160, 176); if the leftists among them could take comfort from a belief in their own ruggedness, this was an advantage; but many of the poor were not left-thinking.

Certainly, some of those who had formerly been comfortably off were eloquent in expressing the painful humiliation that they now experienced as refugees. The interview which follows was recorded in the autumn of 1975 with a previously prosperous farmer called Kalloirkou:

> You know how much property I had in the village, I had many orange plantations and I was completely occupied in working them. I was concerned with my kids and not interested in party politics in the slightest. We left the village on that Thursday early morning, with nothing, and I sat idle for two or three months. I looked for work because the ration-food they gave us and the tiny allowance weren't enough. I wanted to live with more dignity so I kept trying until I found work with the chromium mining company here at St Nicholas, and I'm taking twelve pounds a week. From the day I got work they took away both the rations and the allowance, we haven't been getting a thing, apart from my wages.
>
> I was forty-nine years of age and I'd never gone once in my life to work for other people. I used to work *my own* lands. The first morning I set out for work, with my lunchbag in my hand, I started weeping. I set out in tears. And my wife was standing there in the doorway in tears too, and me out there setting off, the same. I was feeling ashamed in case my fellow-villagers (or even the locals) should see me on my way to work for others. I went on like that for about a month, feeling this shame, trying not to be seen, going around behind the bus station so that no one would see me as I got into the bus. Bit by bit I got used to living an unskilled labourer's life.
>
> To have been economically independent and one morning to find yourself with just the clothes you've got on, with no job, with no property, it's a little difficult to get over. You suffer. To be asking for a labouring job, and not to be given something to put your hands to, is terrible. It wounds the spirit. And for the foreman to insist authoritatively that you haven't been working hard, that you've done nothing, that you haven't done it right, that *really* hurts.

Drink? I didn't drink before the war, a drop of wine now and then, a beer; I never cared much for strong drinks like brandy. I don't think drinking relieves the feelings. There is no point in drinking to relax, it won't work for me, I won't get away from my problems or my feelings for the village. I don't find it logical to do that, though others might.

Wherever I go, don't suppose I can forget Cyprus or the village I grew up in. Until the moment of death I shall remember my village and my native land.

I haven't taken one of the government loans to refugee farmers that are on offer because I am completely disheartened by the situation here today. I am in a state of complete uncertainty. That is, *no one* knows from morning to night what will happen each day, or what to expect from the barbarous Turkish conqueror. Tomorrow he may start the slaughter again and take the whole of Cyprus. Because he is unopposed. The Turks are not conforming to the UN decisions. I've neither courage nor appetite to find land to cultivate. I prefer a plain daily wage which gives just enough to eat, to live for today, since I don't know what will happen tomorrow. I have no inclination to make farming my life again. I must be sure that we are going to stay refugees in the long run, that we have no future in going to find our properties again, then perhaps I would be able to decide. I feel we have a one-in-a-hundred hope of going back. That's my estimate: at least one in a hundred. So even if it is only a 1% chance, we have a hope, which *binds* us.

The citrus trees? They were my occupation, and how shall I explain to you what I feel about them? I was taking money from them, and lived comfortably, with dignity. They were my enterprise, my profession. Hard work? However much work I had, the trees were refreshing to me. When I went in among them and saw the greenness all around, and the fruit, the redness everywhere, it was refreshment. I didn't get tired from my property because it *was* my property. The more tiring it was, the more I got out of it. For the trees repaid my labour twofold and threefold.

So I had a taste for sweating in my field, for working in my field for it would make a better return to me. Were I to go and rent a field now and work it, perhaps in a year's time the government or the owner will want it back, so I lose whatever I invested in it. I have no taste for working another's land. That's what the word 'other' means, isn't it? It isn't *mine*, and that's what it's all about.

I'll certainly say this – the women have a worse time of refugee life because they are isolated in houses or tents from morning to night and they think all the time about their homes and property. The men on the other hand are either at work or in the coffee shop or some bar and when you get together in a crowd you tend to forget a little bit while chatting and laughing, you forget temporarily and relax a little. The women, isolated in their houses, suffer much more than we do.

There were several important themes in what Kalloirkou said: one was the pride which villagers all over the Christian Mediterranean felt if they had achieved economic independence (a goal for which urban small business-men also struggle with great vigour); another is his loss of self-esteem when that independence was removed, the sapping of both his morale and his initiative; a third was the power of even a one-in-a-hundred chance of return to prevent him from commitment to 'a new life'. These comments exemplify the difficulties of making any simple 'objective' judgement about whether the rich or the poor suffered most from the dislocation; all that is clear to me is that they all suffered, but in rather different ways.

'It takes a refugee to understand one'

Kalloirkou's last remarks, about the greater distress of the refugee women, was more sensitive than might have been expected from a Mediterranean 'patriarch'. His wife, Revecca, described how in the first weeks of dislocation they had slept on the ground, then slowly acquired a little furniture; she then went on to explain the particular hardships she, as a woman, was meeting:

> It's difficult here. I get on with my housework, but being by myself is really hard. I haven't got any relatives here, and that upsets me. We're a long way away from our relatives.
>
> Quite often when we want to talk about our district, the people here criticise us. They say that we didn't have what we say we had. They say we've got into the habit of talking about all the things we had, and that those who didn't have a thing, still talk about all the things they had. Well, I keep right out of these situations. I don't say a word. But the word got out, from one of our co-villagers, who told the people here that we had property before. I found out when I was talking the other day, and she said to me, 'Your cousin Schienga told me that you are important people, that you had a great deal of land in your village. That you were the most important people in your village.' I haven't said a word about such things, up here, but it got out nevertheless . . . But in any case, whether I talk about what I had or whether I don't, will anyone feel sorry for me? I don't talk about it. No one is sorry for us, and only if we speak among ourselves do we get any comfort, so it's better not to talk to others about it. The people here don't know our district, and so they don't understand.
>
> Those who aren't refugees do not understand the pain of those who are – it cannot be shared. But the refugee *can* talk about his suffering to another refugee, and between the two of them, the suffering is controlled. The one understands the suffering of the other, but the non-refugees don't feel things, they aren't affected in the least.

This theme, 'it takes a refugee to understand one', was one very frequently expressed to me, and Revecca's complaint was immediately taken up by her two young daughters, who sat demure and attentive throughout the interview with their parents. They were secondary-school girls, and after the invasion had been sent off to Greece to avoid risk of rape, should there have been a 'third round' of fighting. They had less to say about the hospitality of the mainland Greeks than about their own feelings that their hosts did not understand them, and they expressed themselves rather formally:

> A stranger can't understand you like your mother and father, no matter how hard he tries to lighten your sorrows. They tried at first to show us some warmth but later on things changed and they came down quite heavily against us, saying we were giving them a lot of extra problems, and that they'd had enough of us.
>
> At school some girls were patronising though others were more open; we met all sorts but many times rather than giving us courage, they upset us more. To give you an example: once the girls were told to bring a little money for Mother's Day, so that they could give gifts to Cypriot mothers, and some of the girls behind us started saying, 'Collecting for Cyprus *again*? Have we got to *adopt* them?'
>
> As for us, we knew what we'd had before and to what a sorry state we had been reduced. We were really deeply hurt since if we got no support or sympathy from our fellow-students, where were we going to find it? They hurt us many times, perhaps without meaning to, but when they knew we were so deeply affected, they should have tried to help us get over it, at very least.

Her sister added, about her experiences at another mainland school:

> All the Cypriot girls there were like sisters – we understood each other, and when we had a problem, we would tell one another, because we were all refugees, and we got on really well.

By the time I met them, the refugees had been told a very great deal about themselves in newspapers and broadcasts, and the formation of their view of themselves was not simply a direct result of dislocation, but was also caught up in the political process. Their insistence on not being understood by non-refugees was an element of their emerging identities *as* refugees, and this included their role as an interest-group in Cypriot society. But there was more to it than this; it also represented their strong feelings about their relations with the rest of society, about the unique and irreversible effects of a shattering experience. Such feelings have been commonly reported by survivors of other catastrophes, and the media were more probably reflecting and reinforcing them, than creating them.

Preoccupation with loss

Nothing prepared me for the strength of the villagers' preoccupation with their losses. Although they spoke a good deal about both the present and the future, they returned all the time to the past, to their previous state, even though it distressed them to do so. There was a good deal of inner compulsion involved – they did not seem free to think or speak about whatever they liked, or about what would make them most comfortable. The preoccupation showed up in several ways: people would recite long lists of the things they had had in their homes; they would talk with great feeling about the superiority of the village and their way of life in it; women from Argaki, if meeting for the first time since the war, would fall weeping into each other's arms, weeping for the unnatural separation they had suffered, and because meeting reminded them forcefully of a rich social life now in tatters.

Petris HajiChristodoulou, b. *c.* 1934, with his wife Maroulla Pelekanou (see p. 140). As a bachelor Petris worked as a tailor for several years in London, with his brother. Both returned to marry Argaki girls. Petris married Maroulla in 1962. By 1969 they owned more than 600 citrus trees, a combination of dowry, purchased land, and judicious squatting on government-owned land. Petris worked as a tailor in Morphou, which fitted well with the part-time work needed in the orchards.

Petris, an Argaki tailor who also had had some citrus orchards, explained to me how images of village life kept intruding both into his waking mind and in his dreams:

At first we said to the children, 'Never mind, it's all right; and later when we came up here to the mountains we said, 'We'll go back to our houses in a little while, we'll go back.' The kids go on about the things they had at home . . . their toys, they don't forget *them*. They want to go home just as much as we do, which is very, very much indeed.

It isn't a question of your getting another house and them giving you the same amount of land you had before. It's quite different. It's about going back to the home where you grew up and got married and had your family. How can you ever start *that* all over again? You can't forget your home – it keeps coming into your mind in vivid images. O, I've been back to the village. I've been back to my shop. I've been back in the coffee shop, chatting with fellow-villagers. Two or three times I've had dreams. Once I was watering a field. Once was about a day when my brother lent me a tractor. When I woke up it took me an hour and a half to get back to sleep, thinking about it. You remember, you see, that you were back in your village, on your own property, even though mostly I tend to push that sort of thought out of my mind. I want to forget, not to remember. But you can't forget completely, you just can't.

Petris and Maroulla had married in 1962. She had received a dowry-house and 200 citrus trees from her parents. Later the young couple had bought another piece of land, and planted 200 grapefruit trees on it, and they were working a third piece of land, also with 200 grapefruit trees, to which the government had not yet granted them title. Petris had a steady income from tailoring in Morphou, and the trees had matured, and started to make them really prosperous, so just before the war Maroulla had decided to refurbish her dowry-house. She had bought a new fridge, a new cooker, and a new sewing-machine. She had also started laying aside things for the dowry of her eight-year-old daughter, Doulla – sheets, silver spoons for candied fruit (a traditional offering to all visitors), 'things for which the fashions don't change', she explained – safe investments. Her grandmother now added with some bitterness, 'The Turks won't want for a thing. They'll find it all ready to hand.'

As they were telling me these thoughts, their four-year-old caught the gist and started to cry for a toy motor car and bicycle left in Argaki. To comfort him his mother said that they would buy him new ones, and that the Turks wouldn't have broken his toys. 'We'll find them there, just as they were. The people there now haven't got any children.' She then explained to me that the children got particularly distressed at the idea of other children using their things. 'It's better not to think about the things we have lost', she added.

But the refugees were constantly reminding each other of the old life. That same evening, in Petris and Maroulla's house, another Argaki woman started things off by asking, 'What would we be doing now in

Argaki? Myself, I'd be picking grapefruit and lemons.' Petris replied, 'Yes, and on Saturday I'd be up the whole night watering my trees.' Daily life continually reminded them of what they would have been doing at home, and their shared preoccupations made them comment to each other, each making the others more sensitive, a collective activity which was certainly an expression of grief, and which at times made me think of a wake. Indeed, the process of mourning increasingly impressed itself on me as metaphor for understanding what the refugees were feeling. They were like people bereaved, but they could not obtain from custom or religion the conventional assistance to assuage their grief (see Appendix 2, pp. 196–200).

The Greek Orthodox Church, like many other religions, specifies formal ceremonies to commemorate the dead. Three days and nine days after a burial there are special prayers. Forty days after the burial there is a memorial service; then others after three months, six months, nine months, and a year. From then on, the memorials are yearly. The gradual increase in the intervals between these memorial services seems to tell people not to allow a preoccupation with the dead to dominate their lives, and to set limits to their mourning. Because a death can remove all meaning from the survivor's life, it has to be dealt with pragmatically, and a completed mourning allows recognition of the fact that a death hurts the living, but that, in *due course*, they will get over it.

The refugees, however, were not in a situation where their emotions could be directed by religious ceremonial and a body of customs. Their loss was outside the provisions of conventional social structure and social organisation. The ceremonies appropriate to a 'steady state' offered no guidance to them. There was no mourning ceremony for the loss of home, fields, village, and way of life. Not only that, but the public world of politics gave no support to the idea that the loss of Argaki might be a permanent one. It would have been political suicide for any Greek Cypriot leader to say, 'Better to forget your villages, for the Turks will never surrender them.' So, if the refugees were something like bereaved people, they nevertheless lacked certain crucial supports that the bereaved might normally have expected.

Meanwhile, some villagers were very clear about the nature of the loss. While I was groping to understand what had been lost (over and above material things), old Dionysios (from whom we heard on 'encouragement', p. 121) put the matter very simply:

> You ask me, what is the essence of the village, if it's the fields and the houses, which we've lost, or the people, our fellow-villagers? My answer is that it's the people *and* the houses and fields – *all together*.

Chapter 8

POLITICS
August 1974–December 1975

When a society experiences an upheaval as massive as an invasion, there is a moment (which may not last very long) when many people are forced to stop and think, for many of their habitual assumptions will have been called in question. At such a time various institutions and groups – government, the Church, the mass media, and the political parties – offer their interpretations of the central event, and in so doing interpret the past, present, and future.

The theme of this chapter is the political interpretations put upon a number of issues: the *coup* and the invasion; the plight of the refugees and their incorporation into Cypriot society; relations within the Greek community and with the Turkish Cypriots; and hopes for the future. There is an attempt to distinguish certain themes and styles in political discussion and to see how certain philosophies served to sustain people in a most difficult period.

The state of the parties

As has already been mentioned, between 1945 and 1949 the mainland Greeks had endured three rounds of brutal civil war, and in subsequent decades thoughtful Cypriot Greeks feared a repetition of this in Cyprus. Many of them had sought to avoid political involvement, but had found themselves forced by the pressures of public life to declare themselves opposed first to the British, as colonial 'oppressors', and later to the Turkish Cypriots, as 'rebels'. Then, in 1972, the earlier fears of a civil war in Cyprus looked as if they might be realised when the EOKA B campaign against Makarios started and Greek fought against Greek. The six days of the 1974 *coup* were, in fact, a civil war in miniature, which was stopped only by the invasion by Turkey. After the war the Cypriots had to explain to themselves how these events had come to pass, and with whom the responsibilities rested. Those who had previously turned their back on politics had now found that political events had stolen up behind them and smashed their certainties flat, killing or maiming their children, and destroying their property. No one could any longer pretend that politics could be kept at arm's length. Politics saturated Cypriot life, and everybody needed to know about them for their own future. These were not the abstract politics of Aristotle and Plato, but simply the pursuit of interests, and the need to make sense of how public life was to be managed.

The men tainted by the *coup* were very naturally on the defensive, for after the war the parties of the left were calling for a complete purge of the civil service, and the trial of activists. In a sense, every family which had lost a member in the *coup* had a case for revenge, although nothing comparable to, say, the hunting down of Nazi collaborators in liberated France occurred. The EOKA men had been in power for only six days, and there were no official figures for the number of their victims during that time. They made a serious attempt to argue that these had been very few, and that all casualties had been due to Turkish bullets. This was the crucial assertion that helped them to disclaim responsibility: it was Turks, not Greeks, who had bombed the civilian population, raped women, and created a mass of refugees. The way the press inevitably focused on the consequences of the invasion helped divert attention from the *coup*, and later the EOKA sympathisers declared to all who would listen, 'We were all to blame', a phrase of portentous ambiguity, adding in sententious tones that the 'Anglo-Americans' had betrayed Cyprus. Many years of leftist polemic had predisposed the Cypriots to accept this latter view, so the self-defence of the EOKA men seemed more plausible than it should have done.

Finally, with a belligerent Turkish force in control of two-fifths of the island, neither leaders nor most citizens felt it sensible to take a course of action which might lead to further fighting between Greeks. On his return to the island Makarios himself gave the lead in this by announcing that he offered 'an olive branch' to all those responsible for the *coup* who 'truly repented'. In most cases they were quick to accept his offer.

AKEL, the Cypriot Communist Party, was also subdued but for very different reasons. In 1970 it had polled over a third of the popular vote in national elections, but in late 1974 it experienced a loss of both face and support. In spite of many statements of support for the territorial integrity of the island, AKEL's longtime patron, the Soviet Union, had failed to prevent Turkey invading Cyprus. In the eyes of many Cypriots the USSR now appeared convicted of the same kind of super-power indifference as did the United States. True, it was not tainted by being the senior partner in the NATO Alliance, and Turkey was not under its political wing.

Nevertheless, AKEL had very faithfully supported Moscow for fifty years, being one of the very few communist parties to condone the Soviet invasion of Czechoslovakia in 1968, and AKEL leaders had for many years assured the faithful, both in print and in conversation, that the mighty USSR would not stand idly by and allow the partition of Cyprus. But the mighty USSR had done precisely this, and now the line had to be that the risk of thermonuclear war with the USA was too great to expect the socialist commonwealth to indulge in sabre-rattling and brinksmanship; and that while the moral, economic, and diplomatic support of the socialist camp was unwavering, the Cypriot people could not reasonably ask this military sacrifice of their great friend.

The centre-right people who had supported Makarios considered that the *coup* had been brought upon their innocent heads through the clashing fanaticisms of EOKA B and the militant socialists of the EDEK party. Such a view left them with several intellectual problems. Why had the Western Alliance, which they had always preferred to the left's Eastern Alliance, abandoned them when they most needed help? Why had the Cypriot middle class left things to Makarios and Clerides for so many years, while themselves concentrating on providing for their families? Why had they not heeded those leftists and assorted eccentrics who had argued that generosity to the Turkish Cypriots should be national policy? Why had Makarios not made a generous offer to the Turkish Cypriots during the five long years of Inter-Communal Negotiations from 1968–73? Why had he been so stubborn? Why no 'olive branch' to the Turkish Cypriots in those years? 'What wouldn't we have given the Turks, just to stay in our properties?', they now said. It was this sense of the crucial questions having been blindly neglected which tormented the more sensitive, and enabled the EOKA catchphrase, 'We were *all* to blame', to make sense to them.

The only political group which could avoid personal recriminations and retain a buoyant morale was the EDEK socialists, led by Dr Vassos Lyssarides. Numbers of their militants had fought gun-battles with the 'fascists' during the coup (as well as in the years before it). They were not 'disappointed'; they had never expected much from the USSR, or anything but harm from the USA, and since the mid 1960s they had been appealing for the Cyprus government to arm the people, so that the masses could defend republican democracy against 'fascist *coups*' and 'imperialist plots'.

They had now the ambiguous satisfaction of having had most of their positions justified. In Dr Lyssarides, Makarios' personal physician, and HajiDimitriou, a deep-voiced jovial dentist, they had two of the most persuasive rhetoricians in Cyprus, and in the political arena they were, as a party, in a situation where their strategy apparently had to succeed. Before the war the fact that virtually all families in Cyprus had some minimal property, or the prospect of acquiring some, had undoubtedly been an impediment to socialism. Now, there was a large group of potential EDEK supporters among those who had been deprived of their property and security. Were the socialists to act as a pressure-group, demanding a redistribution of existing wealth in favour of the new 'have-nots', they would perhaps amass support and push Cyprus in the direction of progressive taxation, a welfare state, and an acceptance of redistributional policies. If this was firmly resisted by the 'haves', then class antagonisms would become more apparent, and for the first time large numbers of people in Cyprus, the refugees in particular, would be made to question the social justice of private property and market economics. In any event, the socialists would be likely to attract new supporters and keep faith with themselves.

The politics of refugee incorporation

The Cypriot elite were shrewd enough to see the implications of the situation – the tinder-box quality that a large number of destitute people might have. Of the refugees from Asia Minor who flooded Greece in 1922, thousands had starved to death, some had fought their way to new security, but large numbers had turned to the left. In 1970, the communists and socialists had commanded close to 50% of the popular votes in Cyprus, in a period of economic boom. What could they *not* do now? Compassion for the refugees was widespread, and for the first year after the invasion, many acts of real generosity were reported by the refugees. But the long-term problem they presented required something more than spontaneous compassion and generosity: it needed a policy. I spoke with prosperous, non-refugee, Cypriots who realised that institutionalised generosity would be an essential self-defence for people like themselves. If they neglected this provision, a slogan the socialists had borrowed from some Latin American revolutionaries might be heard on many more Cypriot lips: 'Either this country belongs to all of us, or to none of us.' The counter-slogan of the establishment might well have been – had they known of it – 'Things are going to have to change here, if things are going to remain the same.'

To prevent either 'anarchy' or a lurch to the left, the rapid incorporation of the refugees into society, economy, and polity was essential. They had to be given a stake in what remained of Greek Cyprus. In the short term, private property, profits, and *laissez-faire* economics would have to be sharply modified if they were to survive as principles or practices.

Consequently, a number of welfare-socialist measures were rapidly made law, reminiscent of Britain in the Second World War: empty houses and rooms were requisitioned, rents fixed at low levels, ration-food given free to the refugees, small cash allowances, and later loans, made to farmers and businessmen to get them restarted. Refugees were permitted by the government to squat in abandoned Turkish houses and cultivate Turkish fields, and a corps of social workers were recruited (often from prosperous families) to minister to the social needs of the refugees. This programme of incorporation was a humanitarian one, and was efficiently mounted by the civil service. But it inevitably contained a number of political assumptions about the sort of Cyprus that would emerge from the war; clearly this was to be a continuation of the prewar mixed economy, with a strong co-operative movement, loans to farmers, effective trade unions, and a fairly unfettered private sector of light industry, import–export merchants, and the rest. There was certainly no suggestion of setting up a socialist, centrally planned economy.

The way the refugees were recognised socially, and represented politically, was part of the process by which they were to be incorporated. There was one major formal organisation, the umbrella for all official refugee activities, the Pan-Cyprian Refugee Committee (PRC). This included representatives of the communists, socialists, centre, and centre-right groups, but no known extreme rightists. The body negotiated with ministers and civil servants over refugee rights and benefits, and, while there was inevitably political manoeuvring within it, its usefulness was clearly perceived by all its senior representatives, and its constituents. All refugees were automatically members and I heard of no one arguing that it was unrepresentative.

A young Argaki-born lawyer called Pavlos Papagiorgiou became prominent in the PRC. Before the war he had been all set for the good life: on returning from Athens with his law degree, he opened a small office in the market town of Morphou, married the daughter of one of the wealthier citrus-farmers, and, being bright, personable, and ambitious, might have gone into politics. Now he was involved in the politics of representing the refugees and as secretary of the PRC was very active, continually making public speeches.

On 24 November 1975, Pavlos introduced me to the PRC. Michailides, a communist MP, very properly wanted to know who the stranger was that Pavlos had brought to the meeting. Pavlos replied, 'A relative and fellow-villager of mine, a sociologist. He teaches at the London School of Economics and he's doing research on the refugees.' 'Are you sure?' 'He's a cousin of *Tomas*', Pavlos insisted, knowing that the MP could check on me with Tomas, his trusted comrade of many years' acquaintance.

At the meeting there was a decision taken about the forthcoming National Congress and how the refugees should be represented at this. Those present decided that refugees should be represented through the local branches of the PRC nearest to the community in which *they were now living*. There was little discussion, and at first I did not see that there was a power struggle behind this apparently innocuous question of refugee representation. It seemed that a number of refugee pressure-groups had formed, based on the prewar communities of origin. They were called 'Free Morphou', 'Unvanquished Kyrenia', etc. Apparently the EDEK socialist party had been active in the formation of these clubs, and most of the PRC's central committee came from the other main parties, all equally mistrustful of the socialists. Pavlos, a moderate conservative, gave me the following interpretation:

> You've noticed those associations, 'Free Morphou' and the rest of them? Well, I call them 'the guerrillas' because the socialists have got hold of them and want to use them to set the world on fire and start their revolution. In my view the PRC should represent all the refugees, regardless of where they are from, through its local branches, and control these clubs as well.

The socialists, for their part, hoped to get the associations on to the PRC national committee in their own right, thus increasing socialist voting strength in an organisation where it was otherwise badly outnumbered. At the next PRC meeting Phrydas, an EDEK militant, said he was speaking as a representative of the Free Morphou Association and that this was the first time it had been officially represented at a PRC meeting. Paraskevaides, the chairman, took a tough line. Dismissing the claim to 'official representation', he insisted, 'That is not settled, and will have to be the subject of a future meeting.'

Pavlos reckoned that the socialists dared not split the refugee movement by taking too hard a line over getting their clubs recognised. But it seemed to me that the clubs looked as if they were there to stay, and they were built on that most durable, flexible, and serviceable element of Cypriot social life – the sense of local identity and, albeit limited, solidarity. It was administratively convenient to have refugees represented through local committees which were formed in the places they now lived in. But clearly, also, the clubs were based on the prewar localities and could easily become political interest groups which could support or oppose any particular settlement between Greek and Turkish Cypriots. If, as seemed likely, whole areas of former Greek residence remained in Turkish hands, then a club based on such an area might make itself felt in opposing the agreement. But this was probably looking too far ahead. At the moment, it was a matter of immediate tactics; since the socialists were strong in the clubs, the right and the communists were unwilling to recognise these.

A socialist rally

I soon had a chance to see one of the clubs meet. The Free Morphou Association had a Sunday meeting in Peristerona on 16 November 1975. There were 300–400 persons packed into a school hall, with a long list of guest speakers. The agenda started with a Morphou headmaster; then came Toumbazos, the Morphou-born Minister of Roads and Commerce; then a message from the Greek Ambassador read out by the headmaster; then the Metropolitan of Morphou spoke; then Paraskevaides, chairman of the PRC; then a communist spokesman; then a socialist; then a spokesman for the Unvanquished Kyrenia Association; then Phrydas, a socialist journalist, read out a message of solidarity from the Palestinian Liberation Organisation; then the headmaster again; then Phrydas again, a lively, informal speech in his own right, as a socialist.

The walls were plastered with the usual slogans:

WE SHALL TAKE BACK OUR LAND

CYPRUS LIVES

A CURSE ON FASCISM

PURGE – UNITY – STRUGGLE

'NO' TO IMPERIALISM

'NO' TO THE NATO SOLUTION

Why, I wondered, had Paraskevaides decided to speak if, as Pavlos said, the clubs were so left-wing and inflammatory? Perhaps the right could not afford to split the refugee movement either, and the chairman of the PRC could no more afford to stay away than to recognise the Turkish partition. The flavour of the meeting was certainly left-wing: the EDEK socialists had more or less set their seal on the event, and it was poignant to see how the politics of the refugee situation (created by the Turkish army) required that conservative businessmen such as Paraskevaides, and moderate centrists such as Toumbazos, had to seem at ease in the public company of passionate socialists and communists.

The most powerful speech, and by far the longest, came from the deputy leader of EDEK, HajiDimitriou. He started by stressing the foreign occupation, and the painful condition of men who could see their villages but could not enter them. He praised Morphou people for their decency and democracy, and their pioneering example in setting up the 'Free Morphou' association. They all faced a bitter struggle, he told them, but the position of Cypriot refugees was not a matter of 'human misfortune', or a turn of Fate, but a pre-meditated crime – attempted genocide. This the Greek Cypriots would militantly oppose, refusing both to be demoralised and to be divided into 'refugees' and 'non-refugees'.

As the chief victim of a national tragedy, the refugee had a *right* to full economic and moral support. This was not charity, but the *obligation* of society; for there was no reason why the refugees should pay twice – first by being made homeless, and secondly by being condemned to perpetual poverty. He therefore insisted on the need for a far-sighted national *policy* towards the fullest incorporation of the refugees, to avoid a deep social cleavage.

HajiDimitriou drew prolonged applause when he spoke of the difficulties the refugees endured as they trudged from one government office to another in search of their rights. Yet powerful interests had opposed the creation of a single Ministry of Refugees. Today's meeting was to help the refugees express and eradicate their problems, and to avoid repetitions of recent friction between refugee and civil servant.

He next turned to the question of a purge of the body politic, of those persons implicated in the *coup* against President Makarios. Some highly placed traitors were still among them, and still constituted a danger to the future of the island. Those guilty of crimes against the Cypriot people had to be punished.

There was a common line that all must follow: the people must remain united behind the UN's demand for the full withdrawal of all the occupation forces, while activism, consultations, and negotiations to achieve this continued.

But no one would undertake the Cypriot people's liberation struggle for them. They would have to do it for themselves, with every person mobilising for the defence of the homeland and its liberation. But they were not mobilised, as yet, he was sorry to say.

> Why? Because they want to keep us weak until the time when *they* are ready to impose their solutions on us. That is why our slogan is, 'Every citizen a soldier, every household a stockade'. This must be foremost in our minds, it must be our policy, it must carry our conviction and we must advance it, for there is no other road open to us, except that of a militant struggle.
>
> If we do not face up to the enemy, then we give him a free gift. My friends, in the midst of our tragedy, people come up to us and say, 'You're only a small nation. How can you take on this campaign?'
>
> Friends, what if they *do* have 300 tanks and 40,000 troops? We can stand firm against the army. Why should it be 'realism' to believe in our defeat? I say to you, it is more realistic to believe in our victory. We can *fight* and we can *win* and we have no other choice when it comes down to it, but struggle and victory. That is all.

A contrasting rhetoric

It is instructive to compare this speech, tailor-made for the Free Morphou Association, with the kind made at another sort of meeting, that of a district branch of the PRC. This meeting had taken place on 28 September 1975 in the village of Lower Polemidhia, where numbers of Argaki and Morphou families were living in abandoned Turkish houses. There was a large Greek population here before the war, and they, of course, had remained.

The speaker greeted his audience on behalf of both national and local Pan-Cyprian Refugee Committees, and on behalf of Cypriot refugees generally. The local secretary would address himself to the hundred-and-one practical problems they all faced; he himself merely wished to restate the importance of their unity in support of President Makarios' government, as the best method of securing the return to their homes.

The refugees were *guests*, he reminded them, befriended, hosted by local men. As heads of families their first duty was not to compromise their hosts. All thoughts of evil had to be set aside; moral uprightness was the order of the day. They all had to help each other towards better conduct.

Therefore there had to be no vandalisation of Turkish properties, as proposed by certain outside elements, the very ones who had brought Cyprus to her present state. Refugees were not wild men – they were civilised. They invited the Turkish Cypriots to return to their homes; meanwhile, the government was holding their property in trust. Shepherds were to have a care where they grazed their flocks. He continued:

> Let every Greek among us become better than he was before so that our hosts, the people of this community which has taken us in, will love and esteem us. There is no doubt that men's tears are not all of one and the same water – some of us are good men, some less good, some better, and probably some of us are no good at all. Let us then help the sinners to become a bit better, but let us turn our backs on them if they try by their attitudes or actions to sow tares among us or start any trouble in this community. This is a fundamental duty owed to our locality, to ourselves, and to the struggle we are waging. Brethren, both men and women, I shall say only this: only when we refugees and non-refugees join together can we understand one another and come to grips with our problems.

The speaker then recalled that the British Foreign Secretary James Callaghan had said, that the isolation of Turkey had begun from the moment she invaded Cyprus, and, although somewhat academic, that the UN resolution had called for Turkey's withdrawal, a call they all stood by.

In closing, he thanked the community of Polemidhia, and hoped that the refugees would repay its help by making their relations with the local people an example to all Cyprus, so that when the time came to leave, they would be asked to stay on.

This speech contrasted sharply with that of the socialist speaker HajiDimitriou to the Free Morphou meeting. At first sight it looked 'non-political', which was exactly what the speaker wished. He stressed conventional themes – the need for unity, for discipline and order, for support of Makarios. But it also stressed the host–guest relationship, the family, respect for property (even abandoned Turkish property), and for law and order. It was a traditional speech, of the kind which earlier writers report Greek village schoolteachers making on feast days, exhorting people to lead better lives, to treat each other like Christians, and so forth. In the matter of the things it stressed, and the things it passed over in silence, it was anodyne and quietist, for there was no call in it for social justice, for a fair economic deal for the refugees, still less for a purge of EOKA B, a basic restructuring of society, or arming the people.

Greek perceptions of Turks

A major political upheaval must be accompanied by some reconsideration of the past, even if in the end people are merely confirmed in their old prejudices. The Greek Cypriots could not have been characterised before the war as having a single view of Turkish Cypriots, and the invasion did not make their views, influenced as they were by particular political parties and other considerations, any more unified. That these views were political in essence, however, there could be no doubt; for nearly twenty years Greek Cypriots had been presented with Greek–Turkish relations as the single most important issue in their world. There could hardly be a conversational reference to a single Turkish Cypriot which did not provide a hint of the speaker's views on relations between the two ethnic groups in general.

After the war the refugees had to assimilate not only their own individual direct experiences, but also both what other refugees claimed to have seen or heard, and the far more abstract but influential 'experiences' to be had from newspapers and broadcasts. In its official statements, the Cyprus government was always careful to distinguish between Turkish Cypriots, with whom it had certain local differences, and the mainland Turks, who were an invading army; this distinction was crucial, since the Greek diplomatic campaign insisted that partition of the island was not a just or necessary part of any solution to the Cyprus problem. Greek leaders insisted that if the Turkish army would withdraw, they could live at peace with Turkish Cypriots, within a unitary state. The frequent repetition of these views was bound to influence ordinary people.

Greek Cypriot intellectuals looked anxiously for signs of disagreement among the Turks in the north, as reported by the Turkish press, and re-reported in the Greek papers. If Turkish Cypriots expressed dissatis-faction with life under martial law, or with the allocation of occupied Greek property, then the Greeks took new hope. If, as was often the case, the opposition groups criticised Denktash, the Turkish Cypriot leader, for favouritism, autocracy, or other vices, the Greeks quickly imagined the growth of this opposition to proportions which would remove Denktash from power, and then produce new leaders who would perhaps take a more favourable negotiating position with the Greek Cypriots. Such hopes were frequently dashed when the Turkish Cypriot or mainland politicians made emphatic statements supporting a tough line with the Greeks, but within days the hopes were reborn. Intellectuals, too, were prone to remember the past selectively: 'Why, we lived with the Turks very well before. It was only the British and that lunatic Grivas who made a little trouble between us ... The Western Powers have carefully *manipulated* our differences.'

Ordinary people, Argaki villagers among them, often repeated versions of these views and hopes, as well as details of the killings, rapes, and humiliations which had followed the Turkish invasion. But they also sought eagerly for any specific news of Argaki, and its new condition. There were some strange rumours. In April 1975 I was told by a number of people that the Argaki Turkish mayor had shot and killed a Turkish soldier who was attempting to rape one of his daughters, but in September I was told the story was now known to have been untrue.

Argaki people were persistently anxious about their citrus trees, and whether or not the Turks would water them. Some believed that the Turks were inferior to themselves in abilities and energy, and so feared the worst: 'They won't be able to understand the irrigation system, which field flows into which other field. Besides, they're lazy.' Others said that the Argaki Turks knew the water-ways and would be able to explain them to others and, besides, it would be madness to let the trees die, for next year, and in the future, the Turks would want to sell the fruit. 'But we won't find anything in our houses', they added, referring to the reports of systematic looting. Such a remark always contained the built-in assump-tion that they would *eventually go back* to those houses, and that they must accept that they would find them gutted. But never mind that, if the trees had survived and the houses were still standing. As time went on the 'when we go back' became 'if'.

The rethinking of the past raised the stock of the British, as colonial

Iottou and Hambis Pelekanos, m. 1943. Had two daughters, whom they married to Argaki men, and a son who studied food chemistry on a party scholarship in Czechoslovakia, in recognition of Hambis' years of staunch support, which did not, however, prevent him serving on the church committee. He worked as a bulldozer driver. The couple had a small orchard, of 1·1 hectares, in 1969. One son-in-law was owner-driver of a lorry, the other a tailor (Petris HajiChristodoulou, see p. 129); both were keen party men. Iottou is a sister of the author's father. The photo is prewar.

antagonists, but greatly reduced that of the Turks. My aunt Iottou recalled the 'politeness' and 'decency' of the British in the conduct of their curfews during the EOKA insurrection. They even kept an eye on her children while she went out for water. But the Turks had lived up to the worst accounts she had heard from the history lessons at school. Just as a hundred years ago they had roasted Deacon Athanasios alive on a spit, and raped Christian girls, so they had now assaulted a ninety-year-old Argaki woman, who had herself publicly told of it. A poor return for the way the Greeks had treated the Argaki Turks: when bread had been short the co-operative salesman had always kept the last few loaves for the Turks, rather than the Greeks. She continued:

> It would have been a thousand times better if the British had stayed here. We thought we'd be better off with Independence and now the Turks have utterly destroyed us. Our people started the *coup d'état* (Oh, we're in the wrong too, all right) and gave the Turks just the chance

they'd been waiting for. And will they leave now? Not a hope. I'm telling you things the way I see them, understand. I think we'll stay partitioned like this. And we'll see what else happens. Maybe they'll take the whole of Cyprus, that's what I reckon. There isn't a country which will help us. Not one. Who, for example? We'll stay like this.

It will be like this for a long time, and it's our children who will suffer. We've lived our lives, your uncle and me. But the children?'

Having given me a full-blooded account of Turkish 'barbarities' my aunt then started to talk with some sympathy of the Turkish Cypriot refugees:

When we first came here, to the Turkish Quarter [in Paphos], I got really low. This black mood took hold of me and for eight days and nights I cried and cried, and wouldn't eat a bite. Then your uncle told me that he had felt the same. But he hadn't shown me how he felt. It had taken him hard, too.

We came and found a house here the day the Turks were leaving. We'd been three families in two rooms, up in Stroumbi. How long can you go on like that, under the feet of your grown-up married children, and them with five small kids of their own? So we decided to come down here, to the Turkish area.

But we wept to do it. I'm pretty used to it now, but sometimes that grieving takes me and I have to cry again. I remember, and I feel sorry for the people who had to leave these houses. For *they've* left *their* homes, too. It's so sad, what's happened to them. They aren't to blame, either. They said their leaders told them to leave or else the mainland Turks would come and shoot them. They had their orders. The day we arrived here, the Turkish women who were leaving told us this. They didn't want to go and they took earth from here so that they would come back again. Earth in tin cans. They have a custom like that – when you take earth from your home, and go off somewhere, it helps you to come back home again. We didn't think of doing that – we thought we were only leaving Argaki for a few days, two or three at most.

Had the Turks but known it, the mythologising power of history was working for them by eating into Greek morale. Survivors of earlier Turkish feats of arms testified to the potency of the images from the history books that possessed my aunt Iottou and others. Two particular stories were repeated to me by a number of Argaki people. Some of them had met an old Armenian pedlar of watches who roamed the island and who said to them, 'Ah you're refugees are you? Well, let me tell you, I have been *five times* made a refugee', and he told them how. The other episode was even more poignant and demoralising. They met an old man who had become a refugee in the Asia Minor disaster of 1922, and when he heard them talking about their houses and how they would be when they got back, he put his hand in his pocket and pulled out an old iron key. 'With this key I locked up my house in Smyrna, fifty years ago. *I* never went back to it, and nor will you, so forget about your houses.' They digested this, then asked him another question. 'Compensation? *Pah!* Not a copper-*bakira*.' Other people said to me, time and time again, 'The Turks never give anything back and they never withdraw.'

As if this were not enough, there was Radio Bayrak ('The Flag'), the Turkish propaganda station dubbed 'illegal' by the Cypriot Government, but in to which many Greek Cypriots occasionally tuned. People claimed they didn't take it seriously, and would switch it on saying apologetically, 'Let's just see what silly old Bayrak is saying. We might hear something new.' But the fact that they *did* sometimes listen was important. It was another obsessive strand of their relationship with the enemy, who could through it speak directly to them, playing on their fears and countering their arguments with his own. Many people agreed that the main announcer spoke excellent Greek and that the propaganda was highly intelligent.

One day I was visiting Argaki people in a village near Paphos when a farmer called Krittikos switched on his radio. This is what he listened to – a parable on alleged Greek misrepresentations of the Cyprus problem:

> . . . For example consider the following incident. It is recounted to us by someone who asserts that he is the *victim*.
>
> 'I was walking along the road and this man cursed me. We came to blows . . . At that moment another man appeared, a giant of a man with a huge cudgel. With the cudgel he hit me, innocent and unfortunate as I am. He cracked my head open, gave me black eyes, broke my arms and tore my clothes. I lost my wallet. Please punish those who assaulted me.'
>
> What should a judge do now, if he has to decide? Naturally, he ought to examine *the whole case in detail*, to seek out the *real* reasons of the whole matter, to see how far the complainant is speaking the *whole* truth, *and nothing but the truth*. If only the complainant is heard and not the accused, then surely the following facts will not come to light: in reality the complainant is a killer; he never leaves his house without having two pistols and a knife with him; the man he described as a giant is the brother of the man he had set upon; the 'victim' had entered this man's house, and the orchard they had in partnership, by force, and by force and guile had got hold of all the money which the big brother had sent to support his younger brother, beating him into the bargain.
>
> The giant sends him messages dozens of times, telling him to stop harming and insulting him and his brother, to be satisfied with what he has, and has embezzled, and to behave decently. But this adventurer keeps trying by pressure and assault to get the man he'd put upon out altogether. He squeezes him into a corner of the house, and wants to embezzle the entire orchard. He wants his victim to work for him like a helot. Eventually, he has grasped him by the throat. If the weaker man hadn't a strong arm, he would have been killed by suffocation.

Onto the scene comes the giant, gives the adventurer one with his cudgel, and pushes him into the other side of the house. He suggests to him that he settle down quietly, like a man.

Beloved listeners, Greece is exactly like that adventurer. All her efforts are aimed at hushing up her terrible past. The Greek Cypriots are trying to get international opinion to take their side in Cyprus, with the following argument: 'The Turks had no reason to invade Cyprus, whose inhabitants are innocent, defenceless Greek Cypriots. Two hundred thousand Greek Cypriots have been uprooted from their homes, and thousands killed. We want an independent Cyprus, the withdrawal of Turkish military forces, and all refugees to return to their homes.'

The Greek Cypriot side is right up to a point, but tells only *a portion* of the truth. Only those who know the terrible difference between 'facts', and *the truth* can avoid falling into error . . . Simple truth cannot suffice, since a clever man can conceal a lie in three small truths.

A radio personality is known to his audience as a disembodied voice. In Cypriot culture people like to have direct personal evidence for events if possible, and stories are often introduced like the Islamic *hadith*: 'I heard this from X, who heard it from Y.' If the following story had been passed between Turkish Cypriots, it might have been effective in adding fuel to anti-Greek feelings. It was told to an Argaki Greek refugee by a Turkish Cypriot woman shortly before she left for the north. The setting was Polemidhia village:

A woman from your village, Argaki, and her daughter recently arrived here as refugees, and rented a house from me. They paid £40 for two months' rent. When the time was up I went to say that more rent was now due, and they said: 'Go away, and don't come back again. What's mine belongs to you *and* what's yours belongs to you? How can that be?'

When the Turkish woman had protested that she had taken nothing from the Greeks, the Argaki woman had riposted: 'But your daughter is sitting in *my* house.' The reference to her daughter was, of course, rhetorical hyperbole, a kinship metaphor, such as often occurs in nationalist discourse. For 'your daughter' her listener would have understood 'one of your people', with the implication that she was held responsible for their doings, just as in a kinship group one member stands for another. This in embryo is the logic of much class and racial warfare: when the blood is hot, *any* member of the enemy group will do for a reprisal, no matter how remotely connected to the specific issue.[1]

I do not wish to leave Turkish–Greek relations with a negative case, so the reader is advised that in the next chapter (p. 171) an Argaki villager

---

[1] The *feud* is quite different, because it usually involves rules about who may be the proper subject of a vengeance killing (see Black-Michaud 1975).

relates how a Turkish Cypriot retrieved from occupied Argaki something the Greek cherished greatly, and did this as a favour to a friend. But I cannot resist quoting the following letter from a Turk to a Greek, even though the recipient was not an Argaki man. The original spelling has been retained not to make the writer seem unsophisticated, but to convey the charm and poignancy of the *lingua franca* employed:

Nicosia
30/9/75

Dear Toumazos

I received your letter & I was very plased at finding the opportunity to write me a few lines. During the war my wife & I specially my daughter we were worring for you & your family, some time when we were speaking of you my daughter could not stop her tears; Any how I am good in health, but not rich. I am still at the same house. I am without any house & filds yet: as regard of Bambis letter I can do nothing for him. I thing you have learned that the Turkis properties wil be given to refuges, and on the other hand if I singed that letter I shal have to pay a lot of taxes even of the past years: I read this in news papers: I was late to write you awing to the reason that I was away at Famagusta & other villages. naw I am back: please inform Bambis. I hope everything to be settled soon and meat you again:
  Give my regards to your wife & the whole family,

  your sincere friend
[Turkish surname]

Preoccupations with EOKA B

The refugees were obsessed with the Turks, as conquerors whose conquest had somehow to be denied and transcended, even while they were occupying the houses and the fields of the Greeks. This was quite understandable, but so were the two other obsessions shared by most of the Argaki refugees: Who among them had been men of the *coup*, and of EOKA B? And how had America and Britain come to 'betray' the Greek Cypriots in support of Turkey?

The EOKA problem was the immediate, concrete, and most threatening one; for if it were pursued, it could mean confounding kinship, marriage, and other morally charged constraints. The villagers were not organised in large homogeneous blocks, separate kin-groups all of whose members followed the same political line. They were all jumbled up, so that even if a group of brothers and sisters supported the same party, their husbands and wives (or *their* brothers and sisters) were often to be found in different and opposed groups. To punish the men of the *coup* would mean, one way or another, to take a knife to one's own flesh.[1]

But meanwhile, they were constantly meeting people casually whom they felt had a direct responsibility for the invasion. It was not so bad in the case of foolish young men with little brains and no futures – they could be ignored, in effect, as sheep who had been led astray. But there were several prominent Argaki men who had been wealthy before the war, had been EOKA B sympathisers, and who were now clearly getting back on their feet again. For example, there was a merchant, who was renting a large agricultural estate at Mandria village, in Paphos. It was about 100 hectares, and he stood to make a lot of money from it. There was another man who had done something similar with another 180-hectare estate, and who was now having trouble with a lot of poor refugees from other villages, who were threatening to squat on the land he had rented. Indeed, the Communist Party newspaper, *Haravghi*, carried the following item, on 9 October 1975:

REFUGEES DECIDE TO CULTIVATE THE 'GERMAN' ESTATE AT YEROSKYPOS

Paphos, 8 October [from our own correspondent]. A public meeting of refugees and residents of Yeroskypos village decided to cultivate the well-known 'German' estate, since its owners are refusing to rent it out to refugees and farmers.

About twenty tractors and a large number of farmers went to the above-mentioned estate and began its cultivation.

Public representatives of the farmers involved had a meeting with the Paphos District Commissioner concerning the issue, but the formal opinion proffered them was that they should not move onto the land until the question had been discussed by the Council of Ministers.

This story was more than a little misleading, and could have been written up much more forcefully, particularly in a left-wing newspaper. The owners *were* renting the land, and to a refugee. But it was a great deal of land, and the refugee was one man only. He had been known as sympathetic to the anti-government movement, and the money needed to pay the rent for the first year was about £3,200. *Here* was the real story. The man had suddenly found himself surrounded by several hundred angry people, protesting the right of 'one man' to use all this land. He replied that the land would be used to support twenty families, his brothers and sisters, his in-laws, and so on. He also told them that if they threatened him, he would get together 'his people' and they would know how to protect themselves. He might have meant his kin; but he could also have meant EOKA people. He told me that he had been able to pay the

---

[1]   See Loizos 1975:76–83, and chapter 10, particularly p. 282.

rent by means of guarantees at Grindley's bank, plus the help of 'some very rich friends' in Nicosia. Who were they? Harmless businessmen who could see in him a good manager? There were questions to be asked, but the article did not seem to be raising them. How was it possible for those with at least a minor share in the responsibility for the *coup* and the invasion to be doing so well again, so soon afterwards?

Vassilis Karaolis, a communist, described to me his disgust at the continued influence of some EOKA B sympathisers. He had been friendly for many years with a man who had finally come out strongly against Makarios, and who had recently been assiduously courting Vassilis himself, no doubt with the idea that should the left really get a purge going, he would need a friend to speak up for him. This was a very characteristically Cypriot manoeuvre. Now, Vassilis had £2,000 saved in a government agency fund and he could not get it out because the fund had been frozen just after the war to prevent a run on it. His EOKA B 'friend', hearing of this, said, 'Bring me your receipts and *I'll* get them cashed for you.' Vassilis refused, he told me, 'on principle', but he was irked – and this is why he had told me the story – that this man still had the *power* to do such a thing.

People continually pointed at others and said, *sotto voce*,

> He was EOKA B.
> He sent a telegram of support to Sampson.
> He and his brother started walking about the village carrying machine-guns. They said they were demonstrating support for the government, ensuring law and order . . .
> He went and joined the Special Police, when Sampson came in . . .
> He and his friends stole gold jewellery from the Turks after the attack on Ghaziveran . . .
> He was one of the people who set up the road blocks and searched the houses for guns . . .

They spoke of meeting fellow-villagers whom they had known to be involved with EOKA B, and of feeling a cold inner anger towards them, which they often did not show. 'But I've no time for them', they would add. My own meetings with such people were usually conducted through the exchange of slightly barbed, often heated generalities:

> *EOKA man:* Ah, Peter, look what the Anglo-Americans have done to us. What a betrayal!
> *PL:* The Anglo-Americans? Or the EOKA people? It wasn't Americans who attacked Makarios – it was Greeks.
> *EOKA man:* But the foreigners put them up to it, and then betrayed them.
> *PL:* You mean, the EOKA boys sold themselves for £30 a month . . .

One day in Polemidhia an argument began at the next table to mine in the coffee shop. The men were local, not refugees. Three of them were arguing with an EOKA B supporter, who was claiming that the guns held by the socialists had been 'illegal'. To which the reply came that the socialists had been trying to support the elected government, not to overthrow it.

> *EOKA man:* But *we* were trying to bring Enosis, Union with Greece. We believed in our principles. We didn't sell out. We were *idealists*.
>
> *Others:* And to bring Enosis you idealists found it necessary to bury men *alive*? You and your kind are quite simply *killers*.

Tempers were now very high and there was complete silence at the other tables. The EOKA B man decided to leave but not before muttering, 'We'll meet again', a characteristically muffled and ambiguous phrase, an instantly retractable threat. I went over to the table, but no one seemed worried by his parting remark. 'They've done their worst to us now, and they won't *dare* do anything more', one man explained. But another disagreed. 'They are still among us, and so the problem remains with us', he said passionately. And a man in his fifties, a little older than the rest, added, 'The thing that got us into all this trouble in the first place was anti-communism. *That's* where it all started.'

A similar view was put to me in some detail by an Argaki delivery driver, Andreas Tchittonis, a socialist. He was rethinking the recent past, and he now saw the rise of the first EOKA as essentially a movement more concerned to divert the Cypriot masses from socialism than anything else. Such a view of nationalism as 'false consciousness' was favoured by classical orthodox Marxism, but Andreas spoke of it as if it were a very new idea. He did not want to speak too critically of the local communists, but like many Cypriot socialists he regarded their former faith in the support of the USSR as an exercise in self-delusion.

Political philosophies as faith and comfort

In this he was joined by many Cypriots who were not at all left-wing. The theme that the people of a small country had been caught between super-power rivalries and badly hurt was to be heard on many lips. Some drew an interesting conclusion from it: since the super-powers and their supporters will not permit real neutrality then one must take sides. This was certainly the view of Kalloirkou, the farmer who earlier described the pain of becoming a wage-labourer (p. 125):

> The Americans and the Turks together have kicked us out of our homes and are now determined to break down our morale. We go once to the UN and don't get agreement, we go again, and no difference. It will

break down the refugees' morale at least, so that they'll go to the government and all shout together, 'Gentlemen, we want to go home and we don't care if it's partition or not, let's go one hour quicker if we're going, before we completely lose our future, our lives.' That's what is happening . . . they're using us as a lever on the government, that is, they're pressing us so that we'll press the government to accept partition.

The unaligned countries? I haven't much confidence in them. We should be in a major alliance. We should have been with America before the war, but we had those who were against this, and Makarios was. caught between two fires. Once he tried to go in with the socialist countries and the pro-Enosis people were yelling 'Makarios is a communist'. So he didn't join *them*. America asked for military bases, and the whole of Cyprus yelled 'Out with NATO! Out with NATO! Don't let's have NATO in Cyprus! Let it go somewhere else!', so Makarios couldn't do *that* either. One lot wouldn't let him go this way, the other lot wouldn't let him go that way, so he got stuck in the middle, and that's how the present miserable situation came about. What should he have done? I'm no politician to judge what should have been done. If he had joined one major power from the start at least we wouldn't be in the mess we're in now. He'd have given the Americans a base years ago, and we would not be in this mess. That's politics, it's difficult . . . Politicians say one thing and do another . . . We live with the hope that one day we'll go home. Every minute we put on the radio to hear the latest. My wife is waiting for something to happen, and for us to go back.

Kalloirkou was, in most essential respects, an individualist; before the war he had been an independent farmer of substance. Uncle Pelekanos, by contrast, had been from a poorer family, and had been a wage-working skilled labourer all his life, driving heavy earth-moving machinery (see p. 140). He had also been a devoted communist for thirty years, and he had one son studying on a party-sponsored scholarship in Prague. In Stroumbi, in April 1975, he greeted me with the words: 'We're in a pitiful state. We don't know what we want any more or where we're going.' Nothing he said in my presence later suggested he was deriving much support from the party or his membership of it, and a number of other Argaki communists seemed as much at a loss for direction as he was. They certainly did not refer either to the party or to the USSR as possible sources of a solution to their personal problems as refugees.

Other leftists seemed more clear-headed: Parthenis Damianou had been a really wealthy farmer in Argaki; he had never actually become a party member, since he felt he could not spare the time from his land, and he was a man who would do nothing half-heartedly. I asked him if he thought the refugees should demonstrate to make their needs known, and he replied that, since they were represented by their local and national

Parthenis Damianou, b. 1920, Argaki; m. 1943 Stella (b. 1926, Argaki);
seven sons, two daughters. With 10·4 hectares the family is among the
very largest village landowners, but Parthenis is highly sympathetic to
the Communist Party. In 1969 he had 3,500 citrus trees, and several
vehicles. When young he worked in a mine, as a labourer, and as a
carter. He regrets that none of his sons has been interested in higher
education.

committees, they should not do so, and that a demonstration in such a
context must be by its nature anti-governmental and harmful of solidarity. All right, but in these times of dislocation and stress, should not the
left work hard to bring socialism more quickly, turn the situation to its
advantage? This was roughly the line being taken by the EDEK socialists
(see p. 134). He replied 'Socialism has not yet been achieved even in the
USSR, so *now* is certainly not the time to push for it in Cyprus.'
Meanwhile, however, he wanted the government to make sure that all the
refugees were given some land to work, rather than a few big men getting
hold of a lot of land, but he certainly was not proposing any kind of
surprise attack on the institution of private property.

Parthenis' commitment to political discipline and legality was characteristic of the Communist Party's style in Cyprus and he showed no signs
of wavering from this. Meanwhile, though, he faced an important
personal dilemma, which was rather unusual and which underlined his

moral seriousness. He had a small coffee shop open in Polemidhia, but it was doing no business to speak of, and had no future. He had three sons in Canada, and they could easily have sent him £500 or more to open a grocery, but he could not decide if it was worth it. 'It's the uncertainty', he said, to excuse his apparent unwillingness to get started on something serious. But because of these same sons, he could also emigrate to Canada, with the rest of his family, thus ensuring their personal safety. The rape perpetuated by Turkish soldiers had made men like Parthenis, with young daughters, fear any renewal of the war, and many had sent their daughters out of the country if they could. But Parthenis felt he really ought to stay in Cyprus, to do what he could to help save his country. 'And I am ashamed to even discuss the idea of emigrating', he told me. 'Even if the government will allow me to leave, should I do so?'

Like Parthenis in his moral seriousness was Ioannis Zenonos. Before the

Ioannis Zenonos, nicknamed 'the Deacon', b. 1929, Argaki; m. 1953 Eleni Kondou, daughter of a wealthy conservative farmer. At marriage, he received 1·3 hectares, she 2·0 hectares; they purchased a further 0·7 hectares, and by 1969 had planted 1,300 citrus trees. They had four children. Ioannis was an unwavering communist, had visited the USSR on a delegation, a village office-holder, and was popular and influential. Although among the wealthier farmers, he still ploughed by the hour with his tractor. Brother to Pavlos Zenonos (see p. 160), second cousin to the author, close friend of Tomas. (Disguised in *The Greek gift* as 'Y. Tangos'.)

war his brothers had all been admirers of Sampson (see pp. 55–6) and he was the only leftist of the family, having even visited the USSR in a farmers' delegation. Since the war he had rented a piece of land near Limassol and grown vegetables, but prices had dropped to the point where he was not making any real money by prewar standards. He had been living in an abandoned Turkish house in Limassol – quite a good one – and was planning to try his hand at other agricultural enterprises. He had been 'too busy' to go to any party meetings, although he had received written circulars from the central committee, and he knew that if he made the slightest effort he could take up his party membership locally. 'But you don't really need to go to meetings to keep in touch. If you read *Haravghi* regularly, you can keep in touch with party thinking.' He readily agreed that his political philosophy was a source of comfort to him in the crisis:

> You see, I believe that imperialism *cannot* defeat us. 'It shall not pass', as I see it. Sooner or later, we shall defeat it and return to our homes, and our native land. The things we are suffering now are *temporary*.
>
> No matter how nationalistic the Turks are today, justice will triumph, eventually. Other Turks will emerge, who are progressives, and the progressive movement sooner or later must be victorious. We on the left are not in a hurry. I'm certainly not, and I believe the progressives must win.
>
> I can't tell you if this is a question of ten years, or a hundred years, or even longer: that depends on the conditions in each particular country, and I certainly cannot foresee what they will be in Turkey, and how strong the progressives actually are. But to give you some idea, I think the change will come about in between fifteen and twenty years. I *believe* it will be that order of time, but of course it *might* be longer.

I pointed out that his friend and fellow-communist, Tomas, was in the habit of telling people, 'The Turks will leave, eventually, and that is for certain.'

> Of course, he says that to comfort people, as I see it. Look, no one can actually foresee the time – you would have to know the exact conditions in each country to set a time to it. You can easily say that we will go back one day, but the day, the hour, the minute, that can't be worked out. But it's definitely a good thing to offer this kind of comfort that Tomas does – it's something positive for people.
>
> You mentioned the 'militancy' of the socialists. Well, we communists believe we must have the *strength*, we must actually be able to drive the enemy out, before we take up such a posture. Today, we clearly do not have that capability. The Soviet Union? She will only involve herself in our problem by peaceful methods. She cannot go to war over Cyprus, not, as you suppose, out of fear of the USA, but because she has certain

international interests to watch over. Go to war over Cyprus? No. First
of all, it would harm the Soviet Union; then it would set the stage for a
war between the super-powers.

It would be a mistake, in my view, for Makarios to sign a
Kissinger-type plan, involving bizonal federation, but with only half the
refugees going home. The solution that I'll support is one in which all
the citizens of the Cyprus Republic have the right to live together – as we
did before, for many years. I shall wait until the Turks accept such a
solution, and I don't think the party will accept a compromise
agreement. So if they passed a law now which allowed me to go home,
but others not to go, I wouldn't agree to go. It's out of the question.

If a political philosophy is going to meet people's needs even half-way, it
must provide some answers about how an unacceptable present is linked
with an unknown future. Ioannis seemed certain that in fifteen or twenty
years 'other Turks will emerge, who are progressives, and the progressive
movement ... [will] be victorious'. While listening to Ioannis I felt I
understood what kept people within a movement like the Cypriot
Communist Party: it was its ability to propose coherent answers to some
of the problems they encountered.

Much later, I came upon a poem by a mainland Turkish communist,
Nazim Hikmet, who spent much of his life in prison for his beliefs. When
he had been in prison ten years, he wrote a poem on the relativity of time,
which begins:

> Since I was thrown into this hole
> the Earth has gone round the sun ten times.
> If you ask the Earth, it will say,
>   'Doesn't deserve mention
>   such a microscopic amount of time.'
> If you ask me, I'll say,
>   'Ten years off my life.'
>
> The day I was imprisoned
>   I had a small pencil
> which I used up within a week.
> If you ask the pencil, it will say,
>   'My whole lifetime.'
> If you ask me, I'll say,
>   'So what? Only a week.'

Later in the poem Hikmet addresses the masses, and stresses his belief in
their creative ability to act as agents of social change and progress, their
ultimate omnipotence in the 'long march' of history:

> only *your* adventures
>   will be recorded in songs.

> And the rest,
>   such as my ten years' suffering,
>   is simply idle talk.   (Hikmet 1970)

Hikmet found solace during his unbearably long imprisonment by thinking of his sufferings as a tiny part of an immense saga – the progress of the masses towards emancipation. The same view of history as progress comforted Zenonos, its core lying in the belief in transcendence: 'Other Turks will emerge, who are progressives . . .' Such a view explicitly denies that 'history repeats itself', and rejects the notion of an immutable human nature, both expressed in the idea that 'there always will be wars – there always have been'. Once I would have given Zenonos a series of clever arguments to show that evidence for a belief in progress is at best equivocal. As it was I found myself glad for his sake, as I listened to his views, that he had something clear to believe in. My own scepticism was, for once, irrelevant.

Chapter 9

BEARINGS

April–December 1975

An event as final as a death does not affect each surviving member of a family in precisely the same way, at the same time, or to the same degree. No more did the disorientation of becoming refugees affect all the villagers of Argaki in the same manner. In earlier chapters the emphasis has been on the initial impact on them as refugees during the first eight months of displacement; the concern now is with the latter months of 1975, with the awareness that displacement was likely to continue, and that life had to be lived in the present and future, as well as in the past.

Reactions to loss, and the question of economic recovery

Some individuals were much quicker than others to decide that they might continue to be refugees indefinitely, and men, who spent more time reading newspapers and conversing in coffee shops, tended to reach this conclusion without telling their womenfolk; indeed, they did their best to dismiss the idea if it was suggested. They undoubtedly felt uneasy at the prospect of having to comfort dispirited and probably tearful women, and so tended to postpone the moment of disclosure in the hope that the realisation would come upon their women gradually. Only when this realisation was reached was there thought of making provision for the future, and here too there was a wide range of responses.

The older people, if they had married off their children, seemed to feel little pressure to start new economic activities; this was something they could now honourably leave to their grown-up offspring (as Dionysios explained, p. 123). One middle-aged woman said to me about the old, '*They've* married off *their* children. Look at my father – the old chap eats, drinks, sleeps, and enjoys himself. The situation doesn't affect him.' She herself had just come home from a long shift at a factory, the first time in her life she had gone wage-labouring.

Young unmarried men, although often cut off from their previous expectations of an attractive life as citrus-growers, seemed less burdened than their middle-aged parents. They were thoughtful, and some were considering emigrating, since they could see no future in Cyprus. They had survived the war, and had to face the possibility of another one. Although sometimes angry and depressed, they could occasionally take pride in the fact that they had recently risked their lives in fighting for their people. The young unmarried women were equally thoughtful, but far from distraught, for while the war had cut them off from their homes and their properties, it had not denied them the prospect of marriage and motherhood, and, as will appear later in this chapter, the rigours of refugee life had not diminished the attractions of wedlock, if anything having made it easier for the young to enter it.

The most disoriented and embittered of the refugees seemed to be those

Themis married Peva Pipis in 1972, when she was 25. He was the son of a shepherd from a near-by village, had completed secondary school, and held a modest white-collar job with a Morphou firm. She had qualified as a primary school teacher, and taken a loan of £3,000 with which she built an impressive dowry-house in Argaki. They started a family. People like Peva, who had worked and saved hard to achieve a better position in life than her parents could have provided, were among the most deeply embittered of the Argaki refugees. (Disguised in *The Greek gift* as the 'Fanos family'.) (See p. 27.)

like my cousin Peva and her husband Themis, who had completed a long period of hard work and thrift, of Protestant self-denial, only to have its fruits denied them. For some people the task had been the bringing of an orchard to profitable maturity; for others it had been the construction of a dowry-house; and for a few it had been the completion of a professional education, only to find that employment was no longer available.

Peva had trained as a schoolteacher, borrowed the money from her profession's provident fund to build a rather superior dowry-house in Argaki, and had then got engaged to Themis. They married in the early 1970s and started a family. The invasion had made them homeless and destitute, but it had also done more than that. Peva was still teaching, her salary was being cut by 10% 'for the refugees', even though she was one herself, furthermore she had to continue to pay off her original loan to the teachers' provident fund. Before the war, the couple had been mildly attracted to the socialist party, but now they seemed strongly committed to it. Peva talked angrily to me of 'capitalists' and the need for a redistribution of private property in the island. She was quite ready to agree that there were refugees with no salaries, while she and her husband had two straitened ones, but the fact that there were many others worse off than herself seemed not to soften her anger.

It became clear to me that as well as the particular social circumstances of particular families – age, family size, capital assets, education, and marketable skills – there was another linked set of distinctions that helped shape the reactions of the Argaki villagers. They could be divided roughly into those whose prewar lives had mainly been turned inwards towards the village, and those who had faced outwards, to the wider world. The economic interests and social ties of the full-time farmers, who formed nearly 40% of the village, and of some of the skilled workers, village tailors, coffee shop owners, drivers of tractors, were focused on their fellow-villagers, and they had rarely put their heads out of the village, except for the odd spree. As refugees, without their land or the support of their fellow-villagers, they were badly disadvantaged, and were in general slower to start rebuilding their personal fortunes.

The other village men had been merchants, civil servants, teachers, truck-drivers, and those craftsmen who worked away from home. Some of these men had important economic assets, as well as crucial social contacts outside Argaki, and some of the salaried men had been re-employed and continued to draw their salaries, albeit reduced. A man who had been lucky enough to buy a piece of land in the south, or who had money in a Nicosia deposit account, or a reputation for being a good businessman, or some other kind of social credit, could expect to do things which another could not.

The women were mainly concerned with relations within Argaki, the only possible exception being the handful of schoolteachers. Farmers' wives and wives of white-collar workers did not usually take on paid work, and never outside Argaki. Poorer women who laboured in the Morphou citrus-packing factory seemed to have formed few important relations at work. Other Argaki women earned income by work within the village – tailoring, hairdressing, knitting, or labouring in the fields. The effects of the women's commitment to village relations will be discussed a little later (pp. 176ff).

Pavlos Zenonos nicknamed 'HajiPavlis', b. *c.* 1935, Argaki. One of the five most successful merchant entrepreneurs in Argaki, in 1969 he owned only 2·2 hectares within the village, but a very great deal of land outside it, at least 4·0 hectares. He owned a retail clothing shop in Morphou, was an import agent for Sanderson's wallpaper, and also sold agricultural produce in Britain, to which he made frequent business trips. He also often journeyed to the Middle East on business, and having more than once organised a party of pilgrims to the Holy Places in Jerusalem, was entitled to be known as Haji. (Disguised in *The Greek gift* as one of the 'Tangos brothers'.)

Those Argaki men who were concerned to start their economic lives again had tried a range of enterprises. An Argaki merchant, HajiPavlis, had owned a clothing shop in Morphou before the war, had imported wallpaper, and exported agricultural produce. He owned citrus groves as well. After the invasion he had lived for a time by taking on credit shirts from a Limassol factory valued at fifteen shillings each and selling them in the mountain villages for one pound. The factory owner had known him before the war and thought him a good credit risk. By late 1975 he had stopped selling shirts and had acquired a large flock of goats, which he was paying a man to herd. He anticipated high prices for meat.

His brother, Ioannis Zenonos (see p. 153), had been a full-time farmer in Argaki, and by himself would have been quite unknown to a Limassol shirt-maker, but he was able to join HajiPavlis in selling the shirts. He sold 2,500 of them and earned £600, but then decided that mounting petrol costs would make this venture less profitable. Later he added £200 to a sum of £800 pooled by three other men, and together they grew beetroots, beans, and melons. Lots of other men did likewise, there was a glut, and prices slumped. The four partners took £200 profit between them. 'Working for nothing' was Ioanis' comment.

Later still in 1975 he tried to rent an abandoned Turkish orchard near Limassol, but at the auction he was outbid by a non-refugee. The bidding became quite tense, and at one point his rival called out, 'Sure you've really got the money?', since he seemed to know he was bidding against a refugee. Ioannis replied vigorously, 'You think my money is *shit*?', and would have hit his rival if they had not been separated.

There was a third brother, Phytis, who before the war had lived a comfortable life. He himself had acquired a sizeable orchard from his parents, his wife had another one, and the trees did not take up too much of his time. He played cards and went carousing more than was good for him, and people had started to shake their heads over him, saying that he was a drunkard, lazy, and a gambler. When I met up with him in 1975 he was a changed man: he had a small flock of goats and was out all day herding them. His wife Maroulla was clearing the flower-bed of an abandoned Turkish house and planting tomatoes in it; she explained to me how they had set out to become economically independent again:

> By January 1975 our savings had all gone, and we weren't going to sit idle, waiting for help from our friends. Phytis thought we should try rearing livestock in Polemidhia, so we got a bit of money together and bought some animals, and came up here to get started. We didn't want to hire a labourer, because we wanted all the money we could get from the animals, so that both they and we could afford to live. I managed to find some milk and started making *halloumi*-cheese with it, and yoghurt. O, I was doing a hundred and one things, I can tell you. Very slowly we started to get back on our feet, but I found it really exhausting. For nine months I was doing nothing but make cheese. And if there wasn't much milk, I put what there was into the fridge to make cheese the next day.
> We are gradually getting enough money to live on, but to get by, it's

Phytis b. 1935, Argaki; m. 1959 to Zenonos, Maroulla Diakourtis, a half-sister of Tomas Diakourtis (see p. 52) but by a different mother. Phytis received 1·1 hectares at marriage, Maroulla 1·5 hectares. By 1969 they had 830 citrus trees, and Phytis bought another 1·8 hectares in that year. They were as yet childless. A man of the (original) EOKA right, he was also keen on Nicosia night-life. (Disguised in *The Greek gift* as 'Mangaras Tangos'.)

work from the time I get up till the time I go to bed. Non-stop. O, I'm never without something to do, and if one day it's a little easier, why then the next day something 'extra' will turn up to be done. One day it's sacking up the straw. The next day it's fixing up the sheep-fold . . . then it'll be something else. Look, for the last fifteen days we've been working at drying out grape-pressings, for fodder. It'll be fifteen days next Thursday. We've had it spread out all over the place recently, and it has to be turned over every so often so that it'll dry. You see, last year we bought apple-pressings for winter feed, and we were paying about a shilling for three pounds. But these grape-pressings will only cost a half of that, since we bought them wet, and we'll do the drying ourselves.

We don't have much choice. We've *got* to keep at it so that if a time should come when we *do* go home, we can take something with us. Because we don't know what we'll find when we go back – if we'll have our old jobs, a salary, the citrus trees or what. It may be we won't have any of those things, and that we'll have to go on living by rearing livestock. While we are refugees we can get by on bare essentials, but if we go back home and all this trouble is finished, why we'll want to start building up again from the beginning, to get back to where we were at before, when we had our own house with everything in it. If we do go back, that is. We'll see.

As I watched the rehabilitated Phytis go off with his small flock, and his determined wife at her cheese-making, I could not help thinking that some villagers seemed actually to have been strengthened by their adversities.

The refugee entrepreneurs showed an impressive flexibility: some learned new skills, or modified old ones; some did things they knew how to do but had never needed to do; some did something for cash that they had previously done only for the home. Sometimes they literally traded on the name 'refugee' – as in 'Refugees' kebabs' to advertise the roast meat sandwiches they were selling – two Argaki men had tried their hands at this soon after they took refuge in the mountains. Before the war the six main towns of Cyprus had been serviced by two major taxi fleets; now the Greeks had access to only four of these towns, but they had acquired a third fleet – 'Refugee Taxi Lines'.

Two of my cousins, both salaried city-dwellers, were growing fassoleus beans in their flower-beds as a hedge against possible food shortages, not for profit. 'They would supplement a poor diet', Nikos, the chemistry teacher, explained to me. I could not help thinking, though, of the empty OXFAM collection-box in his school's common-room, with pictures of skeletal Africans on it: there were refugees and refugees. The daughter of one of the wealthiest farmers of the village, who had never worked in her father's fields, was now earning piece-work rates by doing embroidery on a sewing-machine. A lot of villagers who had been proud of their genteel life-styles before had now swallowed that pride and were doing unskilled or semi-skilled work for low wages. Petris, a tailor who had divided his time between a citrus orchard and a shop in prosperous Morphou, had found that the village of Stroumbi, in Paphos, lacked a tailor. The villagers had previously had to go to the town for clothes, but he was willing to work cheaply, and soon had a good clientele. Dimos, an unemployed mathematician, was planning to set up a private 'crammer'. He had prepared a leaflet which said that for those who attended his GCE 'Institute' he could secure places at English universities. I raised an eyebrow and he added, '*If* they get good enough marks ...'; his promise boiled down to little more than knowing the technicalities of admission. Each student would pay £7 a month and get three hours of instruction a week, thereby topping up what they were getting at secondary school. 'I stand to lose nothing', he pointed out, and indeed hardly any cash outlay was involved.

Where lack of cash was a problem, there were some government loans available to help the refugees start farming again.

Old Dionysios had explained to me (p. 123) why he was not interested in taking one of these, but the attitude to new enterprise of his son, Takis (the man who had twice returned to Argaki to remove his possessions in the face of the Turkish advance), was very different:

So finally I came and found this house, but couldn't get any work. I started looking for money, since my money had nearly run out. I went to a friend whose ploughing I used to do with my tractor, and when I found him I asked him could he please let me have £100? He knew what sort of a man I am and he gave it me. I wrote him an IOU with my wife as guarantor, and I came back to Polemidhia. The Turks were getting ready to leave for the north, and were selling off their things cheaply. I tried to find a yoke of plough-blades for the tractor. I found one, but I couldn't come to terms with the Turk . . . so I went to the firm of Alexander Dimitriou. My money wasn't nearly enough. The man gave me the plough-rig on credit. I had to really work on him to persuade him. He got my measure and got his boss, who'd been with the firm at Morphou, on the phone, who told him what sort of man I was, so he let me have credit, and now he helps me and does me some really big favours.

So now I'd got the plough-rig fixed, but it was winter by then and there wasn't any work to be done, so I went to work as a labourer up at the Welfare [office] and earned a little bit. We got by for a while. Then it ran out. Nothing left.

The person who helped me was Dimos. *Your* in-law, Peter. The moment when you haven't got anything, along comes the very man you need: 'Hallo, Takis. How goes it?', he says to me. Right, I said to myself: 'Look, Dimos, things aren't too good', I said. 'Got no money?' Actually, it was a Saturday and I couldn't buy any meat for the children. He said, 'I've got nine pounds on me. Here's seven, and when they're all gone, come and ask me for some more.' 'No', I said. 'Where will I find the money later to pay you?'

But Dimos absolutely insisted on giving me the money, and I'm really grateful to him.

After we came I didn't even have enough to pay the rent. I'd got into a house. If the man who owned it had been rich, I wouldn't have minded staying in his house and not paying the rent. He couldn't have got me out, as it happened. But he had six kids, and he had just the one house to rent, at £15 a month. I couldn't stay in it on those terms. *He* was worse off than *I* was, and my fortunes were black enough at the time.

When I first came here to Polemidhia, for a bit I found tractoring work, at £15 a day. The Turks were renting out houses. I rented this house for £10 from a Turkish woman, and I had £3 left. We went through some difficult times then.

Later, when I'd got the plough-rig, I started getting a bit of work here and there, and that's how we've made it till today. Last week I made £2·50. Digging. But one month I took £200. One month, with my brother, Pavlos, we were getting the potatoes up and we took £400. We've had to pay the running costs of the lorry, and the tractor, of course, but till today we've got along pretty well, if you compare us with the others.

I hope God will send us his rain, and that we'll sow some crops and work and get by. We've been through some bad patches and I don't know what is still to come.

That decisiveness which had made Takis go back to Argaki in the face of danger, and which had made him seek a loan when he needed it, was not, as he had observed, shared by everyone. The uncertainty which he voiced about the future, linked with disturbing comparisons with the recent past, clearly held some refugees in its thrall, even up to the end of 1975, fifteen months after they had left the village. Such a person was Sophia Paphiti, who before the war had made a good living by baking some ninety four-pound loaves of superior bread each day in her village

Sophia Paphiti, b. *c.* 1933, Argaki, and married to a man from a Paphos village, who is a lorry owner-driver. They have four daughters and a son. In Argaki Sophia and her children baked 90 loaves of bread a day, which they sold in the village. The family owned two orchards, one of 0·7 hectares with twelve-year-old trees, the other of 0·3 hectares; she received £1,000 a year from the trees. She had married off one daughter and was building the dowry-house of the second.

home. She had sold her bread to the wealthier families who preferred to pay a few coppers more for home-made bread, than to buy that which came each day from Morphou. When I met her in April 1975 she said she was wondering whether to set up an oven where she was, and start again. 'But supposing we go back?', she had mused. 'I can't take the oven with me.' By the winter, she had still done nothing; her explanation why lasted nearly an hour, and was frequently interrupted by sobbing. Her reasons were simple. In Argaki she had worked from her own home, and her married and unmarried daughters had been near at hand to help her. Now, she lived in a draughty room, keeping herself busy by tending five goats and making a little *halloumi*-cheese for sale, when they were in milk. But her daughters were half-an-hour's bus-ride away, in Nicosia, living in a house under the care of her son-in-law. She was obsessed with her come-down, the contrast between her past and her present:

> I did say to you last April that I was thinking perhaps I'd set up an oven here, start baking and sell the bread. And I could easily build an oven for £20. So why haven't I done it? But what I told you wasn't right. You see, it *isn't* just setting up an *oven*. Look, I've got *that* oven, there. The real problem is that I can't set up the bakery properly. I need my own home and my daughters at my side, the family all together before I could get things going.
>
> Going out to work for others is . . . just that. It *isn't* working for yourself, which is quite, quite different.
>
> Why, we used to work in our own home and when Saturday came I'd step out into the alleyway and take a look at the house, and it would be all freshly mopped-out, and clean as the snow. And now I've come here to live in a cave. [Weeping]
>
> When Saturday came round and we took a break from the bakery work, my pocket would be fat with money, the house cleaned from end to end, my daughters at my side. And where am I today? I ask you. In a cave, in a cow-shed.
>
> Oh, you know us well enough, you know I'm not telling you stories, you saw how we lived before and how we are today. Not just us – everyone. You've travelled a lot, so tell me: *are* there people worse off than we are? *Can* there be?
>
> I'm sorry for me and mine, but I'm sorry for everyone, the whole world. At least we are all in good health and my husband's working and he hasn't let us go hungry.
>
> But still, I can't help thinking about what we've lost. We've lost so much. All our possessions.
>
> I had a mature orange grove and I was getting £1,000 a year from it. Twelve years old, in its prime, five *donums*, big trees, each one giving me 800 oranges. First class. The land there was really good for fruit-trees. And I'd got a younger orange-grove, two donums, and the trees were

giving 300 or 400 fruit each. I gave this one to my daughter when she married, but she didn't have the *kismeti*, the good fortune to enjoy it herself for even a year. You see, I was in debt after the wedding, so I used the income for two years, to pay off the debt, and then I was going to make it over to her, last year, the year we fled. She was going to cut the oranges for herself. But her Fate, her *kismeti* didn't let her get a ha'penny-piece from it. She will not get a single *orange*. And my poor son-in-law who used to irrigate it for us, all day and all night, what about *him*?

One summer we made a melon-bed in it, and I built a nice little reed lean-to and took a bed out there and the cooking pots. If I wanted fresh *louvia*-beans, there they were in my field for the taking, as well as marrows, pumpkins, lady's-fingers, tomatoes, aubergines, peppers. We planted all these things so we could eat what we liked when we liked out there. Food tastes so good out in the fields. You could sit out under the stars, enjoying the cool air, humming a tune.

My daughter said the other day: 'The lemons you used to bring us, the bottles of lemonade we got . . . How good you used to smell when you came in from the fields with all those green things, coriander . . .'

I simply pray nothing worse happens. Surely we've had the worst? We won't find anything there if we *do* get back. We've lost so much.

My married daughter used to come in from her house next door, every so often each day. That house of hers . . . she kept it like paradise.

Now, what future have we here? Have I the heart for anything? Look at us, and the sorry state we've come to.

Refugee marriages

In the spring of 1975, soon after reaching Cyprus, I heard to my surprise that there had been a number of weddings among Argaki people. First, I heard about a cousin, Stellios, who had been engaged before the war to a girl from a village about eight miles west of Argaki. Her family had built the couple a £8,000 house in our village, an unusual concession. The wedding was to have taken place in 1974, but the *coup* and the invasion had stopped this. Now the couple had got married in the girl's village, only a couple of miles south of the Turkish front lines. The loss of the dowry-house must have been a serious blow to both families, for Stellios had little to bring to a marriage beyond his modest salary.

I heard a few details about the wedding. Before the war, the whole village was invited to weddings in Argaki, and nearly everyone would come and be offered a substantial meal and plenty to drink. The guests would make cash gifts. At Stellios' wedding, the guests had given gifts, but only close relatives had been feasted. I was also told, by an aunt, about another Argaki wedding which she had not attended and she sounded sorry and a little defensive about this; since she remembered who had been to her own daughter's wedding, she had a lively sense of her obligations, and a wedding was, both for the two families party to it, and for the rest of the village, such an important event (see chapter 2, pp. 27–34). Later in April I went to yet another Argaki wedding, 'left over' from before the war. Even eight months after the diaspora it was attended by perhaps a quarter of the village, but the groom had anti-government connections and a lot of people stayed away because of this, they told me.

During the first months after their departure, many people still had money in their pockets and believed that a return to Argaki was imminent, so it seemed right to go to weddings, and give gifts as if nothing had happened – as if it would all be over soon, like a drought year. It was a chance to meet people one had not seen since before the war, to hear their stories, and tell one's own. But as more months passed, and the weddings continued, it became harder on everyone to attend them. Towards the end of 1975, I overheard one grey-haired man say to another, 'The invitations are getting a bit much', and his friend sadly agreed; on that particular day there were two Argaki weddings in two different villages, and there were not only the travel costs, but the gifts to consider. I heard some of my relatives deciding they could not go to a kinsman's wedding because of travel costs, but they sent envelopes containing gift money by the hands of people who were going. The diaspora and the shortage of money were forcing people to make painful choices, to economise on their social commitments. First, they were forced to stop keeping up ties to all their fellow-villagers and concentrate on their kin. After this, they had to choose when to cut down on help to distant kin in favour of those closer. Then came the point when they had to limit what they could do even for close kin. But under the hard shell of the choice, the kernel of moral and material commitments remained – if a family of five could not afford £2 in bus fares or petrol to attend a distant wedding, it could still send a cash gift. I wondered how long this could be kept up. Would the gifts get smaller and smaller?

The moral pressures towards reciprocity were powerful. In a mountain village an Argaki woman told me to take a message to the Protopapas family in Nicosia. She was about to marry off a child. 'Tell Eleni I expect her to come', she ordered me. I said gently that nowadays people did not always manage to get to weddings, and she replied with spirit, 'I and all my family went to *her* wedding.' That had been nearly twenty years previously. I duly conveyed the message and it was most seriously received by Eleni and her mother, my aunt Stylou Zenona. When the day came, Stylou and I drove up to the village, stayed an hour, and returned.

The thing most puzzling to me about the engagements and weddings of

the spring of 1975 was that they were happening at all. Cousin Tomas
who had two unmarried daughters heard that his old enemy had had an
engagement party for his daughter, and he scoffed, 'What does a man
who's a refugee want with giving feasts?' Tomas never lost an opportunity
to get in a dig at someone with whom he had quarrelled: 'unforgivingly
stubborn' was one way in which he was regarded in the village.[1] But I
could see his point – it seemed oddly rash to splash out in this way, a piece
of bravado which could easily rebound to a man's discredit.

The marriages also seemed hard to understand. They appeared altogether too 'normal'. I considered a number of possibilities. They could be
what might be called an 'affirmation of life' – a denial of the importance of
hardships, an insistence that the diaspora could only be temporary, on the
lines of 'if we ignore it, it will go away'. Another possibility was that the
weddings were a sign of the refugees 'returning to normal', but there
seemed to be so much other evidence against such an interpretation.
People were too disoriented and distracted by their losses to revert to
normal living.

There were several other possible explanations that seemed more
plausible. The first was related to wealth and poverty. Many of the
marriages seemed to be between people who would not have been well-off
before the war, and so it was now to their advantage to marry before the
old social system had a chance to re-assert itself. Before, they would have
had to scrimp and save for many years to build the essential dowry-house,
but now that no one could provide such a house, they could marry off a
daughter without anyone else being able to say 'That's a poor people's
wedding.'

Another possibility was that it was the young people, rather than the
poorer parents, who were forcing the pace. This is quite compatible with
the previous point, and could simply intensify the trend. Now that parents
had no fields or houses, they were less able to veto a love-match, so
youngsters could press to marry girls who might have been 'too poor'
before. This would not have applied to those marriages 'left over' from
1974, but it would help explain some of the new engagements, and
marriages which took place with no engagements at all.

There was a third, equally compatible, possibility: youngsters now
faced rather bleak material prospects, if they did not get back to Argaki.
The boys might find themselves fighting another war, and everyone felt
uncertain about where, or how, they would be living in the future. Could
the boys not argue that there was no reason to postpone for another three

---

[1] By late 1975, Tomas had been reconciled with this man. They met at a wedding,
and started talking again over a drink. Tomas emphasised in relating this that the
other man had started talking *first*.

or four years the pleasures of physical companionship? And would not the girls welcome this too, although without being able to say so? On top of this marriage would enable boys and girls to make the transition from being 'kids' into adulthood. Here was something they could have which would be comforting, and which the Turkish invasion and the loss of material prospects could not deny them.

I could see instances which supported each of these points, and which convinced me that a postwar refugee marriage was not a sign of a 'return

Klykou Ioannou, b. *c.* 1946, Argaki; sister of Lefteris (see pp. 5, 174). Completed secondary school and worked more than ten years towards her dowry-house, latterly as a living-in general assistant in a doctor's practice. By 1974 the house was ready, and it would have been larger and better-appointed than those of her four sisters, just because of the rise in village standards. First cousin to the author. She is seen here with a niece as her bridesmaid.

to normality', but implied something rather different from a prewar marriage; acts took their meaning from contexts.

Meanwhile I noted many small points in connection with the marriages. One of the early Argaki weddings had cost the young couple, both from quite poor families, £600. Before the war it might have taken three or four times this amount. Then, the April wedding which I had attended had nearly been called off at the last minute because the groom demanded a written agreement from the bride's family that if they returned to Argaki they would build her a dowry-house, but that if they didn't, they would provide £4,000. The young man who told me this piece of gossip thought it very funny, and that the boy was being ridiculous. He himself wanted to marry a girl from Argaki, and from nowhere else. He would take one 'with nothing, if need be. But Kyriakos wants it in writing', he said.

In September I visited my cousin, Klykou, who had married an Argaki boy two months earlier. In her spotless house which was formerly Turkish, she shyly showed me her wedding photograph, and for a moment I was completely confused. It was a handsome colour print, showing her in an elaborate white wedding dress, and her husband in a very smart Palm Beach suit, looking more like a millionaire playboy than a young refugee. I looked quizzically at her. 'All hired', she said, with a sigh.

This puzzle was not hard to solve. Klykou had worked and saved for more than ten years to get married, and since everyone knew this the wedding clothes were not meant to make people think she was wealthy. They were designed to be photographed, to make the event endure, in a tangible form. Perhaps, too, the clothes and the photo were to make the wedding auspicious, as when a woman puts on perfume not because it will make her irresistible but because it creates the right atmosphere for a good evening out.[1]

This importance of wedding photographs was confirmed from an unexpected source. After an interview about politics with one young villager, Andreas Tchittonis, he rummaged in a drawer, and handed me something much as a wine expert might pass one a glass of a particularly rare vintage. He then added, as I peered at his wedding photograph, that very few refugees still possessed these, and explained how he had come by his. When he arrived in Polemidhia, he became friendly with a Turk who had not yet left for the north. Finally, when this man, too, was leaving, the Greek asked him to visit his house in Argaki, and retrieve the photo, which he did. (In spite of the military situation, some Greeks and Turks could still meet on the British bases, if they wanted to.) The Turk had

---

[1] I owe the perfume analogy to Alfred Gell, who used it to explain Melanesian love-magic (see Gell 1977).

Andreas Y. N. Tchittonis, b. *c*. 1945, Argaki; formerly a delivery driver (and part-time farmer), who by 1969 had become a strong supporter of Lyssarides' Socialist Party. He observed an Argaki EOKA B group set off to attack a police station (the raid was cancelled at the last minute), and later quarrelled with this group, in the coffee shop, when they sought to define their ultra-conservative nationalist club as 'non-political'. In 1975 he was shepherding. He is seen here with his wife.

done this out of friendship, and had asked for nothing, although some other Turks were charging £15 or more to do the same sort of thing. 'After all, you can't get married a second time, be a bridegroom again', said my informant, gazing at the photograph.

The moral economy of kinship

After many conversations and interviews, I was able to see that the first year after the war could be divided into a number of distinct phases: first the unplanned flight, the chaos of dispersal; then a period of crisis overcrowding, in which people found themselves confined with strangers whom chance had placed next to them; then a regrouping phase, in which people joined up with close relatives, preferring to be overcrowded with people of their choice; and finally, there was a new separation, when the overcrowding could no longer be borne, and huddling close to kin had served its purpose.

It is hardly surprising that people preferred to suffer in the company of those whom they knew and trusted. Greek culture enjoins a strict separation, a social distance which is expressed in physical distance between unrelated men and women; and strangers cannot be trusted to resist the temptation to improper intimacy. Furthermore, the tensions of bad overcrowding are best endured with people who are committed to tolerating and forgiving you your petty trespasses. In this situation people had continually to remind each other of 'first principles' (how blood is thicker than water, and so forth) just to make life bearable. Also, the villagers told me that they had had a colder winter than usual; it is far colder in the mountains than in plains villages like Argaki, and they were usually living in dwellings greatly inferior to those they had left. They made sour but truthful jokes about how being crowded helped with the cold, like the jokes people make about governments they have no hope of changing.

Eventually, six to nine months after the flight from Argaki, it began to look less and less likely that there would be a rapid return to the village, and people started to make plans which looked beyond a literal tomorrow. The period of overcrowding had led to some quarrels and this made separation more appropriate. It seemed at the same time both a small failure and quite inevitable.[1] As heads of families came to hear of better dwellings, or of the chance of a job, it no longer made sense to stay together at any price. The interests of the smaller constituent units came to the fore. But once they had moved, people started to think about the separation and compare it with the easy contacts of village life. I asked one old friend, Andrikos Polyviou, about the strains of being over-crowded.

> It's not a question of whether or not you get on well with your relatives or with anyone else. But understand what it's like if I've got three kids, you've got one, the other fellow has four, some big and some little. The women have been cooking and we sit down to eat. Someone's kid says he doesn't like the food, then another one says . . . well, there are a *lot* of problems. For a month, or two, OK. But to live continuously with other families in the same house, it's . . . well you can't . . . it is *very* difficult. After all, even in one family, the kids quarrel, so what can you expect when there are ten kids all at once? It starts with the kids, not the women. Then there's the other thing. How many people can share a room? How many married people? You can imagine.

Andrikos' younger brother Ttoolis, a truck driver, was more outspoken:

> You cannot get through the experience well, and those who say they did

---

[1] Elizabeth Colson (1971) discusses a similar process in a similar situation. See Appendix 2, p. 205.

and that they didn't quarrel are *liars*. Under these conditions you'll deny both the milk and the breast it came from!

The separation could be passed off less painfully if the quarrels were attributed to the children, and not to the adults. But the manner in which the refugees had been treated by their hosts also influenced the spirit of their separation. A group of my cousins, married sisters from Argaki, had taken refuge with their husbands and children, in the home of their older brother Lefteris, a police sergeant in the city of Limassol. My cousin Maria said:

> As you know, there were thirty of us in one house. We got on very well, very affectionately. But later on the children started to quarrel. They played all day and they wouldn't study and we had a lot of trouble over that. [My brother] Lefteris said, 'Maybe you'll all be able to go home tomorrow, but while you can't this house is yours.' But thirty people, ten grown-ups and twenty kids, can't stay together for long. One kid would be studying *here*, other kids would be playing *there*, they'd get on top of each other, they couldn't study, they'd fight. So we wanted to split up. Lefteris gave things to us like a parent dowers children for marriage back home, that's how he treated us. Merope left first. He bought her beds, mattresses, beds for the kids, household utensils of all kinds, cooking pots and all, big ones, little ones, down to the last thing. Then later I left and it was the same thing all over again. Beds, mattresses, chairs, tables, cooking pots, down to a coffee pot, and down to a bread-bin. An iron, glasses, coffee pots, teapot, knives, forks, cups, ashtrays. You name it. Even two or three ashtrays.

Lefteris also described to me the period when he had his relatives all under his roof. He knew he had done the right thing by them, but he could not conceal the element of strain involved:

> Thirty persons in one house, do you know what that means? You wake up in the morning and you want a piss (or the other), and the first one goes into the lavatory at six o'clock, and it takes till nearly nine for the last one.

But when the refugees were no longer living in such crowded conditions with their close kin, they began to feel isolated, and to compare their present dispersion with the compactness of their social relations in Argaki. Revecca Kalloirkou explained this to me:

> There is a woman in the neighbourhood here who keeps me company a bit. She's from [another village] and we got to know each other because her son and my son are in Athens together. Fortunately I can go to her place and pass a few hours, and she and her female relatives come to my house and spend a bit of time. I see a bit of another co-villager, Maria, but she can't stay long, because of her kid, who wants to be off. I sometimes drop by on her a bit.
>
> In the village it was different. One brother lived really close to my house

and I got on very well with my sister-in-law and with her mother. I was really at home with her and got on with her just like with my own mother, so only at nightfall did we part. And when your mother and father are living in the village, you see them every day too. At night time I'd come back from my work and I'd go along to my parents to see them. Now? I see them about once a month, or whenever by chance we meet. When I miss them really badly I go to Nicosia to see them – they are staying with my brother the doctor.

On the same subject, Petris, the tailor, had this to say:

> One more thing I'll tell you. When I was back in the village I was with my family, my father, mother, father-in-law, my brothers and sisters. You leave, you come up here. My father, now, he's in Polemidhia, sixty miles away. My brother's up here, OK. My other brother, who had a lot of property, and mature trees, and a tractor he made money from, well he's had to go to England with his family. My wife's father is in Paphos and it's hard to go and see him. So one large family has been forced to split up, one here, another there, and this is what makes us sad. It's three months now since I've seen my brother Pantelis, and my father. To go and see them would take a lot of time and money, and that's a real problem.

Being refugees put extraordinary strains on kinship relations, and sometimes I had to force myself to get people to talk about things they found very distressing. My cousin Peva's husband (see p. 158) told me that not long ago his sister had died, leaving eight children orphaned. Two had been adopted, one by a relative, the other by a 'stranger', i.e. a non-relative. I timidly raised the question I felt I had to ask: was he thinking of taking one of them? He was normally a mild, quietly spoken man, but his response to this was as to a fool: 'Can't you *see* the state we're in? *Look* at how we live – we barely get through to the end of the month, and there's *nothing* to spare.' My question thoroughly deserved this response, and afterwards I wished I had not asked it, or at least had done so better, but I told myself that his vehemence was probably because he felt very strongly that he *ought* to have taken one of the children.

There were other dilemmas created by the politics of the invasion, which I can best illustrate with a personal experience. One of my cousins had strongly supported the military dictatorship in Greece, and we had argued many times about politics. There was a strong suspicion among my relatives that he had carried tales to the EOKA boss in Argaki about our various political views, and people discussing politics tended to change the subject when he appeared. In April 1975, he learned that I was in Cyprus and left a message asking me to meet him. I did not want to meet him and was surprised at how much anger I felt towards him and to others who shared his views. But on reflection there seemed no way to avoid the meeting without snubbing a young man who had already been snubbed too often. Indeed, that was probably at the root of his politics. We met in a refugee's coffee shop called 'Morphou', where he swore he had completely rethought his views. He seemed to have changed from having been a man who went to church because it was his duty as a Greek, to being a passionately evangelical Christian, talking earnestly about love for his fellow-men.

The meeting took the edge off my anger towards him, and I found I could be civil to him. Although he had very good reasons (in terms of saving himself from retribution) for saying the things he said, I felt he was not play-acting, but sincere. It was easier for me to be polite to him than it would have been for someone who had been made destitute and homeless by the war. He himself was suffering the common fate: he had lost his home, his village, and his job. All over Cyprus people were faced with difficult decisions about how to behave to erring relatives, decisions much harder than mine with regard to him. I found it much harder to take a detached view when I met EOKA B sympathisers who were not my close relatives.

The dispersal of close kin and fellow-villagers did not, however, mean that individuals were by any means totally isolated. On several occasions I could track news or gossip as it moved between people. In April, soon after arriving in Cyprus, I sought out my cousin Tomas, in the village where he was residing. He told a mutual friend who lived elsewhere, but commuted to work past Tomas' village, that I had arrived. This man in turn met another cousin of mine in Nicosia, and told him, so that he was able to phone me. As I mused on this I said to my Aunt Styllou Zenona, 'Although we are spread out all over the place, we aren't losing touch.' She replied, a trifle tartly, I thought, 'How *could* we lose touch? We're *relations*.' I had been thinking of the contacts between the villagers in general, but she had interpreted my remark in terms of kinship, with its stronger imperatives. She seemed to be trying to remind me, in her eyes a flighty foreign young man who spoke Greek like a Turk, where my obligations lay.

At a loss: the special pains of women

As the period of enforced crowding came to an end in the spring, women spoke to me very clearly of two losses which they felt particularly sharply, and which affected them more than their menfolk: the loss of their *homes*, in whose contents they had, in the recent boom years, taken such pride, and the loss of the compact community of kin, friends, and neighbours that had sustained their lives in Argaki.

The realisation that women were harder hit came partly from observation and partly from inference. The most noticeable behaviour was the readiness with which women wept when talking about their homes, and how some of them fell into a rhythmic sobbing reminiscent of their wailing for the untimely dead; others came close to fainting. Inferences were drawn from the material and symbolic importance of homes to the women. Almost every Argaki girl owned a dowry-house when she married, and her social standing was largely a result of its quality and contents. It was hers, and because it had often cost her and her family dearly in labour and thrift, it gave her a measure of security and independence within her marriage.

Their dowry-houses gone, women were now more dependent, vulnerable, exposed, like snails without shells. Greek culture (whether one sees this as imposed by men upon women, or as a mutual accommodation between the sexes) places women *in* the home – they are not supposed to spend more time outside it than they have to. If domestic pressures permit, then work among a group of relatives in the fields or visits to neighbours and kinswomen are allowable. When all household tasks are done, women may sit in the company of other women but their hands must not be idle – they spin wool or embroider for the trousseau of daughter or niece.[1]

As refugees, the women were still supposed to stay 'indoors', but indoors was no longer *home*, even when it was a house, rather than a barn or a shed. For much of the day, particularly when cooking or cleaning, women experienced sharp reminders of the homes they had lost, homes with which I would think they were so deeply and intimately involved that they might have felt a sense of amputation. They could not help being reminded: they would point to their makeshift cooking places and cramped quarters, and the *marazin*, the grieving, would take them till they wept.

Because they had been so house-bound, brought up to hold themselves proudly closed off from 'strangers', it was more stressful for them than for their menfolk to make new relationships, to settle down next door to unknown people and start to trust them. Men had always been obliged to spend much time outside the home since it was regarded as womanish for them to prefer the company of women to that of their own sex. Male virtues such as openness to strangers and readiness to explore the unknown were deemed vices in Argaki's women. They were confined to their houses.

An important exception to this general confinement was when women

---

[1] Renée Hirschon (1978) and Juliet du Boulay (1974) provide illuminating accounts of how women are conceptualised in Greek culture. Campbell (1964) has done pioneering work on this theme. Much of their writing applies to Cypriot Greek culture too.

went to work as wage-labourers. This added greatly to their burdens. Before the war many Argaki women had been proud of not ever going out to work for money, and now it seemed degrading to do so. Going out to work did not result in a lessening of their domestic drudgery; although their men might occasionally make shift to cook for themselves, or to supervise small children, they probably did little if any of the cleaning and laundering. Also, women were paid at lower rates than men. Before the war certain tasks, such as weeding and fruit-picking, had been defined as 'women's work', and were low-paid, while men had done the better-paid 'heavy' work such as irrigation and the carrying of laden fruit baskets. In 1975 it was quite common to find a refugee household in which the women

Argyrou Diakourtis (née Varella), b. *c.* 1936, Argaki; m. 1952 Tomas Diakourtis, a farmer (see p. 52). Her father was a sheep-dealer, but one of her brothers became an extremely wealthy merchant. Highly informed about women's activities in Argaki, she shared her husband's pride in the fact that although they had started marriage with very little land, by shrewd borrowing, developing, and reselling of citrus orchards, by 1969 they had over 4 hectares of trees. She had four children, of whom the two girls both obtained party scholarships to study in the USSR.

were out weeding, or working in a factory, but the men were unemployed. This was as humiliating for the men as it was exhausting for the women; but it did not result in a radical restructuring of housework, nor did men show signs of seeking out 'women's work' and competing with women to do it, by offering more work for the same pay as a woman received. Men did take jobs at lower wages than they had earned before the war, and they took jobs lower down the scale of *men's* tasks, but they did not rethink the sexual division of labour.

There was, nevertheless, one benefit that women derived from their roles: if the endless chores, the cooking, washing, and cleaning in improvised conditions, reminded them of their losses, they were at the same time reassured that they were not merely useful, but essential to their families. If they also brought in wages, they might be the only providers, and though doubly burdened they might be doubly proud. Many of the men were unemployed for months, with too much time for brooding and feeling useless. They were lucky if they felt they could 'encourage' their families (see p. 121 and Appendix 2, p. 203). Women had no time to feel useless, and no reason to think themselves so.

Argyrou and her husband, Tomas, made me aware of another dimension to the refugee women. Women could extend to each other the very important resources of comfort, sympathy, and solidarity. But these were by no means an automatic gift from any woman to any other; they had to be worked for, and depended on propitious circumstances. In April, at Astromeritis village, Argyrou and her family shared a single room of a two-room shack with a refugee family from Karpoudi village, some ten miles from Argaki. With this family their relations were excellent, and were to remain so. A third refugee family, from another village, lived in the other room, and with them Argyrou and her people were on very bad terms. They were not speaking, and longed to move away from them.

With the Karpoudi family the relationship worked on several levels: first, the senior women liked and respected each other. Their husbands were both leftists (although in different parties), which predisposed them to get on well, and had known each other slightly from meeting in Morphou market. Argyrou felt strong pity for one of the younger women, who wore black for a husband who had not returned from the war and had two small children. The women continually helped each other with chores, as did the men. The women also comforted each other when one of them felt low. By the winter of 1975 they had shared dwellings for over six months, and when the time came to move from their shack to an unfinished house near by, they had chosen to move together.[1]

[1] In September 1980 they were living next door to each other, and were still on good terms.

One day the young widow went off to a demonstration concerning the fate of the 'Missing Persons', that is, those who had not returned from the war. She left her toddler in the care of her sister and Argyrou, but while she was away the boy fell off a verandah and had to have four stitches in his forehead. She returned tired and dispirited from what must have been a harrowing demonstration, to find her son with a dressing on his head. She fell at once to crying piteously 'My child, ah my child . . .', as I had once heard a mother do at a young child's funeral. The other women tried their hardest to calm her down, restraining her as she hugged her child, and insisting that the child was all right, that the wound was nothing. They felt sorry that she was so distressed and that the accident had happened while the child was in their care, but no one suggested that the widow's reaction was excessive. They remained concerned, even though her crying took a long time to subside.

A few hours earlier, this group of women had been working together and had started to laugh about something. Argyrou had caught my eye, and sought to interpret the event for me: 'We're having a laugh at the mess we're in', she said. That they could make each other laugh, and comfort each other when weeping, was the strongest expression of the bonds they had created between 'stranger' families; whatever the men's relations with each other, a very great deal depended on the diplomacy of the women.

There was another particular dilemma which women had to face. The men often spoke of the possibility of another war – this time between Greece and Turkey – and, although few of them talked with enthusiasm or optimism, they seemed to find some outlet for their frustrations in the thought that a war might result in their return to Argaki. But this prospect turned the women's thoughts to the possible loss of their sons. Revecca Kalloirkou (see p. 127) put it like this:

> I don't think we'll go back. I don't know. I'm scared of the Turks – they are hard people . . . Do we expect them to leave our villages? I don't. We rack our brains over what we should do about this. Sometimes it gets so my nerves are ready to snap. I'm filled with grief when I remember the things I had, the property we left behind. But I'm afraid of war. We cannot start one. I'm afraid of war – war is so difficult. Must the children who have survived up till now be killed? Must all the children in the world die? Can you *imagine* what we suffered during the war over our son, until he came back? Thank God the boy escaped unharmed – nothing else matters.

In face of such feeling it is easy to see why revolutionary leaders invariably tell their followers that they must 'harden their hearts', and why revolutionists are often ambivalent to the family.

In spite of their particular hardships, women never complained that they suffered more than men – there was no special pleading on their own behalf. The men could have done much more for them by taking on more domestic chores or releasing them from the house, but if they were in fact becoming more considerate to their wives, it was in ways too private for me to observe. A number of them said, when asked, that they thought the women were having a harder time of it, and I cannot leave this topic without one example of a man's sensitivity to his wife's feelings. My cousin's wife, Argyrou, recalled in some distress how during the war she had stopped her son Pavlos, then about fourteen, from bringing a tractor out of Argaki as they were leaving. Although he was an expert driver, she feared being parted from him in the turmoil, or through an accident. 'And now, what couldn't we do with that tractor', she said, 'What a fool I was.' Tomas heard this, and said, firmly but gently, 'We agreed we wouldn't brood about what we left behind, and who should have done what.' In the circumstances, it was the best thing he could possibly have said.

Identity and community

When the villagers stopped living closely crowded with their kin, and set up as individual families, they did not disperse at random, but went wherever their particular circumstances made attractive. For example, in the winter at Peristerona village, about ten miles from Argaki and close to the cease-fire line, I found some fifteen families. They were, in fact, several clusters of related families (but no longer densely crowded), and they were mostly shepherds, attracted by the plentiful though risky grazing in no-man's land, and by some empty Turkish farm-houses with courtyards for penning the animals.

It was quite common to find a village in which three or four related families were living, but no one else from Argaki. Such a group would usually involve an elderly couple, with some or all of their married daughters, sons-in-law, and grandchildren. The girls declared that they wanted to be close to their mothers, a feeling that the mothers reciprocated; while fathers- and sons-in-law seemed to get on as well together as they had before the war – which was often very well indeed, and better than adult men tended to do with their own fathers, with whom they were often rather reserved.

Most people who had migrated from Argaki before the war had gone to live in Nicosia, and no other Cypriot town had received more than a handful of them. In 1975 perhaps a hundred Argaki refugees were dwelling in Nicosia, but they were not concentrated anywhere. They were living in rented accommodation wherever they could find it, or in the homes of relatives. By the winter of 1975 there were four concentrations of

Argaki families, all in places from which the Turkish Cypriots had departed: the Turkish quarters of the towns of Limassol and Paphos, and the villages of Upper and Lower Polemidhia on the outskirts of Limassol. Sometimes the Turkish Cypriot owners were on the point of leaving for the north, in which case they commonly made formal rental agreements with the Greeks. If the Turks had already left and not designated an agent, it was simply a matter of entering an abandoned dwelling. Sometimes a non-refugee Greek had already taken over an empty Turkish house; in one such case an Argaki woman boasted to me that she had driven out the non-refugee with a broom.

The gossip network kept providing reports that particular families had moved into one of these four areas, and this would often lead to a discussion of what houses were available. Some of the Turkish houses were as new and well built as anything in Argaki, while others were very simple, old, and dilapidated. Those who moved fastest would get the best houses. Women had often heard that the Turkish houses smelled bad, and some said that they feared catching diseases.

It came to look a little like chain migration. Those who were the first to move got the pick of the houses, but they were the pioneers, moving into the unknown. Those who came later had to take what was left, but were moving into an area already populated by their fellows, and for some this was the decisive attraction. By the winter of 1975 I counted fifty-one Argaki families (nearly a sixth of the entire village) in the two Polemidhia villages. But there was an interesting sidelight on this. There were also in the villages a further fifty-six families from near-by Morphou and its satellites, and nineteen from Upper Zodhia, one of Argaki's richer neighbours. The men of these three communities had known each other by sight all their lives, the women knew the families by name, and both sexes might have kin or in-laws in the other villages, or have been to secondary school with their children. Before the war, relations had sometimes been rivalrous, particularly between Argaki and Morphou, but this was now forgotten. I would often now find a group of men who had originally come from neighbouring villages playing cards or talking politics. The diaspora separated Argaki people from each other, but it also put them into closer and less antagonistic contact with many of their prewar neighbours (see Colson, 1971 for similar behaviour, and Appendix 2, p. 203). One old man put it rather succinctly to me, although it is quite possible that he was in fact adapting a thought from an editorial or political speech:

> Now that we are refugees, we are all from *one* village. Whether we're from Argaki, Zodhia, Avlona, Kato Kopia, we're *fellow-villagers* now. It's the same for all of us.

This comment expressed the notion of new identities, fused here in a concrete, local metaphor. First, the war had created a refugee identity, summed up by those who insisted that 'It takes a refugee to understand one', and reinforced administratively by special identity-cards, cash and food allowances, the Pan-Cyprian Refugee Committee, and all the attention given by the mass media. But there was also the growth of a new *regional* identity. Before the war the village was the key administrative unit of Cypriot society, and there was little sense of regional loyalties or identifications. Neighbouring villages were often competitors for resources, and rivals in matters of prestige.

Now, there was no context in which members of a single village were required to stand together, and at the same time the interests which had previously opposed them to neighbouring villages no longer existed. They had been thrown together with their neighbours from their region, in the literal sense of finding themselves, as clusters of refugees, in closer contact than previously. As refugees their political futures appeared linked, for it seemed probable that in any settlement with the Turkish Cypriots, refugees would be included or excluded in regional blocs. For example, the people of Famagusta town might 'go home' while the people of Morphou might remain refugees. One of my cousins put the problem very crisply when she said: 'There cannot *be* a settlement. *You* will sign that *I* cannot go home? Impossible.' When the socialist party started to build up regional clubs among the refugees (see p. 137), did its leaders realise that by controlling such clubs they would hold a veto on any possible agreement?

For most of those who made the move to one of the new settlements of Argaki people, the desire to be near fellow-villagers was important, but not, I suspect, the driving force. It was rather an added attraction, or the item which tipped the balance, the argument sometimes used to persuade reluctant wives: 'And there will be friends and neighbours there as well.' The need for houses, rather than sheds or shacks, was crucial, as was the necessity of finding employment.

However inadequate and improvised, however much a shadow of the original, it was a great boost to morale to be living in one of the several colonies of Argaki people. A young Argaki matron walking in the formerly Turkish quarter of Limassol at the end of 1975 could see behind her the house of the priest and his family, while to her right was a coffee shop with fifteen or twenty Argaki males in it, and to her left a small grocer's run by another Argaki villager. When she bumped into me she exclaimed, 'It's just like the village here – fellow-villagers on every side.' Of course, it wasn't at all like Argaki in any other respect, nor did she mean me to think so.

Facing the future

In April 1975 I had seen people carrying out small actions which looked like metaphors, implying states of mind which could not be probed too bluntly. For example an Argaki woman, dwelling in a half-ruined mud-brick house, only a few miles from her own village, was sun-drying citrus seeds on a sack. I asked her why she was keeping the seeds, and she replied, 'To plant later'. Since she had no land what exactly did she mean? Were the seeds a talisman, to take her home again? Similarly, Tomas had a seedling lemon tree in a one-gallon oil tin, which he watered. All I could get from him on the subject was that it had been left there by the previous owner and that it would have been a pity to let it die. This seemed a curiously tender-minded response from a man who in other moods had wished he had been armed, to fight EOKA B, and who had lost several thousand citrus trees to Turkey.

Between spring and winter there was a marked change in the way the refugees thought about the future, which became evident in styles of greeting. At first, if two people had not met recently, their typical greeting was, 'Well, when are we going back?', asked with the head cocked sideways, and an upturned palm circling an inquiring index finger. Eight months later it was more common to hear: 'So – are we going back, or do we stay as we are?' To which the common reply was: 'Makarios said we are in for a *long-term* struggle. It may take years . . .' I met only a very few men and women who felt sure that there would be no return to the village, but many others felt that the international diplomatic prospects were poor, and that the Turks were not people to make concessions. Most people simply did not know what to think, and there was a continuing tension between what their political leaders felt was acceptable as a public statement, and their own private perceptions about their plight. The public face had to be optimistic and, if necessary, belligerent: the private utterance often belied such a posture.

As with those metaphorical seeds, there were traces of similar hopes in some of the villagers' other acts. For example, an Argaki farmer had rented a shop and two flats from a departing Turk in Limassol. He paid £400 for the properties, and their agreement stated: 'The rental shall continue from today until the day when the Cypriot Political Question is resolved.' A further clause added that if this were to happen within one year, the Greek would get half his rent money back – a canny piece of thinking, containing a scrap of hope. Another similar agreement suggested that some Turks were also not immune from such hopes:

> I, the undersigned, Eminé Osman, declare that I authorise Vassos
> Georgitzis of Argaki to stay in my house in Lower Polemidhia, with his

family. Whenever I return he must hand the house over to me in the same condition as when he took charge of it. He has given me £10 for his sojourn. 21–ii–75.

But many other people kept suggesting, in various ways, that they were trapped, and had lost their usual energy and purpose. A shepherd's wife in Peristerona said, 'What we've lost is priceless. How long d'you think it'll take us to find our wits again?' Another woman, living quite near to her, explained to me at some length that if they were to go back, they would have to be determined to start again from scratch, and that they would never regain the same living standard. 'The only thing is that our children may one day manage it, so we have to educate them. We *cannot* leave them uneducated'; and so she continued for some fifteen minutes. As I listened I was puzzled by some elusive quality about the way she was talking to me. It had a mechanical, rehearsed note, as if she knew exactly what she was going to say before she said it, even though the words themselves were vivid:

> We left the village as if we were going out for a stroll . . . we haven't a
> stick of furniture here . . . we'll go back to a dry, empty place . . . I shan't
> be able to build a dowry-house for my daughter.

All at once I grasped what had eluded me: she was not really speaking to *me* at all. I was merely overhearing an inner monologue, thoughts she must have expressed many times before, or spoken to her husband. She was reaching the completion of a period of mourning, of blurred focus, caught between a past life she could not give up and an unsatisfying present and future, and she was struggling to bring all the images into a single sharp picture, and to find a clear purpose. It was a hesitant, painful process, and I felt uneasy at having been virtually an eavesdropper on her thoughts.

On all sides people were having to come to terms with loss and to cope with the constant reminders of their loss. But they did not try to forget the village. In Polemidhia I was eating in a cousin's house, together with a neighbour of hers. She looked out of a window and saw a bus marked 'Argaki–Morphou'. 'Should we take those signs down, so that we don't feel sad?', she mused, and her neighbour replied, 'No, we shouldn't.' The village name was still used in new coffee shops and was kept alive in other small ways. As I drove to Nicosia one evening, with the radio on, I heard a record requested by a niece of mine, then studying in the middle of Russia, '. . . for her parents Tomas and Argyrou Diakourtis *of Argaki*'.

There were many other examples of how people clung to the village. One of my cousins was living very close to the cease-fire line, so close that she said, 'I could almost smell the village', and she stubbornly refused to go off to Paphos and get a much better house in the formerly Turkish quarter there. There was also a young policeman who had found a vantage-point from which, with binoculars, he could see the village, very faintly, and he told me that he went and gazed at it almost every day. One day in a coffee shop, in the formerly Turkish quarter of Limassol, the young proprietor spied a photograph of the village among my papers. He began to stare at it, and remained rapt for some minutes. 'It's almost as if I was there. I could stare at it for days, and still not have my fill.' Other villagers one day identified all the houses they could in this photograph, and, if they could not see their own house, seemed disappointed. From many people I also heard how at night they dreamed either of returning to the village, or of simply being there, 'as usual'.

It was clear that, however the villagers might get a grip on economic independence, and whether they found themselves dwelling with or without Argaki neighbours, they would never be free of the village. I had a friend in Nicosia whose father had left a village in Asia Minor during the 1922 population exchange between Greece and Turkey. He had run a grocery in Nicosia most of his life, and now his children were grown up. More than fifty years had passed, but he was always thinking about the community of his childhood; he had even written to some of his former companions, who had settled in Greece, and seemed set on finding a way of joining them again, although he died before he could do so. If the refugees of the 1970s felt as he did, there could be no 'getting over' their loss, however much they 'came to terms' with it.

As I prepared to leave Nicosia in late December 1975, there were disturbing signs of a troubled future. The Greek Cypriot soldiers had painted a big sign near the cease-fire line, on the road to the airport: 'THESE are NOT our FRONTIERS.' A cousin of mine, who had been driven out of a good business in Kyrenia, declared vehemently one evening, 'We shall return to Kyrenia – *at the double.*' The image was of an infantry assault.

Such thoughts and slogans were ominous. It was unwise to assume that the threats were entirely hollow, even though, if the Greek Cypriots confronted Turkey, they were outnumbered by more than a hundred to one. The Armenians were still bitter over blood the Turks had shed more than fifty years earlier, and Armenian groups were occasionally responsible for the assassination of Turkish diplomats. Mere pinpricks, or the first payments on account? The most frequent comparison made by Greek Cypriots was with the Palestinians, despite the enormous differences in the two contexts. It had taken the Palestinians fifteen years as refugees before they turned to a violent struggle to regain their lost homes. Were they now any nearer to a return? Should they be emulated?

The news that Greece was now re-arming at full speed was deeply disquieting, as were tiny portents such as the following conversation:

I hear your wife just gave birth.

That's right.

May the child live for you.

Our thanks.

Boy or girl?

A boy.

That's good: another fighter for the village.

By the end of December 1975 very few people spoke as if their return to Argaki was even probable, let alone imminent. A thoughtful villager who had always followed politics closely said to me, 'Surely it's a peculiarity of the Cyprus invasion that the refugees haven't been allowed to go home yet? After most wars, the refugees usually go back, don't they?' From his own knowledge he could easily have supplied the answer to his question. I found it hard to say to him that after many wars the refugees had not gone home, and that partition had become a commonplace 'solution' to both super-power and regional conflicts. Poland, Ireland, Germany, Korea, Vietnam, were all testaments to this. I was sad for him, for his innocence and hope.

Appendix 1

METHODS

To make the general reader's progress through this book less difficult, questions of research methods and of presentation have been confined to this appendix, while matters of general theoretical interest are included in Appendix 2. The style and content of the first chapter will have made clear my personal involvement with the people of Argaki. The partition of Cyprus and their uprooting made me wish to do something more enduring than demonstrating, signing petitions, and lobbying politicians. To this end I published a contribution to the Minority Rights Group's Report No. 30, *Cyprus*, written because of my complete dissatisfaction with the first part of that report; I have now written this book.

My doctoral research had concentrated on the first decade of Cypriot independence (1960–70), and how Argaki had been affected by the politics of the period. The thesis was examined in 1972, and a monograph based on it was published in 1975 as *The Greek gift: politics in a Cypriot village*. In that book Argaki was disguised as 'Kalo' village, and the villagers were all given pseudonyms too. The book was already in page proofs when the invasion of Cyprus took place; overnight, almost every fact in its pages had been rendered untrue.

So in addition to the usual debt an anthropologist feels to those who have enabled a study of their lives to be made, redoubled for me since I was especially close to the Argaki people, I felt an obligation to document their experience of becoming refugees. The most difficult question was how to proceed. The initial idea was to make the book as far as possible the direct product of the villagers themselves, so that tape-recordings were very much to the fore, supported by popular songs, folk poems, newspaper and broadcast texts, police statements, and a good deal of material about the village and villagers in which names were prominent. In successive drafts, and acting on advice from friends, the literal empiricism of 'told in their own words' has given place to a stronger role for myself as narrator and interpreter of their experiences. My initial desire to commemorate

Argaki made me forget for a while that facts – even when they are experiences rather than statistics – rarely speak very eloquently for themselves.

The Nuffield Foundation granted me funds for a reconnaissance visit to Cyprus in April 1975, which led to the Social Science Research Council's supporting a four-month visit from September to December of the same year. I sought their support for an essentially exploratory and descriptive study. During my first visit, I made my base in the Nicosia home of a cousin, and drove out by day to the villages and towns where the Argaki people were to be found. They were not hard to find, because of their interest in each other, so each new discovery led immediately to several more, the small scale of Cyprus and its good roads doing the rest.

For the second visit I thought it best not to impose on relatives, and shared a flat with an old friend, Michael Attalides, a sociologist then writing a book on the power politics of the partition of Cyprus (Attalides 1979). He had counselled me to my great advantage in my original research, and now did so again, as well as introducing me to various officials, and helping me make sense of the turmoil that was then Cyprus.

My most systematic research was a mini-census of 151 Argaki households, drawn from my 1969 sample. I asked about where and how people had lived since they had left Argaki, and what they had brought out with them. My main concern, though, was not with systematic data of this sort, but more with the nature of refugee experiences (both exceptional and more representative). My 'field methods' were chiefly a flexible opportunism; that is, a readiness to follow issues or persons wherever they might take me. It was very clear that the future of the Argaki refugees would not be decided by them. This involved following the issue of the incorporation of refugees generally into the wider Cypriot society, and I therefore attended political rallies, meetings of national and local refugee associations, sought interviews with civil servants, politicians, journalists, and contacts with the UN agencies, as well as spending a great deal of time with Argaki villagers, wherever they were. I had few reservations about this piecemeal approach, even though it had a restless, bitty aspect, for I was not burdened by formal hypotheses or an exacting research design. I noted down everything as it impressed me, and could thus take advantage of a roving commission.

It was usually 'day-return' research. I would leave the Nicosia flat early in the morning, and return late at night, usually to discuss our respective working days with Attalides; sometimes, though, I stayed away for several nights at a time. Sometimes I slept and ate in refugee households, for many were as determined to be hospitable as they had been in their better days; at other times I would bring a meeting to a close, to avoid burdening a family either by accepting a meal they could hardly afford or by refusing it.

During the second visit, I made much use of a tape-recorder, since many people seemed to have dramatic experiences they were ready to talk about at length. Here again, there were lessons to be learned or remembered. There was an initial barrier; since they were being recorded, many villagers felt that they had to speak carefully, or properly, as if in a public recitation. This was partly a consequence of schooldays, and their teachers' insistence on speaking 'proper' Greek (i.e. not dialect), and partly of their sensitivity to the idea of a permanent record being made of something important to them. I had to assure them that a relaxed and spontaneous discourse was the thing to aim for, that there were no 'wrong' ways of proceeding (except, of course, stiltedly!), and that all I wanted was their own words and thoughts in their normal language. I would then use certain methods I had learned when recording interviews for documentary films. I would find a quiet place for us to sit, place the tape-recorder to one side of us, and handle it as little and as calmly as possible. I would ask short questions, designed to elicit sustained narratives (rather than short factual answers), such as, 'Tell me all about the day you left the village.' As they talked I would hold their gaze, and nod from time to time, making it clear I was attending to their every word, and would smile approvingly if they seemed hesitant. I would try never to interrupt them; if they seemed to have reached the end of what they had to say, I would wait without speaking, nodding and looking attentive, and these cues often helped them continue with more experiences. It was not unusual for people to talk without stopping for ten or fifteen minutes at a time in such circumstances.

Sometimes, villagers heard that I was interviewing people, and sought me out. Several women sent me messages that they had composed poems, and that I should come to record their *paraponon* (complaint) (see Appendix 3, p. 207). At other times, people told me that someone had suffered a particularly dramatic experience, and that I should visit them to record it; it was in this way that I heard of Androulla Batsallou's diary.

Polly Hill (1977) has described how difficult she found it to study poor people, and suggests such difficulties may have seriously retarded such areas of research. It seems sensible to mention the ways in which I found it difficult to conduct even brief field research among refugees. First, because I had seen them at their best, it was inevitably distressing to witness their distress, to be highly aware of how far they had fallen and how little they had left of their former ebullience. Further, to meet them day after day in its cumulative effect was depressing, because almost every meeting contained its charge of anger and grief, and my outlook soon became as grey and narrow as theirs in its natural but obsessive concern with Cyprus and the burdens of being refugees.

In my own right I missed Argaki and other favourite parts of Cyprus; many of my pleasantest hours had been spent in these places and now a hostile army stood between them and me. Attalides and I had been enthusiasts for the Cypriot landscape, and he bitterly remarked that in this respect the Turks had seized the best of the island for themselves. From his flat there was a fine view of the Kyrenia mountains, on whose northern slopes I owned a beautiful old village house; but I could no more visit it than I could the orange grove in Argaki, the land which my father had given me, and his father had given him. There were also certain painful separations from people I loved, and although these had not been produced by the partition of Cyprus, the original relationships had been partly nurtured by the island. This involvement of private affairs with public affairs undoubtedly made me more sensitive to the refugees' feelings.

There was another kind of difficulty which did not in any way facilitate my research, and that arose from the anger I felt (as did most Cypriots) towards those held largely responsible for the partition of the island, the men of EOKA B. Once, they had been a puzzle to me, and as such had forced me into some of my best intellectual work, an attempt to explain how they saw the world, the reasons for their resentments and militancy. But the practical harm they had done us all now extinguished any residue of curiosity, and this meant that as an observer I was rarely capable of the restraint needed to learn anything of value from them. There were occasional exceptions, such as the interview with Kajis (pp. 66, 89), and a direct admission from another activist that he had been paid £16 a month while underground. But more often, I found myself exchanging sarcasms with men I should have been pumping hard for information.

There was one other difficulty in working with refugees, which was evident in my reluctance to do a certain kind of systematic 'facts-and-figures' interviewing. In 1969 I had interviewed 200 male household heads, and, with an expansive informant, these interviews had sometimes lasted two hours, and yielded much detail. In retrospect, I found I had tended to avoid administering this census interview to most of my close kin, for reasons which are unclear to me, but which probably had something to do with an awkwardness, an artificiality I felt about formally interrogating people about whom I knew so much by informal means, coupled with a feeling that I could always fill in any tedious details about *them* at my leisure. With the refugees, the mini-census I contrived could hardly have been shorter – it took about ten minutes to conduct and avoided details about their personal economics in the years between 1969 and 1974. Most of the refugees presented themselves as destitute, and I was reluctant to make them specify much about what they had salvaged, for the homes and orchards lost made the retrieved goods seem trifling, like asking a man who had just lost both legs about what he could still do with his hands. (I had felt this reluctance with the Argaki poor in 1969, when asking them detailed questions about ownership of consumer goods.) Sometimes, refugees volunteered crucial information, but a question of great interest – how they dealt with prewar debts between individuals – was not systematically pursued. It was clear that some men agreed to repay such debts by instalments, as and when they could, while others, even decent, upright men, decided that the time was out of joint, and refused to start repayments even when they had the means to do so; but I cannot say how many there were in each of these categories.

There was an opportunity missed in a different area – that of religion – which simply repeated a weakness of the prewar research. I could see that the diaspora might have generated a new interest in religion among many refugees, and although the question cried out to be asked, I did not ask it. By the time I set out to work with the refugees, the weight of my ignorance and the pressures of time made me decide that I would not pursue the topic, but merely note it when it impressed me 'empirically'. Therefore only a few fragmentary insights found their way into my notebooks. I offer no excuses for this, merely crumbs of explanation. I myself had never quickened to the study of religion in general, or Orthodoxy in particular; it had simply been a dead issue for me personally. For most of my life I had in gross form both a secular and a positivist outlook, which made it hard for me to come to grips with religion. I do not know why so many other anthropologists of the Christian Mediterranean should have fought shy of this topic, an omission for which Davis (1977) has rightly taken them to task. Had I known of William Christian's superb study of Spanish Catholicism (published in 1972), I might have faced this issue more squarely when the opportunity was present.

Much material in this book, as well as in *The Greek gift*, has come from my close kin, but a very great deal has also come from people to whom I was not related, or only distantly. To some extent my kinship status in Argaki made me cautious about describing actions which Argaki villagers would prefer strangers not to know of. However, most anthropologists seem to have been scrupulous in this way. Inevitably, my access to much information was greatly eased through my kinship connection, and at times, because I felt a quasi-insider, I took liberties in reporting things that others might have held back. Kinship, after all, allocates rights as well as duties.

To study one's own kin, even if they are achieved and not ascribed, can make for certain tensions. In 1968, while I was aware that every conversation I had might end up in my notebooks, my relatives did not appreciate this, and some of them later, although without obvious rancour, said as much. As I wrote up my notes I often felt uneasy, that I was a kind of spy, betraying a trust and living an alienated life. I countered such feelings by reminding myself of the high regard I felt for the discipline of social anthropology, and the people who had introduced me to it, such as Raymond Firth and Maurice Freedman. I was not much troubled by doubts about the 'relevance' of anthropology, or its possible abuses, issues which engaged one of my fellow-students as he took cover during the bombing of a Thai village, and another who was distressed by the poverty of northern Morocco.

The strain of playing a dual role ended naturally on my return to London in 1969. Although there were some twenty Argaki families, including some of my kin, resident in Britain, very little about their lives found its way into my notebooks. While this was partly through laxness, it was mainly because I preferred to have an uncomplicated relationship with them, to be a kinsman and fellow-villager, rather than impersonating these to further my anthropology.

There are two ways in which these books seem to have been affected by my special status – two 'silences', as a structuralist might say. In the first book I barely hinted at the irregularities of sexual conduct which had reached my ears, and this blandness is reproduced in the second chapter of the present work. It does not apply to the postwar material, for here nothing requiring my discretion came to my attention or, where it did, I have made this plain enough in the text. For the prewar material it must suffice to say (as any anthropological reader will have guessed) that the men and women of Argaki were not, if their gossip about each other is to be believed, all perfect exemplars of the honour code; and they were certainly a good deal less high-minded than the Greek shepherds immortalised by John Campbell (1964). This makes little difference to my account of politics and social structure, but for those concerned with comparative sexual mores it leaves the record obscure. This can be remedied by a careful reading of Cypriot court records and the newspapers of the time, which, while they make little reference to Argaki, supply the elusive detail in a general sense.

The second silence is perhaps less defensible, but less within my conscious control. How far did the particular social positions of my kin influence my account of Argaki? I reckoned some twenty-five households of close kin – uncles, aunts, and first cousins, in the English senses of those terms – but they did not form a faction, a solidary corporate group such as an Arab *hamula* or an Anatolian *kabile* might do. Some of my close kin are (or were) wealthy, others highly educated as well; some poor, some middling in wealth; there are a number of teachers and civil servants, some labourers, some farmers. From my point of view they form a large kindred, and they range across the entire political spectrum. They are fairly sociable people, so through their friends I made many contacts, and yet was not required to take up any enmities. I was therefore not *asketos*, a Greek Cypriot word meaning 'a person without connections', a state which invites from others both suspicion and condescension.

The Greek gift was essentially a study of political *leadership*, the doings of a village elite; the poor appeared mostly as statistics, and quite 'small numbers' at that. Had my kin connections been with a small and poorly off set of people, my account of Argaki might have been somewhat different in emphasis, if not in the actual selection of matters presented. In my view, 'man bites dog' is an *event* which either did or did not take place, regardless of the 'class allegiance' of the man, the dog, or the reporter in question. But the *attitudes* of the three parties are obviously much harder to pin down, and one or another might even deny that the event had taken place at all.

There is a third silence in the earlier book which has been disturbed, if not completely broken, in this one. Women were almost invisible and quite inaudible in *The Greek gift*, even though I was better placed than most male field workers to explore their situation, for I had kinswomen with whom to converse. The explanation for this omission is, of course, one of 'male bias' – not mine alone, but also that of the men of Argaki, who made it clear to me that the kind of kinsman they wanted was the kind who spent his time with other *men*. The difficulty with one's own biases is becoming aware of them, and in 1968 it did not occur to me that in a study of politics the relative absence of women was in itself a challenging problem. By 1975 my ears were open to the sirens of women's studies, and I hope that Argaki's women are now both more prominent and in better voice.

Appendix 2

COMPARISONS

War in anthropological studies

While historians and strategists have written a great deal about war, anthropologists have tended to ignore it, with some honourable exceptions (Goody 1971, Fried and others 1968, Lison-Tolosana 1966, Nettleship and others 1975, Wolf 1969). One suspects that most scholars have been preoccupied with generalisation, with self-regulating systems, or those which contain the seeds of their own change, and have tended to treat wars as contingent, external, and interruptions of 'normal' social processes. It is almost as if they have assumed the normality of peace and the abnormality of war, which is surely to confuse prescription with description?[1]

Robert Nisbet (1969) is one of the few authors to have criticised this tendency, in his analysis of evolutionist assumptions in what he calls 'the Western theory of development'. Arguing that events that many theorists would treat as either unique or external to the system they wish to understand *are the very essence of social change*, Nisbet declared (p. 279):

> If, as is so often argued today ... events, 'unique events' as they are called, are not amenable to the systematic needs of social theory, so much the worse for the theory. The objective, after all, is not the illumination of concept and theory. It is the illumination of reality as mind and sense reveal this reality.

He adds that once one stops discussing such lofty abstractions as 'mankind' or 'civilisation' ... 'significant change is overwhelmingly the result of non-developmental factors; that is to say, factors inseparable from external events and intrusions' (p. 280).

I do not wish to labour the point, because this book is chiefly concerned

---

[1] Marxists have hardly avoided these weaknesses. Empiricist marxists (for example, E. P. Thompson, E. Hobsbawm) have a better record than the rationalist and structuralist marxists inspired by Althusser.

with a very short period of events following a war, and is not a critique of other studies. But I do want to remind the anthropological reader that, with the exception of some small islands, every country with a Mediterranean coastline has either had a civil war, or found itself at war with another state, in this century. To some countries, this has happened more than once. Have anthropologists of the region taken sufficient account of this?

How would a concern with war affect my own work, were I to start with hindsight at the beginning? Very simply, I would have given much more thought to the international political context in which the Cyprus dispute developed (see, for example, Attalides 1979, Crouzet 1973, Windsor 1964), and also to the bitterness, from 1958 onwards, of relations between Turkish and Greek Cypriots. The fragile solidarity maintained between Argaki's Greeks was perhaps more the product of their communal stance towards their Turkish Cypriot fellow citizens than I had realised (but see Loizos 1975:131, 158). I might also have given more weight to the way that ethnic mobilisation tends to damp down class antagonisms. For a considered view of the issues, the reader may consult Loizos (1976).

There is another rather different sense in which war has been neglected by anthropologists. Because they have been primarily concerned with systems, structures, and the like, they have tended to neglect war as a disruptive experience suffered by their informants. More particularly, war usually produces refugees, and they have rather specific experiences; it is to the understanding of these that I now turn.

Refugees as bereaved persons: a useful analogy?

During my second field research trip, in 1975, I read Peter Marris' study, *Loss and change* (1974), and this made me think that in their early reactions to dislocation refugees might be like persons reacting to the loss of a dead loved one. With essential modifications, this view still seems helpful. Marris is not concerned with refugees, but has attempted to apply the insights he gained from the bereavement of widows to a number of other situations of deeply disruptive change.

Building on the work of previous writers, particularly Bowlby, Fried and Murray Parkes, Marris describes grief as the reaction that occurs to the loss of a loved person. It may take normal or abnormal forms, and may vary in intensity and duration. Some bereaved people show no grief for days, or even months, but then experience an unusually severe reaction; others remain in a state of obsessive grief for months or years.

Grief may be shown in a number of ways: outbursts of weeping; an obsessive preoccupation with the lost person, including an inability to believe that s/he has really died; dreams about them, and sensations (amounting almost to hallucinations) that s/he is present; sleeplessness, loss of appetite, apathy, depression, restlessness; and outbursts of violent, unprovoked anger, often directed to well-intentioned helpers (Murray Parkes 1972: 29–76). The experience of grief is normally modified by the personal history and age of the bereaved, and the nature of his or her relation to the dead person. Marris is primarily concerned with the cognitive implications of our attachments, whether to persons or to patterns of meaning. But he does not neglect affective commitments; indeed he insists that 'we cannot command our feelings', and one of his virtues is his attempt to consider cognition and affect together.

Marris argues that in many reactions to disruptive change there seems to be a defensive, 'conservative' element. There appears to be a sense in which the ability to adapt and the wish to conserve meaning depend on each other. He chooses a dramatic example to illustrate this – Bettelheim's observation that those who best survived the capricious unpredictability of a Nazi concentration camp were the two most ideologically dogmatic groups, the communists and the Jehovah's Witnesses. He suggests that 'the impulse to preserve the thread of continuity is thus a crucial instinct of survival' (1974:17).

Grief, in Murray Parkes' phrase, is 'the price we pay for love, the cost of commitment' (1972:20). Marris sees in it a struggle between two contradictory impulses – to preserve the past from loss and yet to accept the loss and re-establish a meaningful pattern of relationships. In several situations which were undergoing radical change he identified 'a characteristic ambivalence, which ... always seemed to inhibit any straightforward adjustment', and he insists that 'the anxieties of change centered upon the struggle to defend or recover a meaningful pattern of relationships' (1974:1).

The grief analogy has to be handled with care, as both Marris and Murray Parkes remind us, for the proper social control of grief is to be found in the institution of mourning, through which society, by custom, ritual, and ceremonial, attempts to regulate the destructive possibilities of uncontrolled grief, and to limit the time which grieving takes. But Marris successfully uses the analogy to analyse a variety of apparently very dissimilar situations: the social backgrounds of Kenyan entrepreneurs; the expulsion of Asians from Kenya and their uneasy incorporation into Britain; the rise and fall of Igbo tribal associations; Fanon's violent rejection of the European culture which had professionally trained him; and, significantly for my argument, a slum-clearance project. Similarly, in his last chapter, Murray Parkes seeks to extend 'bereavement' to contexts wider than the death of a loved person, and he includes in this Fried's

(1962) study of 'slum' clearance also cited by Marris. Fried found that after being relocated against their wills the residents of a low-rent district in Boston experienced a range of reactions which he, as a psychiatrist, wished to describe as grief. While grief is usually associated with loss of a person, it seems reasonable that it may result from the loss of a thing, a place, or a way of life. Auden's lines:

> When I was a child, I
> Loved a pumping-engine,
> Thought it every bit as
> Beautiful as you.
>
> (Auden 1966:153)

are suggestive here, as is Psalm 137:1:

> By the waters of Babylon we sat down and wept: when we remembered thee, O Sion ...
> If I forget thee, O Jerusalem: let my right hand forget her cunning.

But the aftermath of the loss differs in each case. First, how final is the loss? Marris states that the analogy with bereavement does not fit disruptive changes, however severe, if the loss is obviously retrievable (1974:148). Would people in cultures where there is a powerful belief that one rejoins a lost person in the next life qualify as 'bereaved' or not, one wonders? And are the old apparently less affected by bereavement because they expect to follow soon, as indeed they often do (Murray Parkes 1972:31)? But, more to the point, the Argaki refugees were told throughout 1974 and 1975 by their political leaders nothing to suggest that their loss was irretrievable, and much to indicate that it was temporary. Certainly, for the first weeks or months of their dislocation, few of them thought that they had lost their village for ever, so their grieving, if grieving it was, started rather later than normal grieving for someone who had just died would have done. The second problem is that most grieving proper involves mourning, the ceremonial social regulation of grief. In relation to the Lagos slum-clearance Marris has commented (1974:57):

> A situation is created which resembles bereavement in the sudden and irretrievable nature of the loss, yet provides no process akin to mourning, by which the loss can be assimilated and the essential continuity of life restored.

The reader may wish to ask at this point, what specific behaviours of the refugees does the bereavement analogy clarify? My list is rather long: the frequent outbursts of weeping, particularly by women, when they spoke of their homes, the village, and their former way of life; the obsessive recitations of *things* lost; the rapid oscillation between optimism and pessimism about the possibility of a return, from people who tended in the past to state all their opinions about events with a dogmatic certainty; outbursts of anger often apparently unrelated to the specific context; the angry attribution of blame to rather remote agencies, such as the UK and the USA, when to accuse more obvious candidates (EOKA B, Mother Greece, Turkey) would have involved drastic revisions of past views about crucial relationships; the unwillingness of previously energetic, hard-working, and enterprising men to take up cash offers for their economic recovery, even though they had always been very quick off the mark in competition with their fellow-villagers; and actions such as that of my cousin, Eleni Kaourma (p. 185), who insisted on dwelling as close to Argaki as possible, even though it was possibly dangerous to do so.

These are all items of behaviour which could, of course, be explained in other ways. The most subtle benefit of Marris' approach, however, perhaps accrued while I was interviewing people, and listening to them talking about their past, present, and future. I continually had the sense, elusive as an item of 'hard' data but readily available to intuition, that people were working through a set of powerful emotions, and very slowly reaching new perspectives on their lives. Of course, all change and all learning must involve such adjustments; the peculiarity was the sense of observing the process actually happening and feeling that it was an autonomous process, not under any conscious control of those who experienced it.

If the bereavement analogy is taken up, what might follow from it? I shall suggest only a few possible leads. First, that for the first year or so of their experience refugees may appear unduly critical of *any* provisions made for their welfare, and this because inevitably, for the vast majority, nothing can really replace what was lost. Even if refugees have fled from the threat of death or persecution, they have usually *left homes*, and left familiar patterns of meaning. Marris found that widows missed their dead husbands *even when the marriage had been an unhappy one*, and perhaps this helps explain why a political refugee can feel nostalgic towards a country that has proved dangerous to him.

Neither the bereaved nor refugees react uniformly to their losses; there is always a range of individual variation. But it seems safe to suggest that where refugees have become so without warning, they will generally need at least a year to come to terms with their new situations, and some will require several years. During this time restlessness, apathy, indecisiveness, or even a sense of unreality, may occur.

Within this first year, behaviour which looks at first like 'speedy adjustment' should be regarded with caution. Murray Parkes reports that some bereaved people apparently distract themselves for the first weeks or months of loss by hectic, restless activity, but that they are prone to suffer a delayed reaction, and at an unexpected moment express their grief powerfully.

Relative deprivation: material and symbolic

In most cases the refugees had been made homeless and destitute. 'Homes' could not be replaced by 'dwelling units'; the latter could provide shelter, but not the symbolic associations of the houses in Argaki (Friedsam (1962) has useful insights on this issue). The refugees talked, obsessively I thought, about the *things* they had lost – the orchards, the houses, their contents – and rather less about any disruption of social relations, although they did sometimes talk of the village as a whole with great sadness, and this metaphorically included social relations. I was initially puzzled, because it seemed as if they valued 'things' more than people. Obviously, their destitution gave them every reason to dwell upon material losses; and they sometimes said, thinking of those Argaki families who had lost relatives in the war, 'At least we didn't lose anyone', but this was usually an afterthought, at the end of a recitation about things.

In a normal Cypriot village, people did their best to accumulate fields and cash, and to build superior houses for their children. A commitment to the children was properly accompanied by the eventual transfer of property to them. Poverty was extremely dangerous in the days before old-age pensions, for if someone could not provide for his children in their youth, how could he expect them to provide for him in his old age? This meant that commitment was dual, to persons-and-things, both at once. At two extremes this was easily seen: childless couples tended to turn away from economic striving once they had secured themselves; while those parents who became wealthy tended to form the centre of supportive accretions of kin, affines, and friends.

For the refugees the duality of persons-and-things had been destroyed. Most villagers had not lost a close relative (I recorded eight deaths among Argaki residents as a direct result of the war) and so they could be said to have retained their full range of relations, even in diaspora. If it helps to think of social relationships as invisible, flexible bonds created by the ideas in people's minds, then these bonds had been stretched in all directions, but not broken. But the material interests which had accompanied their relationships had largely gone: parents had nothing to give their children; former neighbours no longer had tasks to share, or fences in common; farmers had no need of labourers; butchers, tailors, and builders had lost their customers.

Evans-Pritchard (1940:19) wrote of the Sudanese Nuer people's preoccupation with cattle:

> I have already indicated that this obsession – for such it seems to an outsider

–is due not only to the great economic value of cattle but also to the fact that they are links in numerous social relationships. Nuer tend to define all social processes and relationships in terms of cattle. Their social idiom is a bovine idiom.

Nuer without cattle would be destitute, but they also would suffer the additional deprivation of living within a symbolic world largely emptied of content. Indeed, East Africa today probably contains all too many pastoral peoples in such a condition. Similarly, after the war the Argaki refugees were fed and sheltered, but they were deprived in a way invisible to casual inspection; certain key elements of their lives – home, marriage, property, independence, village, neighbours – had been damaged. The words for these elements remained usable, but nothing very solid backed them. It was Dionysios who had made me understand this by insisting that the essence of the village was *the relationship between the people and the place* (see p. 131).

Refugees as disaster victims

There is an extensive sociological literature on 'refugees', and another literature on 'disaster victims', mainly of floods and earthquakes, but sometimes of aerial bombing and famine (e.g. Barton 1969). My impression is that there is less common ground in these two literatures than there should be. To make the most obvious parallels, disaster victims are often made homeless at very short notice, rendered destitute, forced into temporary shelter with kin, or into camps. To the shock of a rapid and violent disruption to normal life, bereavement is often added, and there may be traces of 'survivor guilt' (Lifton & Olson 1976), since obsessive thoughts about a failure to save loved ones or images of the violent deaths of friends may trouble the victims.

One way of gaining an appreciation of the common ground is to consider a specific contribution. H. J. Friedsam's excellent discussion (1962) of the experiences of older people in disasters reviews studies of victims of strategic bombing and of natural disasters. It concludes with eleven tentative hypotheses, for which some empirical support could be found. One of these is that older people are often particularly reluctant to leave their homes when a danger threatens – my material from Argaki (p. 107), and from Cyprus more generally, tends to support this.

Another Friedsam hypothesis quoted approvingly by Bolin and Trainer (1978:235) is that older persons experience deprivations more strongly than younger ones, but this is not supported by my impressions. I noted several examples of elderly people who seemed less distressed than their middle-aged sons and daughters (p. 157); this is probably to be understood, as one of the villagers made clear, in terms of the difference in realisation of life goals between those who have married off their children, the supreme achievement of Greek Cypriot adult life, and those who have not. To take up a suggestion of Wolfenstein's, which Friedsam quotes, if the children have been married off, for Cypriots old age is a state of being, not of having.

Friedsam himself notes that most of the distressed older people in the studies from which he quoted were 'those with something to lose' – i.e. their own homes – and he compares them with the less privileged, more isolated old people, already deprived before the disaster struck. 'With so little to lose, there is likely to be no difference between their pre- and post-disaster status.' It seems probable that he is dealing here with a specific feature of the American culture that he was studying – the desire of the elderly to be home-owners if possible and to avoid burdening their children. In rural Cyprus, old people tend to have given their homes over to marrying children, and to live for their last years in much smaller, simpler dwellings, often in the courtyard of their former home. They are not defined by what they possess but by what they have given away, and 'independence' is not a key issue. To quote Wolfenstein, 'the more belongings are included in the definition of the self the more vulnerable one is to losing parts of oneself'; yes, and vice versa for most elderly Cypriots. Friedsam notes also the greater difficulty experienced by older people when faced with the need to 'start a new life', or to rebuild their fortunes (see p. 123). He mentions too the stresses which affect families forced to 'double up' after being made homeless (see pp. 173, 174). The suggestion that at such times people move in with their kin for lengthy periods receives further support from Bolin and Trainer (1978).[1]

New identifications

The readiness with which Argaki people were able to relate to other refugees from surrounding villages, and the emergence of a 'Morphou' regional identity, seem to have general implications. A similar process, albeit on a much larger scale, is described in Emanuel Litvinoff's account of European Jews who were refugees, labour migrants, or both, in London's East End:

> The tenement was a village in miniature, a place of ingathered exiles who supplemented their Jewish speech with phrases in Russian, Polish or Lithuanian ... *People spoke of Warsaw, Kishinev, Kiev, Kharkov, Odessa, as if they were neighbouring suburbs.*[2]

[1]   For a number of general surveys of the disasters literature the reader may wish to consult Baker and Chapman 1962, Barton 1969, and Quarantelli 1978.
[2]   Litvinoff 1972, 1976:24; my italics.

The Argaki folk were doing the same thing but over distances of five or ten miles, instead of five hundred or a thousand. Since any family was cut off from a large number of its usual kin and friends, it had, so to speak, social energy, which would have otherwise been expended on the 'missing' people, to spare. So relations with people who were already on the edges of the local mental map were in order. Furthermore, these people had the great advantage over total strangers of themselves being familiar with and of knowing something about Argaki, its customs, prosperity, and personnel. This is the real point: the refugees did not want mere contacts (they were not 'lonely'), but relationships with people who *really understood* what their prewar life was all about, who shared the same pattern of meanings.

Something similar seems to happen when African tribesmen leave their familiar world and move to a city, a world of strangers. They substitute for the people they have left behind by forming friendships with others they did not know before, but who speak their tribal language. These they call 'home-boys' or 'brothers', and they cherish each other. When Greek villagers migrate to Athens, Sydney, or London, they often form clubs based on common membership in the village back home. People who hardly had time to do more than greet each other in the village now become fast friends and seek each other out. An old Cypriot proverb puts it well: 'In a drought even a hailstorm helps.'

Elizabeth Colson's (1971) study of the resettlement of the Gwembe Tonga provides interesting parallels: after the move some of the Tonga found themselves with new Tonga neighbours, with whom they gradually came to participate in common ceremonials. At first, they sought out their previous neighbours, but the difficulties created by distance eventually made it more practical to make common cause with the new ones. They also strove to maintain the symbols of old identity in new and apparently inappropriate contexts. Colson cites an event which occurred among a group of Upland Tonga now living in a riverain area, eight years after their move: a child had been teased by his older brother for eating a frog, but his mother had said, 'He does not eat frogs ... River people eat frogs. Upland people do not eat frogs.' This is only one of many examples given where the social definition of an identity was maintained when its actual context had radically changed.

Forced migration: two comparable studies

There are many studies that would offer some basis for comparison with the material here, but the difficulties of making such comparisons are great. Much of the work has been done using approaches very different from mine. My own material covers only the earliest part of what (by

1981) has already been a lengthy process, so it is inevitably provisional. Most difficult, and rendering strict comparison out of the question, is the fact that the basic situations tend to differ markedly. I shall discuss briefly two anthropological studies which come closest to the situation of the Argakides; but the reader should reflect that of these two essentially preliterate cultures, one lived chiefly by fishing around a tiny Pacific atoll, and the other by shifting cultivation in Central Africa. Some might argue that such comparisons are better left unmade.

The two studies are Elizabeth Colson's (1971) account of the re-settlement of the Gwembe Tonga people of Zambia, to make way for the Kariba Dam, a richly documented account spanning the first ten years following resettlement. The second is Kiste's (1974) account of how the people of Bikini atoll were removed from it, a saga of their tribulations over twenty-three years.

The 'disasters' literature has a lot to say about warnings, and how people react to them, for they can save lives. The credibility of the source of a warning is particularly important. A common sequence of events involves a warning which is discounted; impact; shock; and gradual stocktaking.

The Bikinians had little warning that they were to be evacuated, nor any previous experience which would have prepared them for the request made of them in 1946 that, to help international peace, they leave their homes to make way for the testing of an atomic device. So their subsequent 'acquiescence' to the 'request' is probably misleading: they can have had no idea of what they were in for. Two months after leaving they made the first of their many requests to return to Bikini.

The Gwembe Tonga did not believe that the British colonial authorities were serious about the plan to build the Kariba Dam in their home area – they thought it was a white ruse to disguise an attempted land-grab. Not until a number of them had been encouraged to rebel, and were shot down by the colonial police, did they take the proposed move very seriously. Their preparations for the move were rather half-hearted, and finally they were taken by lorries to their new settlement area, set down, and left to get on with life. It seems to have been the arrival of the lorries, the order to pack their things quickly, and the lorry-ride into the unknown, which finally made the government's plans a reality for the Tonga. They were quite badly shocked.

The Argaki people, as we have seen, thought they were leaving their village 'for a few days'. Neither the 'first round' of the invasion, a month earlier, nor the previous fourteen years of intercommunal conflict during which a partition of Cyprus was often discussed, had served to prepare them psychologically for such an event. For nearly all of them, the

Turkish advance had to be *visible* before it was *credible*, and they were hampered, not helped, by the radio broadcasts of their own side, which repeatedly claimed victories, and denied or ignored Turkish advances.

Immediately after the dislocation none of these three groups was willing to do more than the bare minimum to ensure survival. At first the Tonga would not plant anything, and for several years would not try anything remotely experimental with crops or production methods. The Bikinians were, for the first year or more, apathetic and depressed, and even several years after their move were reluctant to exploit the resources of their new environment. The Argakides for some months showed an unwillingness to take up government-sponsored loans for agriculture or livestock, and many adopted a wait-and-see policy. All three groups were highly critical of the new environments in which they found themselves.

There were similarities, too, in the organisation of kinship groupings and residence patterns immediately following the move. The Tonga and the Argakides spent the first months of dislocation residing in *larger* kin groups than they had done previously, although in the Cypriot case this is partly explained by the basic scarcity of dwellings. Later both groups split up into their previous residential units, with a certain embarrassed regret, and with admissions that the period had been a strain on kinship. The Bikinians, who numbered only 170 in all in 1946, were from the start moved all together (unlike the other two groups). They did not elect to reside in larger kinship groupings as such, but did something roughly similar: for nearly five years they organised themselves as a single community (something they had definitely *not* done previously) and allocated labour and land by communal decision. During this period they presented a united front to outsiders.

There were other changes in social and political relations. As one might have expected, all three groups suspended certain longstanding antagonisms as 'irrevelant' after dislocation (p. 169n). Land disputes particularly are not worth pursuing when both parties have lost the land in question, and local 'honour' disputes pale when both parties face a common 'dishonourable' enemy. Other changes were more specific to the particular group. The Tonga's support for their cult wavered since the deities were thought to have failed in their duty to protect the people from incursion and danger. Colson's material on Tonga religious changes is full, but Kiste is silent on this issue. My own material says little about religious beliefs, but in any follow-up study this would be a matter of importance.

The longer-term responses to dislocation among Tonga and Bikinians varied. It took the Tonga several years to come to grips with their new locations, but five years after the move they had accepted and spent their modest cash compensation, and put the move behind them. They started living in the present, and adopting new technologies and economic opportunities. Colson thinks that their previously harsh environment had led them to adopt a 'flexible social system' which allowed them to substitute personnel or symbolic actions when they needed to, to tolerate non-closure, and to postpone all non-essential activities. She places much less emphasis on the finality of their loss: once the Kariba Dam had flooded their former homes, there was no possibility of return. My guess is that this second point is rather more important than the flexibility of the social system, in having brought the Tonga into engagement with the present.

This irreversibility becomes important when we consider the situation of the Bikinians. They never settled down anywhere, always found fault with their several new locations, and never accepted their loss of Bikini as final. Whenever they moved they tried to get the government to build their dwellings for them, and, if this was refused, demanded to be paid to do it for themselves. They became increasingly articulate, and continuously between 1946 and 1969 demanded both a return to Bikini and compensation, which started with very small sums but by 1969 had become a claim for one hundred million US dollars. They changed from a passive, easily cowed population to a self-conscious and highly manipulative political interest-group. Perhaps they received some tuition in this from successive students of their predicament; Kiste was the *third* anthropologist to study them. Their numbers increased three-fold, and, as with the Palestinians, the number of claimants to the 'lost lands' (or to compensation) increased.

The Argakides have been studied for only the first fifteen months of what has already been more than six years' exile. Unlike the Tongans, but like the Bikinians, there is no necessary finality about the loss of their homes.

Appendix 3

FRAGMENTS

The need to provide a concise, coherent account of the villagers' experiences has inevitably sliced many details from the body of this book. But the four brief items which follow seemed to demand a place in a proper chronicle of Argaki.

I

In Stroumbi village, among the Paphos foothills there were five Argaki families resident in winter 1975. Eleni Pitsillou was wife of one of the Argaki butchers, and she sent word to me that she had 'a song' about the village. The reference to 'roads like oil' is to contrast her plains village with her present situation, where she like the other Argaki people found the steep pathways hard going.

The Complaint of Eleni Pitsillou

I get up each morning and as I cross myself
I ask my Maker, 'Please send me to my village.'
How are you now Argaki, with your roads like oil
What dog is now your President, and gives the orders?

Argaki mine, you were the best village in Cyprus
Deprived now of your inhabitants.
I had so many orange trees, if counted thousands.
But now those dogs of *agas* take their pleasures in them.

II

My beloved and unforgettable Xenia,

I got your letter today and it made me very glad. Today as I write to you, Xenia, I'm very tired. I got up this morning and milked the goats, I did the milk and then I took them out to graze. Later Nikos came back from school, and we

207

went out together and brought back green stuff for the goats. Before going back to the house I asked Petros if we had a letter. As soon he told me we had I went to the house, read the letter and had a rest. I asked Nikos to make me a coffee, and he brought it to where I was sitting, on the bed. I started feeling really low, and weeping in my heart. Four daughters I've had and not one by my side.

Last Sunday was Sikosi [Shrove Tuesday] and we had a really good time. We went to Pretori village – Maroulla, Nikos, Sophoulla, your uncle, your aunt, Nikos, Petros, Phroussou and Eleni. They'd been staying with your uncle Andrikos in Nicosia.

Today your father's been keeping Yiangos company. I told him to write you a letter himself and he said to me, my Xenia's all right (being in Athens). I'm sending you a photo which Nikos took just after he came down from the snows of the mountain. We were on this outing. I was sitting with your grandma at the dam, and a goat started giving birth.

I read your letter. You have many greetings from your grandma and your dad. I send you greetings by way of the pilot.

> The road so long I cannot come
> Yet want so much to find you
> To have one glimpse of you at school
> And come straight back again.

> I praise you Lord and Master
> Please God do not forget us!
> Speedily to our houses
> Perhaps he will return us.

> Where I was once, beside my house
> I had an orange-tree
> And every day I worked, I filled
> My pocket full of money.

> Now I'm reduced to living
> Upon the mountainside
> And if I do not cry at dawn
> I cry noontime.

I'm not writing these songs down to make you unhappy. I'm setting them down for you to have as a reminder of this time now, when we are refugees. It is enough that we are all very well. The only thing that is wrong is that we are not near one another. Nothing else. Goodnight, my Xenia. The only thing I wish is that you stick to your reading as much as you can. With much love,

yours mother,

Sophoula Paphiti

III

Eleni Kaourmas' song

Now it was close to daybreak on the twentieth of July
The Turks began invading the isle of Cyprus nigh.

Eleni Kaourmas, b. 1928, Argaki; m. 1951 Giorgios Kaourmas, b. 1928, Argaki, after a five-year engagement; five children. She received 1·1 hectares, he ·4 hectares from their respective parents. They later bought a ·4 hectare plot near Morphou, and by 1969 had 920 citrus trees. Giorgios had a small wage as a nightwatchman. Eleni is a sister of Tomas Diakourtis (see p. 52), a first cousin to the author, and the mother of Christos Kaourmas (see pp. 74, 211).

I see a mother weeping, her grief she feels it sore,
To have to wake her sleeping son, now, and send him to the war.
'Wake up, son, you must wake up, and get you gone to war
The Turks they are invading, they stand upon our shore.'
Just like the hare he starts up, just like the bird he moves
And asks from his sweet mother to fetch his soldiers' clothes.
'Give me my clothes, now, mother, the ones that are khaki,
And now that I must leave you, your blessing give to me.'
'I bless you, child, I bless you, now you must be away
May you devour the Turks like bread, for this I'll surely pray.'
From out of every doorway see mothers coming fast
For they can hear the thunder of Turkish cannon-blast.

Look, there are our young lions, the lads of Cyprus' birth
Firing upon the Turks so hard the houses fall to earth.

But Turkish planes are coming, their planes are coming fast
And raining bombs upon our boys, who get the awful blast.

But bravo to our soldiers, who held the line for days
And shot down all of twenty-three attacking Turkish planes.

But later now come over the Yankee aeroplanes
And from them pour the napalm bombs to burn us in their flames.

The composer, Eleni Kaourmas, is a sister of Tomas, and, like him, of the left, so she used the melody of Theodorakis' very popular 'To Yelastó Paidhií' (The Laughing Lad). She left the listener somewhat in the dark by describing the aeroplanes as 'American'. They were made in the USA, and supplied to Turkey as part of her NATO armaments. The US Congress subsequently decided that they had been used illegally in Cyprus.

A great deal has been written about Greek folk-poetry, and the curious reader may have an excellent short introduction from the chapter 'Lamentations' in Patrick Leigh Fermor's *Mani*. In Argaki particular women were said to have the gift of 'singing' and in 1966 when I pressed a kinswoman to show me how well she could sing, she responded by composing a couplet which celebrated my arrival. She was the same Eleni who wrote the previous song.

In Argaki songs were composed by women sometimes at banquets, by both women and men at weddings, and by women at funerals, where they were known as *klámata*, half-shouting, half-sobbing laments which praised the dead person. If the death was untimely the emotion was very strong, the praise hyperbolic, and the custom accompanying her grief required that the bereaved woman attempted to throw herself into the grave.

Women were normally highly self-controlled in their speech, gestures, their sexual conduct, their thrift, and many other things. It seemed that only in certain public crises were they allowed a more free expression of emotions and creativeness, and here they were still loosely constrained by the forms of verse, however simple. It is not very hard to produce rhymes in Greek and one does not want to make the production of these verses sound like a difficult achievement. They do not seem in the same class as the splendid lament quoted in *Mani*. Rather, they are offered here as another example of the refugees' legitimate obsession with their situation. The 1922 exchange of populations between Greece and Turkey had produced several million refugees, and Greek literature and music seem to have been nourished as a result. In Cyprus, within two years of the war there were major exhibitions of refugee poetry, and of paintings by refugee children, while every second intellectual one met was writing a book about some aspect of the war, its causes, its trauma, its outcomes. Schoolteachers certainly encouraged the children, and the newspapers and broadcast media also hammered at refugee themes, but these emphases were from the heart, and not the results of more self-conscious and manipulative cultural commissars, who, although they may have approved, could not have succeeded in stimulating what was not, in an important sense, already there.

IV

Christos Kaourmas (Eleni's son) we last heard from (chapter 4, p. 74) as he spent three days pinned down by the Turkish Army at the central prison in Nicosia. He was then released from duty for a few hours' leave and set out for Argaki. On the way he was taken prisoner by an advance party of Turkish soldiers, and at first he thought they were discussing whether or not to shoot him on the spot. Later he was sent to Turkey as a prisoner-of-war. There were periods of intense discomfort, due to heat, hunger, and thirst. During one journey in great heat in a closed truck, some of his comrades became so thirsty that they drank urine. 'Leave some for me' one said to another. But his worst moment may have been when he feared he was to be lynched, during the triumphal procession in central Turkey, to celebrate the victory of Turkish arms:

> On the morning of August 19th, 20th or 22nd, I'm not sure, it was really burning hot. Doors and windows were shut, no water or food, well you can imagine what it was like in the train when things are like that. Again the long journey and again the real misery of it; afterwards night falls and its just the opposite, covered in our sweat, sodden from the day, all our clothes sopping and then the cold night, that's how we got to Amasia, after about a thirty-six-hour journey. Well, we'd just about done half the trip when the train broke down near a town called Tockhat, six miles outside what's really quite a large town, with about 50,000 inhabitants. Some of them got word that the prisoners-of-war were passing through, and they started massing on the main boulevard of the town. When the train broke down, they decided to bring buses and put us in them. Standing there, for those four hours in the middle of the noonday heat, was the nastiest experience of my life, I'm telling you. Those days, I thought every day worse than the one before. About two they brought the buses, then, and put us in them.
>
> As we were going through Tockhat there were really huge crowds of people and they were so fanatic that they seemed capable of eating us alive. The soldiers were standing shoulder to shoulder to keep the crowd back from the road, where the buses were. The townsfolk had hold of stones, sticks, anything you can think of and they hurled them at us. Of course, they bounced off the buses.
>
> Finally, at 7 in the evening we got to Amasia.

At Amasia things were OK again, as they had been in Adana. They put us in the cells and gave us food and water. The food didn't really satisfy us. It just about kept you alive, that's all. Can you imagine waking up at five and thinking about when they'll bring the food at seven. It was the only good thing you had to think about, because you've got no news, and everything that passes through your mind will be unpleasant, fears about your family, and what is going on in Cyprus, how are all my people, my family, my friends, so food was about the only good thing to think about, it makes you forget, so at seven the food used to come, some pretty awful soup it was, and by eight, or nine or ten at the latest, you were hungry again. Twelve o'clock comes. Well, you know that we Cypriots have got into the habit of eating till our stomachs fill out a bit before we say we've had enough. Really, the food was all right to keep you alive, but not much else.

There was even some medical treatment there, not exactly top rate. They'd bring a doctor to check on the men who had toothache, some of our people went and saw him and asked him to do some fillings, and he told them, we can't fill them for you in here, wait until you go home and have them done. If you like, I'll take them out to stop the pain. Some had them out, some waited. Whatever we had we went to the doctor and he gave us pills to make us feel better. We didn't get any beatings at Amasia, well, nothing at all systematic. On a few occasions, we got it from some particular soldiers who were really more fanatic than need be, and if it chanced that our barracks was in the prison and on the way out to the exercise yard, with winding corridors, this fanatic bloke would try to have a go at us, when the officer was looking the other way. The officers kept a watch out for this sort of thing, and sometimes they beat the ordinary soldiers for having a go at us. This man I was telling you about managed to get in the odd one as we went by, a kick or a punch, but we used to move very fast, one at a time at the double, and he couldn't catch that many of us, and it didn't hurt us that much anyway. If we'd complained to the officer (since it got at us psychologically), he might have beaten up this man, but then he would have come at us later, when he got a chance. There were three or four others like him out of the fifty we were guarded by. The rest of the soldiers were decent fellows. They told us that the news programmes in Cyprus were saying that Makarios was coming back, that EOKA B had made it up with him. They didn't know a great deal, and we managed to make out the bits they knew. When they started exchanging prisoners-of-war, these kids told us this, but we didn't believe them at first. They told us once, 'They're going to let you go tomorrow! They're going to let you go tomorrow!' Naturally later on we realised that they didn't know exactly when, but they were well enough disposed to give us what news they had.

But as I said to you before our only real problem, the thing that really weighed us down was the agony over our families and homes, and what had happened over there. It was a real anguish and we felt we were being tortured. Well, about October 16th we heard that the Turks were going to let the older men go. That is an order came down to the Turks to let a certain number of us leave Amasia. And the Turkish officers thought it right to let the men go first who were over 27, who were likely to have families, their own wives and children, for whom it was more urgent to get back quickly; so they gave these men preference and the rest of us knew that we would be leaving in ten or fifteen days. When that first lot had left, they started giving us better food, that is more of it, because now there were fewer of us, and they looked on us with a better disposition.

When the decision was taken for us to leave, the return journey was really quite pleasant. The Turkish officers sat opposite us on the train and chatted with us, joked, laughed; there were some officers who knew some English, and some of our lads knew Turkish, or some other language, well, we managed to make ourselves understood. They went over the whole situation as they saw it; and the Turks told us everything they'd heard, in turn. We got to Nicosia and they took us and handed us over at the Hilton Hotel, no, I mean the Ledra Palace Hotel, and from there our people took us to the Hotel School where all our relatives were waiting. My mother had been coming each day for fifteen days expecting my release.

WORKS CITED

Amir, M. 1971. *Patterns in forcible rape*. Chicago: University of Chicago Press

Attalides, M. 1979. *Cyprus: nationalism and international politics*. Edinburgh: Q Press

Auden, W. H. 1966. *Collected Shorter Poems*. London: Faber and Faber

Barton, A. H. 1969. *Communities in disaster: a sociological analysis of collective stress situations*. Garden City, New York: Doubleday

Black-Michaud, J. 1975. *Cohesive force: feud in the Mediterranean and in the Middle East*. Oxford: Basil Blackwell

Bolin, R. and Trainer, Patricia. 1978. 'Modes of family recovery following disaster: a cross-national study', in E. L. Quarantelli (ed.), *Disasters: theory and research*, pp. 233–50. Beverly Hills, California: Sage publications

du Boulay, Juliet. 1974. *Portrait of a Greek mountain village*. Oxford: Clarendon Press

Campbell, J. K. 1964. *Honour, family and patronage*. Oxford: Clarendon Press

Christian, W. A., Jr. 1972. *Person and God in a Spanish valley* (Studies in social discontinuity). New York: Seminar Press

Colson, Elizabeth. 1971. *The social consequences of resettlement: the impact of the Kariba resettlement upon the Gwembe Tonga* (Kariba Studies, IV). Published for the Institute of African Studies, University of Zambia, by Manchester University Press

Council of Europe. 1976. European Commission on Human Rights Report: *Cyprus versus Turkey* (Application numbers 6780/74 & 6950/75). Adopted by the Commission 10 July 1976 (Declassified 31 August 1979)

Crouzet, F. 1973. *Le Conflit de Chypre, 1946–1959*, 2 vols. Bruxelles: Carnegie Endowment for International Peace, European Centre. Case Studies of International Conflicts, No. 4

Davis, J. 1977. *People of the Mediterranean: an essay in comparative social anthropology*. London: Routledge and Kegan Paul

Evans-Pritchard, E. E. 1940. *The Nuer: a description of the modes of livelihood and political institutions of a Nilotic people*. Oxford: Clarendon Press

Fermor, P. L. 1958. *Mani: travels in the southern Peloponnese*. London: Murray

Firth, R. 1959. *Social change in Tikopia*. London: Allen and Unwin

Fried, M. 1962. 'Grieving for a lost home', in L. J. Duhl (ed.), *The Urban Condition*, pp. 151–71. Reprinted 1963. New York: Basic Books

Fried, M., Murphy, R., and Harris, M. (eds.). 1968. *War: the anthropology of armed conflict and aggression*. New York: Natural History Press.

214

Friedsam, H. J. 1962. 'Older persons in disaster', in G. W. Baker and D. W. Chapman (eds.), *Man and society in disaster*, pp. 151–184. New York: Basic Books

Gell, A. 1977. 'Magic, perfume, dream', in Ioan Lewis (ed.), *Symbols and sentiments: cross-cultural studies in symbolism*, pp. 25–38. London: Academic Press

Gellner, E. and Waterbury, J. (eds.). 1977. *Patrons and clients in Mediterranean societies*. London: Duckworth

Goody, J. 1971. *Technology, tradition, and the state in Africa*. London: Oxford University Press

Gorer, G. 1965. *Death, grief and mourning in contemporary Britain*. London: Cresset

Hikmet, N. 1970. 'Since I was thrown into this hole', in *Selected poems of Nazim Hikmet*, trans. by T. Baybars. London: Jonathan Cape

Hill, Sir George F. 1952. *A history of Cyprus*, vol. 4. Cambridge: Cambridge University Press

Hill, Polly. 1977. *Population, prosperity and poverty: rural Kano, 1900 to 1970*. Cambridge: Cambridge University Press

Hirschon, Renée. 1978. 'Open body/closed space: the transformation of female sexuality', in Shirley Ardener (ed.), *Defining females: the nature of women in society*. London: Croom Helm, in association with the Oxford University Women's Studies Committee

Keller, S. L. 1975. *Uprooting and social change: the role of refugees in development*. Delhi: Manohar

Kiste, R. C. 1974. *The Bikinians: a study in forced migration*. Menlo Park, California: Cummings

Lifton, R. J. and Olson, E. 1976. 'The human meaning of total disaster: the Buffalo Creek experience'. *Psychiatry* 39 (Feb.): 1–18

Lison-Tolosana, C. 1966. *Belmonte de los Caballeros: a sociological study of a Spanish town*. Oxford: Clarendon Press

Litvinoff, E. 1976. *Journey through a small planet*. Harmondsworth, Middlesex: Penguin Books; first published 1972, London: Michael Joseph

Loizos, P. 1975. *The Greek gift: politics in a Cypriot village*. Oxford: Basil Blackwell

Loizos, P. 1976. 'An Alternative Analysis', in *Cyprus*. London: The Minority Rights Group, Report No. 30

Mackenzie, W. J. M. 1975. *Power, violence, decision*. Harmondsworth, Middlesex: Penguin Books

Markides, K. C. 1977. *The rise and fall of the Cyprus Republic*. New Haven and London: Yale University Press

Marris, P. 1974. *Loss and change*. London: Routledge and Kegan Paul (Reports of the Institute of Community Studies)

Murray Parkes, C. 1972. *Bereavement: studies of grief in adult life*. London: Tavistock Publications

Nettleship, M. A. and others (eds.). 1975. *War, its causes and correlates* (Papers from the 9th International Congress of Anthropological and Ethnological Sciences). The Hague: Mouton

Nisbet, R. A. 1969. *Social change and history: aspects of the Western theory of development*. Oxford: Oxford University Press

Patrick, R. A. 1976. *Political geography and the Cyprus conflict, 1963–1971*, ed. J. H. Bater and R. Preston. Waterloo, Ontario: Department of Geography, University of Waterloo

Quarantelli, E. L. (ed.). 1978. *Disasters: theory and research*. Beverly Hills, California: Sage Publications

Salzman, P. C. 1978. 'Ideology and change in Middle Eastern tribal Societies'. *Man*, N.S. 13 (4): 618–37

Turkish Cypriot Human Rights Committee. 1979. *Human rights in Cyprus*. Nicosia: Tezel Press (Copies obtainable from the Public Information Office of the Turkish Cypriot Administration, Nicosia)

Volkan, V. D. 1979. *Cyprus – war and adaptation: a psychoanalytic history of two ethnic groups in conflict*. Charlottesville: University of Virginia Press

Warner, Rex (trans.). 1954. Thucydides: *The Peloponnesian War*. Harmondsworth, Middlesex: Penguin Books

Windsor, P. 1964. *Nato and the Cyprus crisis* (Adelphi Paper No. 14). London: Institute for Strategic Studies

Wolf, E. R. 1969. *Peasant wars of the twentieth century*. New York: Harper and Row

INDEX

217